Chimariko Grammar

Chimariko Grammar
Areal and Typological Perspective

Carmen Jany

University of California Press
Berkeley • Los Angeles • London

University of California Press, one of the most distinguished university presses in the United States, enriches lives around the world by advancing scholarship in the humanities, social sciences, and natural sciences. Its activities are supported by the UC Press Foundation and by philanthropic contributions from individuals and institutions. For more information, visit www.ucpress.edu.

University of California Publications in Linguistics, Volume 142

University of California Press
Berkeley and Los Angeles, California

University of California Press, Ltd.
London, England

Printed in the United States of America

Cataloging-in-Publication data for this title is on file with the Library of Congress.

ISBN 978-0-520-09875-6 (pbk. : alk. paper)

The paper used in this publication meets the minimum requirements of ANSI/NISO Z39.48-1992 (R 1997) (Permanence of Paper).

To my parents

Contents

List of Tables xiii

Acknowledgements xv

Abbreviations xvi

Abstract xvii

1. INTRODUCTION 1
   1.1 Ethnographic setting 1
   1.2 Genetic and areal relationships 3
   1.3 Fieldworkers and speakers 7
   1.4 Possible dialectal variation 10
   1.5 Sources and publications 10
   1.6 Grammatical sketch 13
   1.7 Organization of this work 14

2. PHONETICS AND PHONOLOGY 15
   2.1 Phoneme inventory and orthography 15
      2.1.1 Consonant inventory and allophonic variation 15
         2.1.1.1 Consonant inventory 15
         2.1.1.2 Stops, fricatives, and affricates 15
         2.1.1.3 Lack of voicing distinction 15
         2.1.1.4 Nasals, liquids, and approximants 15
         2.1.1.5 Orthography 15
         2.1.1.6 Phonetic realizations 15
         2.1.1.7 Allophonic variations 16
         2.1.1.8 Retroflex phonemes 16
         2.1.1.9 Speaker variation 17
         2.1.1.10 Minimal pairs 17
         2.1.1.11 Phonemic status of sounds 19
         2.1.1.12 Gemination 19
      2.1.2 Vowel inventory and allophonic variation 20
         2.1.2.1 Vowel inventory 20
         2.1.2.2 Minimal pairs 20
         2.1.2.3 Vowel length 20
         2.1.2.4 Diphthongs 21
         2.1.2.5 Creaky voice 22
   2.2 Syllable structure and phonotactic restrictions 22
      2.2.1 Syllable structure 22
      2.2.2 Structure of roots 23
      2.2.3 Phonotactic place and co-occurrence restrictions 24
         2.2.3.1 Phonotactic restrictions 24
         2.2.3.2 Possible consonant clusters 26

2.2.3.3 Geminate consonant clusters 26
2.2.3.4 Summary of phonotactic restrictions 27
2.3 Stress and prosody 27
2.3.1 Stress 27
2.3.2 Prosodic units 28
2.4 Sound symbolism 28
2.5 Phonetics and phonology in areal-typological perspective 28

3. MORPHOPHONEMIC ALTERNATIONS 33
3.1 Pronominal alternations 33
3.2 Negation and imperatives 36
3.2.1 Negation 36
3.2.1.1 Deletion of pronominal affix with *x-..-na* 36
3.2.1.2 Vowel backing and vowel assimilation with *x-..-na* 37
3.2.2 Imperatives 39
3.3 Other alternations 39
3.3.1 Stem shapes: Deletion of final vowel 39
3.3.2 Aspectual suffixes 39
3.3.3 Locative and directional affixes 40
3.3.4 Metathesis 41
3.3.5 Affixes with initial consonant clusters 42
3.3.6 Suffixes with the initial vowel /a/ 43
3.3.7 Suffixes with initial glottalized obstruents /k', c', č'/ or with /č/ 43
3.3.8 Possessive markers 44
3.3.9 The derivative -V^{ʔ} 45
3.4 Morphophonemics in areal-typological perspective 45

4. WORD CLASSES 47
4.1 Nouns 47
4.1.1 Common nouns and proper nouns 49
4.1.2 Placenames 50
4.2 Pronouns 51
4.2.1 Personal pronouns 51
4.2.2 Interrogative pronouns 54
4.2.3 Demonstrative pronouns 55
4.3 Demonstrative determiners 55
4.4 Adjectives 56
4.5 Numerals and quantifiers 57
4.5.1 Numerals 57
4.5.2 Quantifiers 60
4.6 Verbs 61
4.7 Adverbs 63
4.8 Closed small classes of words 65
4.8.1 Copula 66
4.8.2 Adpositions 66

4.8.3 Particles 67
4.8.4 Evidentials and discourse markers 68
4.8.5 Connectives 69
4.8.6 Interjections 69
4.8.7 Clitics 69
4.8.8 Other word classes 70
4.9 Word classes in areal-typological perspective 70

5. NOUN MORPHOLOGY 71
5.1 Inflectional morphology 71
5.1.1 Possession 71
5.1.2 Definite suffix 73
5.1.3 Locative suffixes 74
5.1.4 Nominative syntactic relations 75
5.1.4.1 Instrumental suffix *-mtu* 75
5.1.4.2 Comitative suffix *-owa* 75
5.1.5 Modal suffixes 75
5.1.6 Other nominal affixes 76
5.1.6.1 *-a* of uncertain meaning 76
5.1.6.2 *-ita* of uncertain meaning 76
5.1.6.3 *-oq* 'former, formerly' with temporal meaning 77
5.2 Derivational morphology 77
5.2.1 Derivational suffixes 77
5.2.1.1 Privative and exclusive suffixes 77
5.2.1.2 Diminutive suffix *-lla* 79
5.2.1.3 Derivational suffixes *-la, -lla, -lala* 80
5.2.1.4 Other derivational affixes 81
5.2.2 Compounding 82
5.2.3 Reduplication 82
5.2.4 Verbalization 83
5.3 Kinship terms 84
5.4 Placenames 85
5.5 Noun morphology in areal-typological perspective 86

6. PRONOUN MORPHOLOGY 89
6.1 Morphological structure of personal pronouns 89
6.2 Definite *-ot* with personal and demonstrative pronouns 90
6.3 Roots and affixes in demonstrative and interrogative pronouns 91
6.4 Verbalization 92
6.5 Pronoun morphology in areal-typological perspective 93

7. ADJECTIVE MORPHOLOGY 95
7.1 Verbal morphology with adjectival roots and stems 95
7.2 Comparatives and superlatives 96
7.3 Other suffixes 98

8. VERB MORPHOLOGY 99
8.1 Inflectional morphology 99
8.1.1 Pronominal reference 99
8.1.2 Tense and aspect 103
8.1.3 Mood 110
8.1.3.1 Interrogatives 112
8.1.3.2 Negation 113
8.1.3.3 Irrealis mood 114
8.1.3.4 Imperative and admonitive 118
8.1.3.5 Evidentials 120
8.1.3.6 Other modal suffixes 121
8.2 Derivational morphology 121
8.2.1 Reflexives and reciprocals 121
8.2.2 Applicatives 122
8.2.3 Causatives 124
8.2.4 Indefinite third person plural agent 125
8.2.4.1 *-teʔw/-deʔw* 125
8.2.4.2 *-tta/-ta* 126
8.2.5 Noun incorporation 126
8.2.6 Reduplication 127
8.2.7 Nominalization 131
8.2.8 Instrumental affixes 133
8.2.9 Directional affixes 134
8.2.10 Suffix *-ma* of unclear meaning 135
8.3 Verb morphology in areal-typological perspective 136

9. SIMPLE SENTENCES 141
9.1 Constituent order 141
9.2 Argument structure 145
9.2.1 Agents, patients, and person hierarchy 145
9.2.2 Transitivity 149
9.2.3 Core versus oblique 151
9.2.4 Argument structure alternations and voice 153
9.3 Intransitive sentences 157
9.3.1 Agents and patients 157
9.3.2 Predicate adjectives 158
9.3.3 Predicate nominals 159
9.4 Transitive sentences 161
9.5 Ditransitive sentences 162
9.6 Noun phrase 163
9.6.1 Definiteness 165
9.7 Verb phrases 166
9.7.1 Co-occurrence of pronominal, aspectual, and modal marking 166
9.7.2 Dependency 167
9.8 Sentence structure in areal-typological perspective 168

10. QUESTIONS 171
10.1 Yes/no questions 171
10.2 Question-word questions 172
10.3 Answers 174
10.4 Question formation in areal-typological perspective 176

11. NEGATION 177
11.1 Clausal negation 177
11.2 Negative imperatives and admonitives 178
11.3 Negative existential and possessive clauses 180
11.4 Negative conditionals 181
11.5 Negative questions and answers 182
11.6 Negation in areal-typological perspective 183

12. COMPLEX SENTENCES 185
12.1 Coordination 185
12.2 Complementation 185
12.2.1 Complementation strategies 186
12.2.1.1 Separate clauses 186
12.2.1.2 Verbal morphology 188
12.2.1.3 Attitude words 189
12.2.1.4 *imiˀna* 'to want' 190
12.3 Relative clauses 191
12.4 Adverbial clauses 194
12.4.1 Time, place, manner 194
12.4.2 Conditionals 195
12.5 Complex sentences in areal-typological perspective 197

13. DISCOURSE STRUCTURE 199
13.1 Couplets and information flow 199
13.2 Discourse structure in areal-typological perspective 203

14. SUMMARY: CHIMARIKO IN AREAL-TYPOLOGICAL PERSPECTIVE 205

Appendices 213
i. Narratives 213
i.i Introduction to the narratives 213
i.ii Fugitives at Burnt Ranch 213
i.iii Woman Wanders 215
i.iv Mrs Bussell 220
i.v Hollering at New River 221
i.vi Dailey Chased by the Bull 222
i.vii On Grandmother Getting the Hiccups 223
i.viii Cutting Finger When Cleaning Salmon 224
i.ix Cutting Navel 225

i.x Postnatal Seclusion 225
i.xi Hopping Game 226
i.xii Crawfish 227
ii. Transcript of sound recording 228

Bibliography 235

Tables

CHAPTER 1: INTRODUCTION
Table 1. Chimariko fieldwork in chronological order 7
Table 2. Different symbols used in Chimariko materials 12

CHAPTER 2: PHONETICS AND PHONOLOGY
Table 1. Consonant inventory 16
Table 2. Vowel system 20
Table 3. Characteristics of syllable structure 23
Table 4. Summary of phonotactic restrictions 27
Table 5. Phonemic characteristics of Chimariko and its immediate neighbors 29
Table 6. Characteristics of Chimariko and its distant neighbors to the (north-)west 30
Table 7. Characteristics of Chimariko and its distant neighbors to the east....30
Table 8. Characteristics of Northern California syllable structures 31

CHAPTER 3: MORPHOPHONEMIC ALTERNATIONS
Table 1. Verb stem classes....33
Table 2. Pronominal affixes for all verb stems....33
Table 3. Pronominal affix by verb stem class (following Harrington 020-1109) 34
Table 4. Pronominal affixes including initial stem vowel by verb stem class 34

CHAPTER 4: WORD CLASSES
Table 1. Chimariko placenames (from Bauman 1980) 50
Table 2. Personal pronouns....52
Table 3. Topical and contrastive pronouns 53
Table 4. Interrogative pronouns (Dixon, 1910:322; Harrington)....55
Table 5. Chimariko numerals....57
Table 6. Numeral systems in Northern California (from Haas 1976)....59

CHAPTER 5: NOUN MORPHOLOGY
Table 1. Possessive affixes....71
Table 2. The word for 'bull, cow' 83
Table 3. Possession in areal perspective 87

CHAPTER 6: PRONOUN MORPHOLOGY
Table 1. Definite and contrastive pronouns 89
Table 2. Interrogative pronouns (Dixon, 1910:322; Harrington)....91
Table 3. Pronoun shapes in Shasta and Chimariko 93

CHAPTER 8: VERB MORPHOLOGY
Table 1. Verb templates for inflectional morphology 99
Table 2. Pronominal affixes including initial stem vowel by verb stem class 100
Table 3. Pronominal affixes for all verb stems....100
Table 4. Distinctions in bound pronominal marking....100

Table 5. Person hierarchy in pronominal marking....102
Table 6. Temporal suffixes....103
Table 7. Aspectual suffixes....104
Table 8. Co-occurrence of *-xana* and *-kon* with other suffixes....106
Table 9. Modal affixes and clitics....111
Table 10. Conditional clauses....117
Table 11. Word formation with applicatives (from Grekoff 012.010)....123
Table 12. Instrumental affixes (Dixon 1910:329)....133
Table 13. Directional affixes....134
Table 14. Pronominal reference in Northern California....136
Table 15. Affixing pattern in tense/aspect/mood....137
Table 16. Reduplication in Northern California....138
Table 17. Directional and instrumental affixes....139

CHAPTER 9: SIMPLE SENTENCES
Table 1. Verb stems with first person patient markers (Grekoff 003.005)....157
Table 2. Verb stems with first person agent OR patient markers (Grekoff 003.005)....158

CHAPTER 10: QUESTIONS
Table 1. Interrogative pronouns (Dixon, 1910:322; Harrington)....172
Table 2. Question formation strategies in Northern California....176

CHAPTER 11: NEGATION
Table 1. Morpheme templates with negative affixes....178
Table 2. Negation strategies in Northern California....183
Table 3. Position of negative morpheme....184

CHAPTER 12: COMPLEX SENTENCES
Table 1. Conditional clauses....196

CHAPTER 14: SUMMARY
Table 1. Similarities between Chimariko and its close neighbors and Karuk....210

Acknowledgements

I am very grateful to the various people who have helped to shape this work. In particular, I wish to thank Marianne Mithun for her guidance and many detailed suggestions on earlier drafts of this work. Furthermore, I am especially thankful to Marianne Mithun for introducing me to the Harrington notes and for her constant encouragement and enthusiasm for the subject matter. I also highly appreciate the feedback given to me by Sandra A. Thompson, Matthew Gordon, and Dorothy Chun during the development of this project. In particular, I would like to thank Sandra A. Thompson for many insightful comments on previous versions of this work. I also wish to thank Matthew Gordon for his useful feedback on the phonetics and phonology chapter. Moreover, I would like to extend my thanks to Victor Golla for many valuable discussions in various e-mail exchanges. In addition, I am grateful to Andrew Garrett and two anonymous reviewers for their insightful feedback.

Many individuals I never met personally also contributed to this work. I am thankful to the last Chimariko speakers who worked tirelessly with John Peabody Harrington to leave a rich source of data to examine. I am also grateful to John Peabody Harrington for his collection of the Chimariko materials and to George Grekoff for his valuable and detailed notes on the language. Furthermore, I wish to thank the J. P. Harrington Database Project for sharing their work.

This work would not have been possible without the constant encouragement from my parents. I am mostly indebted to my parents for their continuing support in my education and projects.

I would also like to thank Jose Del Toro for his moral support in all my educational and professional endeavors and for encouraging me to pursue this work on the Chimariko language.

Abbreviations

A	Agent
ACCOMP	Comitative
ADM	Admonitive
APPL	Applicative
ASP	Aspect
CAUS	Causative
COLL	Collective
COMP	Completive
COND	Conditional
CONT	Continuative
DEF	Definite
DEP	Dependent
DER	Derivational
DET	Determiner
DIM	Diminutive
DIR	Directional
DUAL	Dual
EV	Evidential
EXCL	Exclusive
FUT	Future
HYPO	Hypothetical
IMP	Imperative
INF	Inferential
INST	Instrumental
LOC	Locative
MOD	Modal
NEG	Negative
NOM	Nominalizer
NUM	Number
P	Patient
PFUT	Potential future
PL	Plural
POSS	Possessive
PRED	Predicative
PRIV	Privative
PROG	Progressive
PRS	Present
PST	Past tense
Q	Interrogative
RECP	Reciprocal
REFL	Reflexive
SG	Singular

Abstract

One of the tasks typologists engage in is to discover what all languages share and how they can differ. The most striking feature of California and other Native American languages is the amount of information they package into their verbs. But what exactly makes languages the same or different? There are various influencing factors, such as genetic affiliation and language contact, among others. Often, it is difficult to distinguish shared linguistic features attributed to genetic affiliation from those attributed to language contact, in particular if there is an intense contact for centuries and if there are no written records, as in the case of Chimariko, a now extinct Northern California language.

The present work addresses this and other issues related to language contact and brings together all existing sources on Chimariko to: (1) compile a grammatical description, (2) examine language contact phenomena within Northern California, and (3) see how the linguistic structures and phenomena found in Chimariko relate to those in other languages of the world.

Published and unpublished materials on the Chimariko language and culture are limited to a brief grammatical sketch, a few articles, and handwritten notes from data collection sessions. This work combines these sources into a comprehensive grammatical description. The main source of data comes from 3500 pages of handwritten field notes collected by John Peabody Harrington in the 1920s.

The typological features of Chimariko include: (a) head-marking, (b) mainly suffixes, (c) mostly agglutinating, (d) synthetic to polysynthetic, (e) verb-final word order, and (f) no preference in the order of nominal elements. Typological highlights are: (a) the complex system of argument marking and (b) the near absence of clause combining syntax.

Similarities and language contact phenomena between Chimariko and other Northern California languages include: (a) phoneme inventory, (b) stress system, (c) reduplication, (d) distinction between alienable and inalienable possession, (e) noun incorporation, (f) directional and instrumental suffixes on verbs, and (g) agentive and/or hierarchical person marking, among others.

Overall, this work makes a previously inaccessible language accessible in the form of a grammar and examines typologically rare features and language contact.

1. INTRODUCTION

1.1 Ethnographic setting

The Chimariko language was spoken in the nineteenth century in a few small villages in Trinity County, in north-western California. The villages were located along a twenty-mile stretch of the Trinity River and parts of the New River and South Fork River. In 1849, the Chimariko numbered around two hundred and fifty people. They were nearly extinct in 1906, except for a 'toothless old woman and a crazy old man', as well as 'a few mixed bloods' (Kroeber 1925:109). The 'toothless old woman' Kroeber refers to was most likely Polly Dyer and the 'crazy old man' Dr. Tom, also identified by Dixon (1910:295) as a 'half-crazy old man'. The last speaker probably died in the 1940s.

First contact with European explorers occurred early in the nineteenth century, in the 1820s or 1830s, when fur trappers came to the region. However, the tribe was left largely unaffected by this encounter (Dixon 1910:297). During the Gold Rush in the 1850s the Chimariko territory was overrun by gold seekers. Continuous gold mining activities in the region threatened the salmon supply, the main food source of the tribe, and led to a bitter conflict in the 1860s (Silver 1978a:205). The fights between European miners and the tribe resulted in the near annihilation of the Chimariko in the 1860s. The few survivors took refuge with the neighboring Shasta on the upper Salmon River or in Scott Valley or with the Hupa to the northwest (Dixon 1910:297). Once the gold was gone and the miners left the region, the survivors returned to their homes after years in exile (Silver 1978a:205).

The exact boundaries of the Chimariko territory are uncertain, as systematic ethnographic investigations started many years after the tribe's near extinction in the 1860s (Bauman 1980:12). While it remains undisputed that the Chimariko lived along a twenty-mile stretch of the Trinity River roughly from the mouth of South Fork to French Creek, the extensions of their territory to stretches along the South Fork River and the New River have been questioned. Bauman (1980) provides a detailed account of their territory by examining place names and information obtained from Chimariko and other consultants. He concludes that the Chimariko originally extended along the lower New River, the Trinity River, the South Fork River, and the Hayfork River (1980:24). Dixon (1910:297) and Silver (1978a:205) mention six known villages along the Trinity River: Cedar Flat *hotinakčohota*, Hawkin's Bar *ˀamaitace*, Taylor's Flat *čʰičʰanma*, Big Bar *šitimaače*, Salyer *mamsuˀče*, and Burnt Ranch *čutamtače*, the latter being the largest. In addition, the Chimariko had temporary hunting camps on the New River and in other foreign territory (Dixon 1910:297; Silver 1978a:205).

The neighbors of the Chimariko to the north on the lower New River were the Chimalakwe. It remains unclear whether the Chimalakwe were part of the Chimariko tribe or identical with it. Powers (1877:92) asserts that the two groups spoke the same language. Dixon (1910:296) points out that their name is unquestionably derived from the same stem *č'imar* or *č'imal*. Merriam (1930) considered the Chimalakwe and the New River Shasta living on the New River together to form a distinct group based on thirty-five words he secured from Saxey Kidd (see 1.3). Dixon (1931), however, presents evidence against this hypothesis. By the time European explorers entered the region, the Chimalakwe were being conquered and absorbed by the Hupa. Only about twenty-five speakers were left (Silver 1978a:205). The Chimalakwe were extinct by 1872 (Silver 1978a:205).

Two other small tribes were also neighbors to the north: the New River Shasta on the upper New River and the Konomihu on the Salmon River. Both spoke Shastan languages. The Shastan people include four groups: Shasta, Konomihu, Okwanuchu, and New River Shasta (Silver 1978b:211). Dixon (1910:306) believes the Chimariko to be culturally and linguistically related most closely to the Shastan people. This may result from the fact that the Chimariko spent years in exile with the Shasta before becoming Dixon's consultants. Consequently, they had been culturally and linguistically in closest contact with that group.

The Wintu were neighbors to the south and east of the Chimariko. The Wintu, Nomlaki, and Patwin languages comprise the Wintuan family, a family included in the hypothesized Penutian stock. The Wintu suffered a fate similar to that of the Chimariko during the Gold Rush in the 1850s. Yet, as they numbered over three thousand in 1852 (LaPena 1978:324), the Wintu have managed to escape extinction. At the time of contact with European explorers, the Chimariko were on friendly terms with the Wintu. At an earlier time, they may have lost some of their territory to the Wintu (Silver 1978a:205). Kroeber (1925) and Dixon (1910) noted cultural similarities between the two groups, suggesting a close contact. The Chimariko, for instance, followed the Wintu in the manner of playing the guessing game (Kroeber 1925:111). The import of red and black obsidian from the Wintu is evidence of a trading relationship.

To the west and northwest of the Chimariko were the Hupa and the Whilkut or Redwood Creek Indians (Silver 1978a:205). They spoke different Hupa dialects. Hupa is an Athapaskan language of the Pacific Coast branch. The Hupa numbered only about a thousand in 1850 and shared a distinctive way of life with the neighboring Yurok and Karuk (Wallace 1978:164). The Chimariko feared the Hupa and fought against them (Dixon 191:305). According to Powers (1977:92), the Chimariko living on New River paid the Hupa a yearly tribute of an average of one deer-skin per capita. Nevertheless, intermarriage indicates some friendly interaction between the two tribes (Silver 1978a:205). Trading and social relationships existed in particular with the South Fork Hupa who inhabited the South Fork of the Trinity River (Wallace 1978: 177). Kroeber (1925:111) states that the Chimariko followed the Hupa in some of their customs, such as refusing to eat grasshoppers and angleworms, which were considered sufficiently nutritious by the Wintu. Equally, their form of tattooing was more similar to that of the Hupa than to that of the Wintu (Dixon 1910: 295).

Culturally, the Chimariko shared many traits with their neighbors and other Northern California tribes. In terms of social organization, the largest units were village communities, each having a chief. The social status of each person was determined by wealth and birth, as with the Hupa. Yet the Chimariko did not seem to have practiced slavery as the Hupa did. Each Chimariko village had dwelling houses (*awaˀ*) accommodating two or more families and a sweat house (*maˀtta)* where the men sweated and gambled. The houses were similar to those of the Hupa, but simpler. Chimariko clothing showed aspects of both Wintu and Hupa culture. Body ornaments were more restricted than among the Hupa. Tattooing was less elaborate than among the Wintu.

In general, the Chimariko were monogamous (Dixon 1910:301). A wife was usually bought from her parents, and marriage took place within a local group. After giving birth, a mother had to remain in seclusion for a few weeks and was subject to food restrictions (Dixon 1910:302). Seclusion and food restrictions were also part of the puberty ritual. An illness was cured either by a doctor sucking out the object and making it disappear or by a herb doctor who recited formulas and gave medicine internally. The dead were buried, and widows cut their hair short. More information on customs related to marriage, birth, puberty rituals, curing, and funerals can be found in Silver (1978a). The Chimariko practiced four kinds of ceremonies: a doctor-making ceremony, a girl's puberty ritual, a sweat-dance, and an annual summer dance. Dixon (1910:303) affirms that their ceremonies were more like those of the Shasta than like any of their other neighbors' ceremonies. They did not practice the first-salmon rite, the first-acorn rite, or the Deerskin Dance, all typical Hupa ceremonies. Chimariko men engaged in a variety of games, such as the 'guessing game' or the 'grass-game'.

The main food supply of the Chimariko was the salmon of the Trinity River. Eels were also an important source of food. In addition, the Chimariko ate deer, elk, bear, and other animals. Acorns were their main vegetable food. The men were responsible for hunting, using a variety of techniques for fishing and hunting: nets, traps, spears, baskets, and others. The Chimariko did not make canoes. They crossed the rivers by swimming or on simple rafts (Dixon 1910:300).

Little is known of Chimariko mythology. Regarding the creation, Dog was the most powerful being. He foretold the flood. When the flood came, only Frog, Mink, Otter, and one man survived. After the flood subsided, the man found a bone fragment which later came to life as a girl. The man married her, and the Chimariko descended from this union. Coyote also appears in some tales. The tales do not bear any close resemblance to those of the Hupa. There are some similarities to Wintu stories and even more similarities to Shasta narratives (Dixon 1910:305).

Overall, the Chimariko were a very small tribe prior to European contact. They were in close contact with their immediate neighbors, the Shasta, the Wintu, and the Hupa, through intermarriage and trade, suggesting a certain level of multilingualism. They also shared many cultural traits with their neighbors and with other Californian tribes.

1.2 Genetic and areal relationships

The Chimariko language has been genetically and areally linked to various neighboring languages. Genetically, it is considered by some linguists to be a Hokan language, along with its northern neighbor Shasta. Hokan is a linguistic stock based on a series of hypotheses about a distant genetic relationship among several languages of California and others. However, the long history of language contact, multilingualism, and intermarriage in California makes it difficult to distinguish distant genetic relationship from ancient language contact. Furthermore, the time depth of Hokan complicates the process of finding evidence of a relationship. Therefore, Chimariko is viewed as an isolate by linguists not yet convinced of the Hokan hypotheses. Areally, Chimariko is situated within the Northern California linguistic area along with its neighbors, the Hupa, Shasta, and Wintu, and with others. The well-established California culture area

(Driver 1962) consists of at least three linguistic areas: Northern California, Central or Northern-central California, and Southern California (Sherzer 1976b). The Northern California area is characterized by great genetic diversity. Regardless of whether Chimariko is genetically or areally linked to its neighbors, similarities and shared features are expected to occur due to the intimate and extended contact for centuries.

The possibility of a Hokan linguistic stock has generated wide interest ever since it was put forward. It has also been grounds for many discussions, due to the difficulties in finding supporting evidence. The Hokan stock was first proposed by Dixon and Kroeber (1913) who hypothesized a genetic relationship among five languages spoken in Northern California: Chimariko, Shasta, Karuk, Yana, and a Pomoan language. Their hypothesis was based mainly on five presumed cognate sets for 'eye', 'tongue', 'water', 'stone', and 'sleep'. In addition to the cognate sets, Dixon and Kroeber (1913) observed structural characteristics shared among the Hokan languages, such as the absence of a plural in most nouns, verb suffixes indicating plurality, instrumental verb prefixes and local suffixes, as well as affixed pronominal elements. Later, Dixon, Kroeber, Sapir, and others expanded the stock. By 1929, a total of thirteen languages or language families formed part of the Hokan stock: Karuk, Chimariko, Shastan, Achumawi-Atsugewi, Yana, Pomo, Washo, Esselen, Yuman, Salinan, Chumash, Seri, and Chontal, extending from Northern California to Mexico. Opinions on which languages should be included vary greatly. Based largely on lexical evidence, Kaufman (1988) came out in favor of a wide Hokan stock including Cochimi, Coahuilteco, Comecrudan, and Jicaquean, among others. The five languages and language families first defined by Dixon and Kroeber were subgrouped as Northern Hokan and further subdivided into Northern Hokan (a): Karuk, Chimariko, and Shasta, (b) Yana, and (c) Pomoan (Bright 1954). Following this subdivision, Chimariko is expected to be more closely related to Shasta and Karuk than to the other languages within the Hokan stock. Shasta, however, is also an immediate neighbor of Chimariko, and effects of language contact can be expected.

In addition to time depth, the Hokan hypotheses are problematic due to the close and extensive contact among these languages for centuries, making it very difficult to distinguish areal from genetic characteristics. It is almost impossible to apply the comparative method successfully to these languages, as evidence of a relationship decreases over time, and ideally there would be no contact among related languages after their split from a proto-language. Furthermore, poorly recorded materials, inconsistencies in spelling, and lack of materials for some of the languages weaken the Hokan proposals. Nevertheless, many linguists (Bright 1954, Crawford 1976, Haas 1954, 1963, 1964, Kaufmann 1988, McLendon 1974, Olmsted, 1956, 1957, 1959, 1965, Silver 1964, 1976, 1980) have tried to find more evidence for the Hokan stock since 1913, studying sound correspondences and reconstructing the proto-language through binary comparisons. Bright (1954) attempted to establish sound correspondences for the Northern Hokan languages. Crawford (1976) compared several cognate sets for Chimariko and Yuman, finding sound correspondences for vowels and consonants. As a result, he hypothesized a new subgrouping within Hokan connecting Chimariko and Yuman more closely. Despite all efforts and some encouraging results, only very limited details based on a few questionable cognates constitute the evidence available for a Hokan stock. Observed similarities are often unsystematic and occur only in small numbers of words. In view of the problematic issues connected to Hokan and outlined here, this work is not intended to prove or disprove a genetic relationship. Even so, this grammatical description of Chimariko, based on phonemically accurate materials and outlining similarities to neighboring languages, may serve as a basis for future Hokan studies which should also consider language contact phenomena.

Northern California is characterized by great genetic diversity with five major linguistic stocks and over twenty language families represented. Many of the languages were spoken by small groups, and there is a long history of contact. As a result, the languages share traits with their genetically unrelated neighbors. These traits have been studied by many linguists. Haas (1976) examined phonological features, numeral systems, and consonant symbolism, i.e. the substitution of one class of consonant by another related class for the purpose of expressing the diminutive or augmentative or to characterize the speech of myth characters. She concluded that 'most languages bear more resemblance to their adjacent unrelated neighbors than they do to their congeners' (1976:353). Sherzer (1976) provides a detailed list of areal features found in California. He asserts that the California culture area is best viewed as consisting of three linguistic areas: Northern California, Central or North-Central California, and Southern California. His Northern California traits include: lateral fricatives (which are not found in Chimariko), possessive prefixes (possessive prefixes are found on body parts in Chimariko), and tense-aspect prefixes (tense-aspect markers are suffixed in Chimariko). In addition to the features found in Northern California, Chimariko shows North-Central traits identified by Sherzer, such as retroflex apical sounds. This indicates that Sherzer's areas overlap. Conathan (2004) examined the linguistic effects and sociolinguistic context of language contact in Northwestern California. Among the language contact features she studied are diminutive consonant symbolism, similarities in numeral systems and in directional terminology, reduplication marking repetitive aspect, second person prominence in argument marking, the presence of numeral classifiers, preverbal particles marking tense, aspect and mood, verb initial word order, frequent loan translations, and shared euphemisms. Conathan suggests that the effects of language contact can be observed at the level of morphosyntax, but not in lexical borrowing or as local phonological convergence. According to Conathan, the contact phenomena in Northern California show a 'functional convergence', i.e. they involve an increasing similarity in the semantic and pragmatic categories expressed, but not in surface syntax. Analyzing spatial and temporal dimensions in Northwestern California, O'Neill (2001) found that while there is a common geographical orientation with mountains and rivers as primary points of reference, as well as a common orientation to the world of time, the languages of the area differ in how they express these concepts in their grammars. Mithun (in press) examined the diffusion patterns of core argument marking in Northern California and demonstrated how person hierarchies have resulted from language contact. Following Mithun, hierarchical systems did not develop through the direct transfer of grammatical structure; rather they resulted from an increased tendency of choosing one stylistic option, whereby low-ranked agents are eliminated through passivization, over another. Chimariko, one of the languages Mithun studied, has a hierarchical system favoring speech act participants, i.e. first and second person, over third persons. In another study, Mithun (2008) showed how agentive core argument systems could have developed through the reanalysis of nominative-accusative patterns in situations where third person pronominal markers are omitted and where there is no overt marking of transitivity. Agentive systems are rare cross-linguistically but there is a strong areal distribution in North America. They are found in two areas of Northern California: on the Northwest Coast and in the Southeast (Mithun 2008). Chimariko distinguishes between agents and patients for first persons. Apart from Chimariko, agentive systems are found in Karuk, Yuki, and Pomoan languages in Northern California. Overall, California is characterized by much linguistic diversity in a relatively small area where many linguistic traits have distributions which cut across genetic boundaries. Many of these areal traits and some diffusion processes have been described in previous literature.

In addition to the linguistic outcomes of language contact, some scholars (Bright 1976; Sherzer 1976) have examined the sociolinguistic conditions characterizing the particular language contact situation found in California. California had a great population density prior to European contact. There were many small communities, all speaking different languages. Neighboring groups had good relationships with one another, and there was a considerable amount of trade, intermarriage, and bilingualism (Sherzer 1976). While the relationships with immediate neighbors were intimate, contact with distant groups was practically nonexistent (Sherzer 1976). This suggests that shared features due to language contact are more likely to be found in languages of adjacent groups. Bright (1976) studied the processes and effects of bilingualism and linguistic acculturation between native languages and between native and European languages. Following Bright, the outcomes of these two language contact situations differ greatly. Contrary to contact between native languages, contact between native and European languages resulted in little phonological borrowing and almost no grammatical borrowing. The amount and type of borrowing is determined by sociocultural rather than by linguistic facts (Bright 1976). Hence, little influence from European languages (i.e. English and Spanish) is expected in the Chimariko data, while borrowing from neighboring languages may be pervasive. Sherzer (1976) suggests that the intimate contact between immediate neighbors may result in the borrowing of folktales, expressive behaviour, and most aspects of language. Therefore, Chimariko is compared in detail to its close neighbors, the Wintu, Hupa, and Shasta in this work.

Linguistic areas must be internally coherent and distinctive with respect to languages outside of the area. Rather than finding proof for the Northern California linguistic area, this work intends to identify similarities between Chimariko and its neighboring languages and to describe possible patterns of diffusion. Such similarities may appear in categories, constructions, meanings, or in the actual forms used to express them. There are many different types of linguistic borrowing, such as the borrowing of a grammatical system, of linguistic processes, syntactic constructions, semantic patterns, or pragmatic patterns, among others. While the diffusion of forms is unsystematic and may be used for gap filling, the borrowing of patterns tends to be systematic, may serve to minimize syntactic differences, and is often difficult to distinguish from independent development (Aikhenvald 2005). In this work, Chimariko forms and patterns are compared to those of neighboring languages. Contact-induced changes can depend on the structure of the languages involved and on the kind of contact and the sociolinguistic environment (Aikhenvald 2005). With respect to the Chimariko sociolinguistic environment, it is worth noting that at the time of European contact the Chimariko were tributary to the larger and more powerful Hupa, as were many other tribes of the area. This relationship may be reflected in the outcome of this particular language contact situation. Chimariko may have adopted more Hupa features than the reverse. To conclude, this grammatical description lays the ground for future genetic and areal studies involving Chimariko, rather than offering an analysis of the Hokan linguistic stock or of the Northern California linguistic area.

1.3 Fieldworkers and speakers

Fieldwork on Chimariko was conducted in the late nineteenth and early twentieth century when only a few speakers of limited fluency were left. The first known data collection consisting of about two hundred words is found in Powers' 'Tribes of California' (1877:474-7). In 1889, Curtin compiled a Chimariko vocabulary from 'Old Tom' while working on Hupa (Curtin 1940). 'Old Tom', also called Dr. Tom, later served as a consultant for Kroeber (Dixon 1910:363). Systematic fieldwork on Chimariko began with Kroeber in 1901 and 1902 (Bauman 1980:13). Around the same time Goddard obtained data from another speaker, Sally Noble. The materials collected by Powers, Kroeber, and Goddard were later incorporated into Dixon's 'The Chimariko Indians and Language' (1910). Dixon worked in 1906 for two months with Polly Dyer and with Friday, who had also worked with Kroeber. He recorded vocabulary items, phrases, and narratives for a grammatical sketch. Several years later, in 1920 and 1921, Merriam recorded a short wordlist from Sally Noble, Lucy Montgomery, and Abe L. Bush. Some of his notes are published (Merriam 1979). The most extensive fieldwork was carried out by Harrington in 1921 with Sally Noble. Although Merriam and Harrington had planned joint work on Chimariko in 1921, the two researchers travelled to the region at different times and worked separately. Harrington later returned to collect additional data from Lucy Montgomery and others. He never published any of his materials, but his handwritten notes are available on microfilm (Mills 1985). In 1927, Sapir worked for a few days on Chimariko during a field trip to the Hupa. The data collected by Sapir have been edited by Berman and published in Golla and O'Neill (2001). The various fieldworkers and their consultants are summarized in Table 1. More details on the collected data can be found in 1.5.

Table 1: Chimariko fieldwork in chronological order

Year	Fieldworker	Consultants
1875	Stephen Powers	A woman from Martin's Ferry, Trinity River
1889	Jeremiah Curtin	Old Tom
1901-1902	Alfred L. Kroeber	Dr. Tom, Friday
1902	Pliny E. Goddard	Sally Noble
1906	Roland B. Dixon	Polly Dyer, Friday
1920-1921	C. Hart Merriam	Abe L. Bush, Sally Noble, Lucy Montgomery
1921	John Peabody Harrington	Sally Noble
1926	John Peabody Harrington	Lucy Montgomery
1927	Edward Sapir	Saxey Kidd, Abe Bush, Martha Ziegler
1928	John Peabody Harrington	Abe Bush, Lucy Montgomery, Saxey Kidd

In general, the fieldworkers were familiar with previously recorded data, and often re-elicited or incorporated these materials. The largest amount of linguistic data was collected by Dixon and Harrington. Dixon included the vocabularies recorded by Powers, Kroeber, and Goddard in his description, whereas Harrington re-elicited the materials published by Dixon.

Dixon was an anthropologist who published in the fields of ethnography, ethnology, archaeology, linguistics, and folklore (Tozzer and Kroeber 1947). He conducted extensive fieldwork with different tribes in northern California. As a result, his description of Chimariko contains valuable ethnographic data, in addition to the grammatical sketch. Nevertheless, Dixon was not a trained linguist, nor was he rigorously grounded in phonetics. Given this, and the fact that his consultant Polly Dyer was lacking teeth, his data are phonetically flawed.

Harrington documented numerous Native American languages under the auspices of the Bureau of American Ethnology for nearly half a century. He had a good ear for phonetics and left behind many accurate notes on languages now extinct. He first became interested in California Indian languages under the influence of Kroeber and Goddard (Stirling 1963:371), both also Chimariko fieldworkers. During his lifetime, Harrington collected close to a million pages of notes on more than a hundred and twenty-five separate languages of California, as well as many sound recordings. His Chimariko notes, comprising several thousand pages are of great value, as they represent the largest data collection on the language. Details about his Chimariko data are provided in 1.5. More information on Harrington can be found in Golla (1991) and Klar (2002).

The various fieldworkers often used the same consultants, some of whom were related. Sally Noble and Martha Ziegler were half-sisters. They were Polly Dyer's daughters from different marriages. Lucy Montgomery was a cousin of Sally Noble. Abe Bush's mother was a cousin of Polly Dyer. The consultants had varying degrees of fluency in Chimariko, and some had only a passive knowledge. Many were fluent in at least Hupa, Wintu, or Shasta. Following is a detailed description of each consultant's linguistic background and family history where known.

Dr. Tom was a full-blood Chimariko. He was from Burnt Ranch at least on his father's side and maybe on his mother's side as well. Yet, he lived until middle life on the New River (Bauman 1980:14). It seems that after he had worked with Curtin and Kroeber, he suffered some mental deterioration. Dixon (1910:295) described him as a 'half-crazy old man'. At the time of data collection he was living with the Hupa. Curtin (1940) noted that Tom was 'the only Chimariko at Hoopa'.

According to Dixon (1910:307), Friday was not a Chimariko but spoke the language fluently because he had lived with the tribe for much of his life. He was half Hupa and half Wintu by birth (1910:295). Bauman (1980:27) claims that Friday was Chimariko on his father's side and notes that Dixon's erroneous comment came from a misinterpretation by Kroeber. Kroeber seems to have associated Friday's statement that his father was half Hyampom and half Burnt Ranch with Wintu parentage, based on the conception that Hyampom was a Wintu speaking area. However, both Wintu and Chimariko consultants agreed that someone from Hyampom was typically Chimariko (Bauman 1980:27). In any case, Friday was raised primarily as a Hupa speaker by his mother. He spoke very little Chimariko and also knew some Wintu (Bauman 1980:27).

Polly Dyer was a full-blood Chimariko born and raised at Taylor's Flat on the Trinity River. When Dixon recorded his data from her she was a 'failing old woman of about eighty years of age, living on lower New River' (Dixon 1910:295) who was lacking teeth.

Sally Noble was Polly Dyer's daughter. She was probably born at North Fork and raised elsewhere. Apparently she was classified as White, which indicates that her knowledge of Chimariko must have originated with her mother (Bauman 1980:14). When Harrington collected data from Sally Noble, she was living on the New River. Harrington described her as having an almost exhaustive knowledge of Chimariko. She also had some familiarity with Hupa, and she knew some Wintu terms (Mills 1985:49). Sally Noble died shortly after Harrington left in 1922.

Lucy Montgomery was a cousin of Sally Noble. She lived at Stone Lagoon when the data were recorded from her by Merriam and later by Harrington. She had stopped speaking Chimariko at age eleven and had only a passive knowledge.

Abe Bush was born at Hayfork and came to Hyampom when he was four years old. His mother was a full-blood Chimariko raised at Taylor's Flat. She was a cousin of Polly Dyer. When Sapir recorded the data from Abe Bush in 1927 he was about seventy years old and lived at Oak Flat, Hyampom. At that time, he had not heard Chimariko for fifty years. Abe Bush never spoke Chimariko thoroughly, but understood it (Berman 2001:1040). Contrary to Berman, Bauman (1980:16) indicates that Abe Bush had not spoken Chimariko in fifty years when Sapir worked with him, but that he 'undoubtedly heard it spoken until at least 1906 when his mother died'. Abe Bush used Wintu to communicate with other Indian elders in the area. He died in the 1930s.

Remarks about Saxey ('Saxy' in Bauman 1980) Kidd's background are somewhat inconsistent. Bauman (1980:14) describes him as half Hupa and half Chimariko. Berman (2001:1040) provides the most details indicating that Saxey Kidd was born a New River Shasta, was raised among the Hupa after his parents were killed by gold miners, and also lived with the Chimariko. As a result, he was fluent in Hupa, knew only a few words of New River Shasta, and spoke a little Chimariko. Sapir noted that the little Chimariko he knew was 'distorted by his Hupa phonetics' (Golla and O'Neill 2001:1090). Merriam identified Saxey Kidd as a full-blood New River Indian raised among the Hupa. According to Merriam (1930:280), Saxey Kidd had also lived with the Chimariko and spoke their language. At the time of Sapir's fieldwork he lived in Salyer.

Martha Ziegler was Polly Dyer's daughter and Sally Noble's half sister. Her maiden name was Dyer (Berman 2001:1040). As with Sally Noble, apparently she was White, which indicates that her knowledge of Chimariko must have originated with her mother (Bauman 1980:14). Her name has been spelled in various ways: Ziglar (Sapir's fieldnotes), Ziegler (Sapir's letter to Harrington), or Zieglar (Mills 1985:54).

Fieldwork on Chimariko was done after the tribe's near extinction in the 1860s with some of the few survivors. Only two of them, Polly Dyer and Dr. Tom, seem to have been full-blood Chimariko. By the time of the data collection, many of the consultants had not actively spoken the language in years or decades, and they were fluent in other indigenous languages of the area. As a result, the collected data needs to be viewed with caution, given that influence from other indigenous languages such as Hupa, Wintu, and Shasta seems likely due to intense language contact and multilingualism at the time of data collection and prior to it.

1.4 Possible dialectal variation

According to Langdon (1974:18) and based on Powell (1891), there were two different dialects. One was spoken by the Chimariko who lived on the Trinity River, the other by the Chimalakwe on the New River, a branch of the Trinity River. For more information on the Chimalakwe see 1.1.

Possible dialectal variation was also noted by Dixon (1910:309), but he stated that the opportunity for determining it with any certainty was lacking, as one of his consultants did not have any teeth and the other was not a native Chimariko. Dixon mainly observed the confusion between the [l] and [r] sounds. Phonetic differences between the various consultants were also noted by Sapir. They are described in detail in Berman (2001:1040-46).

Sapir was interested in finding evidence for dialectal differences in Chimariko and said in a letter to Harrington that Friday's dialect was 'not quite the same as that of Mrs. Dyer, Dr. Tom, and presumably Mrs. Noble', but that Friday's material 'seems to agree better' with what he collected from Abe Bush (Golla and O'Neill 2001:1092). Sapir concluded that this was a hint of a Trinity River dialect and New River dialect different from a South Fork dialect. However, Sapir used Dixon's phonetically poor data for comparison. Harrington followed up on Sapir's hint and suggested that 'dialects there must have been, at least to some very limited extent', but that they could not 'make much out of them at this late day'. He also mentioned that Mrs. Noble called Friday 'uncle' and used to quote him, and that these quotes sounded exactly the same as her speech, hence contradicting Sapir's hint. Harrington concluded that as Friday and Abe Bush's mother used to 'hang out around the Dyer outfit all the time', they all 'talked exactly the same'.

Kroeber recorded data from Dr. Tom, who affirmed that his language was spoken up to the New River, and that it was different from the speech of Burnt Ranch (Bauman 1980:14). Nevertheless, the scarcity of data available and the limited fluency of the consultants at the time the linguistic materials were collected, given that Chimariko was no longer actively spoken in a community at that period, leave the possibility of dialectal variation uncertain. Recorded differences could also be attributed to possible interference from other languages.

1.5 Sources and publications

A very limited number of publications have resulted from the fieldwork on Chimariko. The only grammatical description is found in Dixon (1910). The grammar treats phonetics, word formation processes, pronouns, verbal and nominal stems and affixes, adjectives, numerals, and word order. Rather than providing linguistic analyses, Dixon often just lists words or affixes in a section of his grammar. Furthermore, the grammar is sketchy and does not treat all grammatical topics. Clause combining, for example, is not described. In addition, Dixon's data are phonemically flawed, as noted by Sapir and others. Due to Dixon's phonemic inaccuracies, his data are used solely in a supplementary way for this work. Nonetheless, Dixon's grammar includes a vocabulary and glossed narratives, which have proven useful. Dixon also examines Chimariko culture and compares it to neighboring tribes. He notes that the Chimariko shared many cultural traits with their neighbors and other Northern California tribes. Berman (2001) describes the Chimariko data collected by Sapir. He mentions phonetic interspeaker variation and provides lists of pronominal, instrumental, and other verbal affixes. These materials have likewise been used in a complementary manner.

The main materials for this work come from Harrington's field notes, thousands of handwritten pages available on microfilm. Harrington worked for five months with Sally Noble in 1921 and later returned in 1926 and 1928 to continue his documentation with other speakers (see 1.3). The field notes from Sally Noble are most valuable and consist of vocabulary items, elicited sentences and verb forms, and textual material with free translations. In addition to that, there are grammatical analyses. Harrington's Chimariko data, 3500 pages on five microfilm reels, are the most extensive and reliable source for the language. The first microfilm reel with data from Sally Noble contains 1168 pages with mainly lexical items and sentences with translations. Much of this information was elicited by Harrington using Dixon's grammatical sketch (Dixon 1910). Also included are grammatical analyses in the form of charts, in particular verbal affixes and pronominal elements. The second reel, with 539 pages, also containing data collected from Sally Noble, consists of a series of texts, some with interlinear free translations. Some of these texts were re-elicited from Dixon's grammatical sketch. The third reel comprises mainly single vocabulary items with translations. The fourth reel, with 1175, pages contains a rehearing of the notes from the first reel with a different and less fluent speaker, Lucy Montgomery. The fifth reel has ethnographic notes and short interviews. For this work, the first two microfilm reels represent the main source. A few of the narratives on the second reel, where provided with interlinear translations by Harrington, have been glossed to the extent possible using all available sources, including the vocabularies and lists of affixes in Dixon (1910) and Berman (2001) (see appendices).

Only a few linguists have studied Chimariko, most using Dixon's grammatical sketch as their source of data. One linguist working with the Harrington data was George Grekoff, who examined Chimariko continuously from the 1950s until his death in 1999. He left a large number of notes, housed today at the Survey of California and other American Indigenous languages at Berkeley. Grekoff meticulously studied Harrington's data and incorporated materials from all other available sources. In addition to Harrington's extensive corpus, Grekoff's unpublished notes, in particular a draft of an unfinished chapter on phonology, have been a valuable source for this work.

Apart from the written materials, there are two short Chimariko sound recordings. One contains a song performed by a Wintu speaker, and the other consists of words elicited from Martha Ziegler (see 1.3). At the time of the recording Martha Ziegler was an elderly woman struggling to remember a few words. Some of the words were re-elicited during the recording, which lasts about 13 minutes (see appendices). Unfortunately, the quality of the sound recording is too poor for detailed phonetic analysis.

The published sources and unpublished handwritten materials available on Chimariko are sometimes problematic. The lack of phonemic consistency across sources and the lack of systematic organization and presentation make it difficult to use them as reference. The incorporation of examples from diverse sources is often complicated by the fact that there has been no accord as to how Chimariko should be written. Each source uses different symbols, and no standard orthography has been established so far. Table 2 summarizes the symbols used in different sources and indicates the symbols adopted here. Apart from the affricates and the retroflex stops mostly IPA symbols are used in this work.

Table 2: Different symbols used in Chimariko materials

This work	IPA	Harrington[1]	Grekoff[2]	Sapir[3]	Dixon
p	p	p	p	p	p
p'	p'	p’	p̓	p’	-
pʰ	pʰ	p‘	ph/pʰ	p‘	p‘
t	t	t	t	t	t
t'	t'	t’	t̓	t’	-
tʰ	tʰ	t‘	th/tʰ	t‘	t‘
ṭ	ʈ	tr	ṭ	tṛ/tʸ	tr
ṭ'	ʈ'	tr’	ṭ̓	tṛ’/t’ʸ	-
ṭʰ	ʈʰ	tr‘/trh	ṭh/ ṭʰ	tṛ‘/t‘ʸ	-
k	k	k	k	k	k
k'	k'	k’	k̓	k’	-
kʰ	kʰ	k‘	kh/kʰ	k‘	k‘
q	q	K	ḳ/q	q	q
q'	q'	K’	ḳ̓ /q’	q’	-
qʰ	qʰ	K‘	ḳh/qʰ	q‘	q‘
ʔ	ʔ	’ (#__, V__)	ʔ	ʔ	’
c	ts	ts	-	ts	ts
c'	ts'	ts’	c̓	t’s	-
cʰ	tsʰ	ts‘	-	ts‘	-
č	ʧ	ʧ/tc (Berman)	č	tc	tc
č'	ʧ'	ʧ'/tc’ (Berman)	č̓	t’c	-
čʰ	ʧʰ	ʧ‘/ʧh/tc‘ (Berman)	čh/čʰ	tc‘	tc‘
s	s	s	s	s	s
š	ʃ	ʃ/c (Berman)	š	c	c
x	x	q	x	x	x
x̣	χ	R/χ	x̣	x̣	x/r
h	h	h/‘	h	h (__V) / ‘ (__C, __#)	h

[1] See also Crawford (1976:177-8)

[2] See Grekoff's phoneme inventory in Grekoff 009.004

[3] The symbols are based on Berman (2001). See also Abe Bush's phoneme inventory (Berman 2001:1041)

As can be seen in Table 2, the sound inventories represented in the different sources vary. Dixon's inventory is less elaborate than the others. He does not distinguish a separate set of glottalized consonants, which makes his data phonemically inaccurate. Grekoff does not list the plain and the aspirated alveolar affricate in his phoneme inventory, most likely due to the absence of sufficient proof for these two phonemes. Overall, the main difference between the sources lies in the representation of the apical sounds and the affricates.

1.6 Grammatical sketch

Chimariko is a head-marking language. Core arguments are obligatorily marked on the verb and possession is marked on the possessed. Case-marking occurs only with instruments and companions. Other nominal syntactic relations are unmarked. With regard to fusion, Chimariko appears to be mostly agglutinating. In general, word-internal morpheme boundaries are easily recognizable. Roots and affixes are clearly separable with one exception: most verb roots have an initial vowel which sometimes fuses with certain prefixes. However, fusion may be harder to detect given the limited nature of the data. It could occur in the tense-aspect marking which is not fully understood. Chimariko is mainly suffixing, but personal pronouns and possessors are either prefixed or suffixed. In terms of synthesis, Chimariko is synthetic to polysynthetic. There are many different verbal affixes, and verbs are often composed of three or more morphemes. Yet, sometimes only two or three morphemes occur in one verb, and there are numerous mono-morphemic words. As for basic word order, Chimariko seems to be verb final, though the limited amount and kind of data does not yield a clear picture. With regard to the order of nominal elements within a noun phrase, the modifier either precedes or follows the modified with no apparent preference or restrictions.

Chimariko exhibits a number of interesting typological features. A typologically uncommon feature is the complex system of argument marking based on agents and patients, as well as a hierarchy favoring speech act participants over third persons. Both, agentive and hierarchical argument systems have strong areal distributions (Mithun 2008, Mithun in press) and are found in other Northern California languages. Chimariko also shares a large consonant inventory, mainly consisting of obstruents, with other languages in the area. Interesting is the absence of a voicing distinction for obstruents, also lacking in many other North American languages. Other areal features found in Chimariko include: a distinction between alienable and inalienable possession, reduplication, noun incorporation, and locative, directional, and instrumental affixes on verbs.

Larger structures and clause combining strategies also show some typologically striking properties. Argument structure alternations, comparable to passives in other languages, shape core argument structure only semantically. They are achieved through verbal derivational affixes. Grammatical structures indicating clause combining surface only minimally. They occur with relative clauses and with adverbial clauses. Relative clauses are internally headed or headless and show a special verb form with a nominalizing suffix. In general, there is no morphosyntactic complementaion in Chimariko. The semantic concepts expressed as complements in some languages are coded using one of four different strategies: (1) separate sentences with no linking morphology, (2) verbal morphology, (3) attitude words, and (4) *imiʔna* 'to want' with a complement clause. The textual material studied exhibits a special style with many word and clausal repetitions, whereby a basic statement is followed by successive elaborations. It seems likely that such elaborations were linked intonationally to the basic clause. However, while intonation may have played a role in discourse structure, clause combining, and elsewhere in the language, it can not be examined here due to the lack of textual sound recordings.

1.7 Organization of this work

The Chimariko grammar is divided into twelve main sections: phonetics and phonology, morphophonemic alternations, word classes, noun morphology, pronoun morphology, adjective morphology, verb morphology, simple sentences, questions, negation, complex sentences, and discourse structure. Given the complex morphology of Chimariko, many different sections of the grammar are dedicated to the functions and forms of morphemes. While there are certainly enough data available for a grammatical description of Chimariko, some topics, such as phonetics, are treated in less detail due to the nature and limited amount of data.

A comparison of Chimariko to neighboring languages, in particular Wintu, Hupa, and Shasta, is conducted for each grammatical topic. This is summarized in a separate section after each of the twelve main parts of the grammar. Similarities between Chimariko and its neighboring languages, as well as the main typological characteristics, are discussed in the final section of this work.

The examples used in this grammar are based on three sources of data: (1) Harrington (1921, 1926, 1928), (2) Grekoff (1950-1999), and (3) Dixon (1910). The source is indicated for each example. The orthography and translations of the examples are kept the same as in the respective source to avoid any misrepresentations, except for the Harrington data where the symbols have been adapted (see Table 2). Incomplete translations, sometimes found in the Harrington data, are complemented with information in brackets. Given that the orthography of the examples is carried over from the source, some examples do not reflect a phonemic writing system; in particular allophonic voiced stops are found frequently in the data (see 2.1.1.7). The glossing of the examples is provided by the author and is consistent throughout the grammar. A number of morphemes cannot be analyzed due to the nature and limited amount of data. These morphemes are glossed with question marks.

2. PHONETICS AND PHONOLOGY

2.1 Phoneme inventory and orthography

The Chimariko phoneme inventory is very similar to that of its neighbors, having a complex consonant system and a simple vowel system. It is based on Harrington's data collected from Sally Noble.

2.1.1 Consonant inventory and allophonic variation

Chimariko has a complex consonant inventory and shows some typologically common allophonic variations.

2.1.1.1 Consonant inventory. Chimariko has a large consonant inventory with 33 phonemes: 27 obstruents and 6 sonorants. Not all phonemes have been attested for all speakers (see Berman 2001 and Grekoff 1950-1999).

2.1.1.2 Stops, fricatives, and affricates. Stops occur in three series: plain, ejective, and aspirated. They distinguish five places of articulation: bilabial, alveolar, post-alveolar, velar, and uvular. There is also a phonemic glottal stop. Fricatives are found in five places of articulation: alveolar, palato-alveolar, velar, uvular, and glottal. Affricates equally occur in three series: plain, ejective, and aspirated in two places of articulation: alveolar and palato-alveolar.

2.1.1.3 Lack of voicing distinction. Noticeable is the lack of a voicing distinction for stops, fricatives, and affricates. In general, voice is not distinctive. While obstruents are always voiceless, all sonorants are voiced. This is a common feature in large areas of North America.

2.1.1.4 Nasals, liquids, and approximants. Nasals occur in bilabial and alveolar position. Liquids and approximants include an alveolar rhotic, an alveolar lateral, and two glides in velar and palato-alveolar position. Grekoff (008.004) classifies /w/ as a back consonant rather than labial based on distributional restrictions which associate /w/ with the back high vowel /u/.

2.1.1.5 Orthography. Table 1 illustrates this inventory. The symbols are represented according to IPA standards. Where the orthography differs from the IPA standards, the symbol is included to the right in cursive. This applies to the retroflex stops, the affricates, the palato-alveolar fricative and approximant, and to the uvular fricative.

2.1.1.6 Phonetic realizations. The actual realizations of these phonemes remain unclear given the scarcity and quality of sound recordings and the limited fluency of speakers at the time of data collection. In particular the post-alveolar phonemes show variation across speakers and in the way they have been described by different fieldworkers (see Berman 2001:1042-3; see 2.1.1.8).

Table 1: Consonant inventory

	Bilabial	Alveolar	Post-alveolar	Palato-alveolar	Velar	Uvular	Glottal
Plosive voiceless	p	t	ʈ *ṭ*		k	q	ʔ
Plosive vl. glottalized	p'	t'	ʈ' *ṭ'*		k'	q'	
Plosive vl. aspirated	p^h	t^h	$ʈ^h$ *$ṭ^h$*		k^h	q^h	
Affricate voiceless		ts *c*		tʃ *č*			
Affricate vl. glottalized		ts' *c'*		tʃ' *č'*			
Affricate vl. aspirated		ts^h *c^h*		$tʃ^h$ *$č^h$*			
Fricative voiceless		s		ʃ *š*	x	χ *x̣*	h
Nasal	m	n					
Rhotic		r					
Approxi-mant		l		j *y*	w		

vl. = voiceless

2.1.1.7 Allophonic variations. Noticeable is the sporadic voicing of plain stops and affricates word-medially in a voiced environment, i.e. in inter-vocalic position and after nasals (Grekoff 008.004). Most frequent in the available sources are instances of the allophonic voiced alveolar stop [d], as in example 1a.

1a.	*č'utamdače*	'Burnt Ranch'	*sunda*	'being' (from 'to be')
	nač^h*idot*	'we'	*wisseeda*	'downstream'

Also worth mentioning is the allophonic status of consonant length which has been attributed to sporadic lengthening of the second consonant in words of the shape CVCV (Berman 1985), as in example 1b (from Berman 1985:348, based on Sapir's data). However, most sequences of two identical consonants are found in hetero-syllabic clusters mostly due to syncope (see also 2.1.1.12).

1b.	*hut·u*	'wing, coarse feathers'	*x̣uw·u*	'bee, yellow jacket'
	hutu	'wing, coarse feathers'	*x̣uwu*	'bee, yellow jacket'

2.1.1.8 Retroflex phonemes. The post-alveolar phonemes show variation across speakers. Langdon and Silver (1984:140) describe these sounds as a 'posterior t, possibly formed with the back of the tongue against the palate and the tip depressed against the lower teeth' that 'almost inevitably rings to English ears like tr'. In fact, Harrington and Sapir used 'tr' in their orthographies. Phonetically, /ṭ/ is classified as an apical affricate and not as a stop for Chimariko (Langdon and Silver 1984). Grekoff (009.004) suggests that the apical retroflex set belongs to the palatal (palato-alveolar here) set rather than to the alveolar. He gives two reasons for that: 1) there is a higher frequency of confusion of the retroflex phonemes with their palatal (palato-alveolar here) affricate counterparts and 2) retroflexion is sometimes manifested in the articulation of the palatal (palato-alveolar here) fricative. Retroflex apical stops are not found in any of the neighboring languages, but are common in Central California (Mithun 2004c, Haas 1976). They occur in Yuki, Wappo, Esselen, Salinan, Pomoan languages, Miwokan, Costanoan, Yokutsan languages, Yuma, Diegueño, Cocopa, and Mojave (Mithun 2004c).

2.1.1.9 Speaker variation. Apart from the apical retroflex stops, some of the fricatives show speaker variation. Berman (2001:1043) mentions the variation in sibilants and even raises the question of a phonemic distinction between the two sibilants and the two affricate series. Grekoff also notes that s and š are poorly distinguished in the data. Bright (1978) examines the distribution of sibilants in California and notes that these sounds have sometimes been recorded inconsistently by linguists due to the influence from European languages. He concludes that the retracted sibilant [ṣ] is not only very common in California, but it is also the 'normal' or 'natural' sibilant of the region, as opposed to [s]. While some languages show a contrast of [s] with [ṣ] (Karuk, Wiyot, Atsugewi), others contrast [ṣ] and [š] (Hupa and Yurok). The lack of a complete understanding of sibilants together with poorly recorded data may have led to the recorded interspeaker variation for sibilants.

One of Sapir's consultants, Martha Ziegler, does not distinguish between velar and uvular sounds (Berman, 2001:1043). Grekoff mentions that the back fricatives x, x̣, and h are poorly distinguished especially in clusters following a consonant. Berman finds similar problems in the speech of Martha Ziegler and asserts that as the second member of a cluster the velar and uvular fricatives are lost.

Inconsistencies are also attested for the distinction between the lateral and the rhotic. Grekoff (008.004) finds that etymological /l/ is always represented by /l/, while etymological /r/ may be represented by either /r/ or /l/. The fluctuation seems to be random, according to Grekoff, except in the following clusters: rr, rl, lr. These are all represented as /ll/. While the phonemic status of some of the sounds in table 3 may be questioned, others can easily be contrasted in minimal pairs (see also 2.1.1.8).

2.1.1.10 Minimal pairs. The following minimal pairs are proof of the phonemic status of some of the sounds given in Table 1. A phonemic distinction between plain, glottalized, and aspirated stops is shown in a set of verbal stems:

2. /k ~ k^h ~ k'/

/oko/	'tattoo'
/ak^ho/	'kill'
/ik'o/	'talk'

A phonemic distinction between a plain alveolar and a plain apical retroflex stop is demonstrated by the following example:

3. /t ~ ṭ/

/hita/	‘lots’
/hiṭa/	‘his hand’

The free and bound pronouns form several sets of minimal and near minimal pairs illustrating a variety of contrasts:

4. /p^h ~ m/   /y ~ $^?$ ~ č^h ~ m ~ q^h ~ h/

/p^{h}a$^?$mot/	3SG, 3PL	/y-/$^?$-/	1SG Agent
/mamot/	2SG	/č^h-/	1SG Patient
		/m-/	2SG
		/q^h-/	2PL
		/h-/	3 (SG and PL)

The following sets of minimal and near minimal pairs represent contrasts between nasals and other sounds, between obstruents, and between liquids and obstruents:

5. /m ~ w/

/$^?$ama/	‘country’	/ama/	‘eat’
/$^?$awa/	‘house’	/uwa/	‘go’

/m ~ p/		/m ~ t/	
/imat/	‘find’	/imam/	‘see’
/epat/	‘sit’	/imat/	‘find’

/n~w/		/č ~ $^?$ ~ w/	
/onu/	‘growl at’	/exači/	‘steal’
/awu/	‘give’	/ixa$^?$i/	‘cause’
		/xawi/	‘Redwood Indian’

/č ~ k^h/		/č^h ~ q’/	
/ičut/	‘hit’	/č^{h}e/	‘say’
/ek^{h}ut/	‘cut’	/q’e/	‘die’

/č^h ~ l/		/l ~ $^?$/	
/pač^{h}a$^?$/	‘what’	/lul/	‘drop’
/p^{h}ala$^?$/	‘be string’	/lu$^?$/	‘be string’

/q^h ~ k/

/q^he/ 'smoke'
/ke/ 'here'

2.1.1.11 Phonemic status of sounds. Words contrasting the two sibilants /s ~ š/, the affricate series /c ~ č/, and the back fricatives /x ~ x̣ ~ h/ still need to be found to prove their phonemic status. Grekoff also questions the phonemic status of the aspirated alveolar and post-alveolar stops given that they have not been unequivocally attested. Attested sequences of their plain counterparts followed by a velar fricative may be interpreted as allophones of these phonemes (Grekoff 008.004). This is illustrated below:

6. /t^h/ => [t^h, t^x] /ṭ^h/ => [ṭ^h, ṭ^x]

7. *txer* 'broad and flat' could be interpreted as /t^her/
tx̣ol 'crawfish' could be interpreted as /ṭ^{h}ol/

2.1.1.12 Gemination. Geminates are limited to [ll, mm, nn, ss, tt] and are found mostly due to syncope (see also 2.1.1.7). They never occur word-initially and are often confined to morpheme boundaries. There is no evidence for contrastive gemination. In the Harrington data, /t/ geminates are represented as lowercase *t* with two strike-through lines instead of one. Other geminates, such as [ss, ll, nn, mm] appear with macrons. Dixon (1910:313) describes *-alla, -ulla,* and *-olla,* all containing a geminate [ll], as derivational suffixes with a diminutive function (see examples below). Berman (1985) attributes gemination to the lengthening of the second consonant in words of the shape CVCV, in particular if that consonant is [m] or [n] (see also 2.1.1.7).

8. [ll] *q^homalla* 'where'
malla 'there'

ˀiṭi-lla 'boy'
man-DIM

xalall-op 'the baby'
baby-DEF

šunuhull-ot 'the old woman'
old.woman-DEF

ˀičinšolla 'dress'
xotalla 'a little'
ˀalla 'month'
čitxa-yamu-lla 'while without a blanket'
blanket-without-DEP

[mm]	*ṭamma*	'salmon meal'
[nn]	*pʰaʔaasinni*	'that way'
[tt]	*h-epat-ta* 3-sit-ASP	'they were living'
	h-iwet-ta 3-hook-ASP	'he hooked it'
	m-uwet-teʔta 2SG-hook-COND	'if he had hooked you'
[ss]	*wisseeda* *kimass*	'downstream' 'today'

2.1.2 Vowel inventory and allophonic variation

2.1.2.1 Vowel inventory. Chimariko has a simple vowel system with one low, two mid, and two high vowels. Phonemic vowel length is questionable (see 2.1.2.3). /a/ could also be a back vowel, as it patterns with back vowels in certain morphophonemic rules (see 3.2.1.2 and 3.2.2).

Table 2: Vowel system

	Front	Central	Back
High	i		u
Mid	e		o
Low		a	

2.1.2.2 Minimal pairs. The following set illustrates the phonemic status of /i~ o ~ u/:

9. /awi/ 'be afraid'
/iwo/ 'sit down'
/awu/ 'give'

2.1.2.3 Vowel length. Grekoff (008.004) notes that vowel length is rare and that it can sometimes be attributed to a sequence of VC(V), whereby C is most often a glide or a glottal stop. According to Berman (2001:1042), transcriptions of Martha Ziegler's speech show no distinction in vowel length, while those of Abe Bush and Saxey Kidd do. Good (2002:10) proposes a system containing six vowels, given that vowel length is clearest for the low vowel as noted by Grekoff: a, a:, e, i, o, u. Good further states that this inventory is similar to a three-vowel system where a distinction in length can be associated with a distinction in quality. The phonetic examination of several tokens recorded from Martha Ziegler reveals instances of final lengthening, i.e. the vowel in the final syllable being longer than its respective counterpart in a non-final syllable.

Final lengthening is not represented in the Harrington data. Yet, sequences of two identical vowels are found for all vowels, often as part of the root and marked for stress (see also 2.4). No phonemic distinction in vowel length has been identified, and it remains unclear whether the recorded instances are structurally two vowels or one long one.

10.	[ee]	*x-ukee-na-tinda* NEG-understand-NEG-ASP	'you don't understand'
		č^h-umeečo-da IMP.PL-watch-DER	'you watch around'
		wisseeda	'downstream'
		p^{h}a^{ʔ}mot h-išee-da Frank 3 3-name-DER	'he is named Frank'
	[aa]	*paač^{h}ikun*	'no more'
		p^{h}a^{ʔ}aasinni	'that way'
	[oo]	*koow-i-dinda* holler-3-PROG	'he is hollering'
		h-uhooida-t 3-?-ASP	'they were here, too'
	[ii]	*č'iim-xana-t* dry.up-FUT-ASP	'it is going to dry up'
	[uu]	*y-ečuuda-n* 1SG.A-lie.down-ASP	'I am lying down'
		n-ačuuda IMP.SG-lie.down	'lie down!'

2.1.2.4 Diphthongs. The low-high and mid-high rising diphthongs, [ai, ei, oi, ui], are found in roots and as a result of affixing. There is also a fronting diphthong [ui]. In the data, the diphthongs appear either as a sequence of two vowels or as a vowel followed by a glide. While the front high vowel [i] occurs as either a vowel or a glide in these sequences, the back high vowel [u] always appears as a glide. Given that the two variants, vowel-vowel and vowel-glide, can be found in different instances of the same word, as in 'sister' in the example below, they are assumed to have the same phonetic and phonological basis. High-low and mid-low diphthongs do not occur; they are always interrupted by a glottal stop as in *mo^{ʔ}a* 'yesterday'. In glide-vowel sequences, the glide always functions as the syllable onset, as in *u.wa.ma^ʔ* 'where did he go' or in *yaxak^{h}onaxan^{ʔ}i* 'we won't kill them'.

11.	[ai]	*xotai*	'three'
		maik	'?'
		ˀama-ida	'her country'
		country-POSS	
		ˀeloh-aikulla	'only hot'
		hot-only	
	[ei]	*n-ikei*	'hear him'
		IMP-hear	
		čʰu-ṭa ṭe-yta	'thumb'
		POSS-hand ?-POSS	
	[oi]	*šitoi*	'mother'
		ˀawa-kunoi	'into the house'
		house-into	
	[ui]	*ˀuluyta*	'sister'
		ˀuluida	'sister'

2.1.2.5 Creaky voice. Initial, final, and intervocalic glottal stops may be realized as creakiness on the surrounding vowels, as phonetic analysis of the sound recording from Martha Ziegler reveals. Sequences of a glottal stop followed by a consonant in coda position are realized as simple codas with laryngealization of the preceding vowel (see also 2.2.3.1).

12.	*ˀaˀa*	[ˀaa̰]	'deer'
	himaˀ	[hima̰]	'head'

2.2 Syllable structure and phonotactic restrictions

Chimariko syllable structure and phonotactic restrictions are similar to those of other Northern California languages. The following description of syllable structure and phonotactic restrictions in Chimariko draws upon an unfinished chapter on phonology in Grekoff's notes.

2.2.1 Syllable structure

The most common syllables are CV and CVC. The maximal syllable template is (C)CV(C)(C). Complex onsets and codas do not co-occur in the same syllable. Hence, the largest possible syllable is either CCVC or CVCC. However, there is no evidence for a cluster reduction in either onset or coda due to having a complex onset or coda. This could just be an accidental gap. The segments that are found in complex onsets and codas are very limited (see 2.2.3.2). Complex onsets are restricted to word-initial position. Complex codas occur word-medially and word-finally. Onsetless syllables are only found word-initially as a result of the elision of an initial /h/ or /ˀ/. The smallest word is CV. Monosyllabic words are rare and include *qʰe* 'smoke' and *ke* 'here' among others. Longer words can include six or more syllables, such as *himaˀqeˀč'ankučʰa* 'stove'. Table 3 summarizes the main characteristics of Chimariko syllable structure.

Table 3: Characteristics of syllable structure

Open syllable	Onsetless syllable	Complex onset	Complex coda	Minimal word
yes	no/restricted	yes /restricted	yes/restricted	CV

2.2.2 Structure of roots

Verb roots are for the most part disyllabic of the structure V.CV(C). Disyllabic roots have an initial vowel surfacing in certain pronominal prefixes (see 3.1), and they carry the primary stress (see 2.4). Monosyllabic roots are less frequent and always begin with a consonant. Instances of trisyllabic verb roots occur and may be due to the crystallization of an older morphology. The same as disyllabic roots, they always have an initial vowel. A small set of verb roots are discontinuous of the form CV(C) . . CV(C). Other morphemes may occur in between the two separate parts. Examples of monosyllabic, disyllabic, trisyllabic, and discontinuous verb roots are given below:

13. *q'e* 'die'
    kow 'holler'
    iwo 'sit down'
    awu 'give'
    oko 'tattoo'
    imat 'find'
    exači 'steal'
    imiči 'kick'
    po . . mu 'sleep'

Nominal roots are mainly disyllabic. They carry the primary stress on the penultimate syllable (see 3.1). Monosyllabic and trisyllabic roots are also common. Nominal roots with more than three syllables are rare and may be attributed to lexicalisation effects. Examples of nominal roots are given below.

14. *ˀirˀir* 'stranger'
    č'imar 'person'
    ˀama 'country'
    qʰe 'smoke'
    šinčela 'dog'

2.2.3 Phonotactic place and co-occurrence restrictions

2.2.3.1 Phonotactic restrictions. All consonants occur as onsets. The rhotic /r/ never appears in word-initial position, and /kʰ/ appears only rarely. The glottalized stop /p'/ occurs only before back vowels in onsets, and the glottalized /t'/ is rare overall. All but aspirated and glottalized phonemes occur as codas. Typologically, glottalized consonants are seldom part of codas. One exception to this is /q'/ which occurs in some codas in Chimariko. However, the data are limited. The retroflex apical /ṭ/ and the plain affricate /č/ are not attested word-finally and only in a few examples syllable-finally. The glottal fricative /h/ is rare word-finally. The two glides /y/ and /w/ can not be followed by their vocalic counterparts, /i/ and /u/ respectively, in onset position. Ejective and aspirated occlusives do not precede /h/ or /ˀ/. Sequences of a glottal stop followed by a consonant in coda position are analyzed as simple codas with laryngealization of the preceding vowel, such as in the following example:

15. *ho-liˀ-taˀn* 'it is not right'
[holiˀta̰n]
CV-CVC-CVC

Some segments can be lost at word edges. Initial /h/ and /ˀ/, as well as any word-final vowel, can be elided. Some examples are shown below:

16.	*hita ~ hit ~ ita ~ it*	'many, lots'
	ˀapu ~ ˀap	'fire'
	qʰomalla ~ qʰomall	'where'
	ˀičinšolla ~ ˀičinšoll	'dress'

The loss of word-initial /h/ and /ˀ/ occurs often after vowels. The following examples illustrate this process.

17. Word-final vowel and word-initial /h/

Elision of both V and /h/:			Rules:
ˀawa + homuta	->	*ˀaw omut*	1. h -> Ø /V____
house collapse			2. V -> Ø /___V, h
'The house collapsed'			
Elision of V only:			
huc'u + hičʰuni	->	*huc' hičʰun*	1. V -> Ø /___V, h
tooth be.long			
'The tooth is long'			

Elision of /h/ only:

čʰuṭanpu + hic'ani -> *čʰuṭanpu ic'an* 1. h -> Ø /V____
my.arm ache (second rule not applied)
'My arm hurts'

18. Word-final vowel and word-initial /ˀ/

Elision of both V and /ˀ/:

qʰapu + ˀuleyta -> *qʰap uleyta*
brush little
'Little plant'

yapʰaˀi + ˀimiˀnani -> *yapʰaˀ imiˀnan*
marry want
'I want to marry'

Elision of V only:

tiˀla + ˀuleyta -> *tiˀl ˀuleyta*
bird little
'Little bird'

sawu + ˀičʰeskita -> *saw ˀičʰeskit*
potato cook
'I'm cooking potatoes'

Elision of /ˀ/ only:

hičxu + ˀama-ye -> *hičxu amay*
Hupa country-POSS
'Hoopa Valley'

Other elisions at word margins involve vowels and consonants, and consonants and /h/ and /ˀ/. These are illustrated below.

19. Word-final vowel and word-initial consonant (other than *h* or ˀ)

Elision of V only:

čʰilintosa + pʰaˀyiaqleaˀ -> *čʰilintos pʰaˀyiaqleaˀ*
Coyote say.so
'Did Coyote say so?'

20. Word-final consonant and word-initial /h/

Elision of /h/:

pʰoˀot + hohuta -> *pʰoˀot ohut*
that.one whistle
'That one whistles'

21. Word-final consonant and word-initial /ˀ/

Elision of /ˀ/:

č'imal + ˀuˀil -> *č'imal uˀil*
person other
'Stranger'

2.2.3.2 Possible consonant clusters. Onset and coda clusters are very limited. Only four clusters are found in onsets in word-initial position: *pq', tq', tx, ṭx*. As mentioned in 2.1.1.11, the two clusters having a velar fricative a second segment could also be interpreted as the aspirated stops /tʰ/ and /ṭʰ/ which are rarely found in the data. Examples of onset clusters are shown below:

22. *pq'iliˀi* 'crooked'
tq'amina 'flea'
txeleˀi 'flat and broad'
ṭxol 'crawfish'

Coda clusters are found word-medially and word-finally. Word-finally only the sequence ˀC is attested, where C represents any consonant except /ṭ, č, š, x, h, l, q', ˀ/. As noted in 2.1.2.5, this sequence can be analyzed as a single consonant with laryngealization on the preceding vowel. In CVC_1C_2 syllables word-medially the following sequences have been attested: *yn, wˀ, wn, wm*, although the latter two only rarely. Examples of coda clusters are given below:

23. *ˀu-x̣ayn-šol-la* 'apron'
ˀew-ˀewˀ-čʰin 'we warcry'

Aspirated consonants are occasionally de-aspirated when followed by another consonant, as in the following example.

24. *haˀaqʰa + tamta* -> *haˀaqtamta* '(deer) went downslope'

This process can be summarized with the following rule: C^h -> C / ____ C .

2.2.3.3 Geminate consonant clusters. Geminate clusters are found mostly word-internally. Only the following consonants occur as geminates: /t, k, m, n, l, y/. Grekoff (008.004) asserts that they are found only at morpheme boundaries or due to syncope. Two examples are shown below:

25. *č^{h}-at-ta* 'he hit me'.
1SG.P-hit-ASP

26. *^{ʔ}iwinq^{h}utta* 'I dump them in (the water)'
^{ʔ}i-win-q^{h}utu-ta
1SG.A-drop-immersingly-ASP

The syllabification of geminates is unclear. With matching morphological and phonological alignment they would be heterosyllabic.

2.2.3.4 Summary of phonotactic restrictions. The phonotactic restrictions are summarized in Table 4:

Table 4: Summary of phonotactic restrictions

Word-initial	Syllable-initial	Word-final	Syllable-final
no r, k^{h} rare y, w not ___i, u resp. h, ^{ʔ} elision possible	all, p' only before o, u y, w not ___i, u resp.	no ṭ, no č h rare vowel elision poss.	no asp., no glott. (except q') ṭ and č rare
	Word-initial (only)	Word-final	Syllable-final
Complex onset	pq', tq', tx, ṭx		
Complex coda		^{ʔ}C (not cluster)	^{ʔ}C (not cluster) yn, w^{ʔ}, (wn, wm rare)

2.3 Stress and prosody

While primary and secondary stress have been marked occasionally in the data and can be described in some detail here, information on prosody is limited to punctuation.

2.3.1 Stress

Chimariko shows phonologically predictable stress on the root or the penultimate syllable of the root in polysyllabic roots.

27. *ápu* 'fire'
éšoh 'cold'
šinčéla 'dog'
mutákweh 'rain'

mála-^{ʔ}i 'my mother's sister'
mother's.sister-POSS

Instances of root stress on the final syllable of polysyllabic roots may occur due to lexicalisation, as in the following example.

28.	*pʰuncá-lla*	'little girl'	*ʔiṭí-lla*	'boy'
	woman-DIM		man-DIM	

Although vowel length is not phonemic, long vowels are found sporadically in the data (see also 2.1.2.3). If a syllable contains a long vowel, it is always stressed.

29.	*pááčʰikun*	'no more'
	wissééda	'downstream'
	y-ečúúda-n	'I am lying down'
	1SG.A-lie.down-ASP	
	x-ukéé-na-tinda	'you don't understand'
	NEG-understand-NEG-ASP	

An acoustic analysis of the sound recording from Martha Ziegler shows that length (in short vowels) does not correlate with stress; neither does intensity correlate with stress. The only acoustic correlate of stress which can be clearly identified in the data is pitch, i.e. a higher F0. The acoustic analysis also reveals final lengthening, in particular in open syllables. Unstressed vowels in word-final syllables are often longer than their stressed counterparts within the same word. This is a common phenomenon cross-linguistically.

2.3.2 Prosodic units

Prosodic units are marked in the data by punctuation. Nevertheless, given the lack of sound recordings of connected speech, they can not be examined in detail.

2.4 Sound symbolism

Sound symbolism is a common phenomenon in languages of Northern California, and it has been described for Hupa, Yurok, and other languages of the area. No instances of sound symbolism were identified in Chimariko, due partly to the nature of the data and probably to the limited fluency of the speakers at the time of data collection.

2.5 Phonetics and phonology in areal-typological perspective

The Northern California linguistic area has been characterized by many shared phonological traits. Haas (1976) identified the following Northern California traits: 1) three series of stops and affricates (plain, aspirated, glottalized), 2) back velar consonants, 3) voiceless laterals, 4) retroflex apical stops, and 5) consonant symbolism.

Except for consonant symbolism, these traits are summarized below for Chimariko and its immediate neighbors: Wintu, Hupa, and Shasta. Furthermore, four more traits have been added to the table: obstruent voicing, labialized consonants, gemination, and vowel length. Obstruent voicing is often absent in native languages of North America and occurs only as a recent development (Mithun 2004c). Labialized consonants are very common in Western North America (Mithun 2004c).

Table 5: Phonemic characteristics of Chimariko and its immediate neighbors

Language	Chimariko	Wintu[1]	Hupa[2]	Shasta[3]
Language Family	isolate	Penutian: Wintuan	Na-Dene: Athabaskan	Hokan: Karuk-Shasta: Shastan
Consonants	33	30 (3 marginal)	34 (6 marginal)	19
Stop series	pl, asp, glott	pl, asp, glott	pl, asp, glott	pl, glott
Obstruent voicing	no	yes (only front)	no	no
Back velar *q*	yes	yes	yes	no
Voiceless lateral	no	yes	yes	no
Retroflex *ṭ*	yes	no	no	no
Gemination	no	no	no	yes
Labialized consonants	no	no	yes (restricted to čʷ, čʷ', xʷ)	no
Vowels	5	6 (marginal æ)	3	4
Phonemic vowel length	no	yes	yes	yes

pl = plain; asp = aspirated; glott = glottal

[1] see Pitkin 1984:24-39

[2] see Golla 1960:24-38

[3] see Silver 1966:22-49

Except for Shasta, Chimariko and its immediate neighbors have large consonant inventories with three series of stops. Shasta lacks the aspirated series, as well as back velars found in the other three languages. Voiceless laterals are attested only in Wintu and Hupa, and retroflex apical stops are only found in Chimariko. Labialized consonants occur only in Hupa. Obstruent voicing is found in Wintu and is most likely a recent phenomenon (Mithun 2004c). Except for Chimariko, all languages show phonemic vowel length. Overall, the phonological inventories and patterns are very similar among neighboring languages. When Chimariko is compared to distant neighbors in the area, there are fewer similarities. These facts are illustrated in the following two tables.

Table 6: Characteristics of Chimariko and its distant neighbors to the (north-)west

Language	Chimariko	Karuk[1]	Yurok[2]	Wiyot[3]
Language Family	isolate	Hokan: Karuk-Shasta	Algic: Algonquian	Algic: Algonquian
Consonants	33	16	23 (1 marginal)	25
Stop series	pl, asp, glott	pl	pl, glott	pl, asp
Obstruent voicing	no	no	no	yes
Back velar *q*	yes	no	no	no
Voiceless lateral	no	no	yes	yes
Retroflex *ṭ*	yes	no	no	no
Gemination	no	yes	no	no
Labialized cons.	no	no	yes	yes
Vowels	5	3	6	5
Vowel length	no	yes	yes	no

pl = plain; asp = aspirated; glott = glottalized; cons. = consonants

[1] see Bright 1957:7-27

[2] see Robins 1958:1-10

[3] see Teeter 1964:12-28

In general, the consonant inventories are somewhat smaller as compared to Chimariko, distinguishing only one or two series of stops and lacking back velars as well as retroflex apicals. The two related languages, Yurok and Wiyot, share two traits: both have voiceless laterals and labialized consonants. Obstruent voicing is only found in Wiyot as a recent development (Mithun 2004c). Similar tendencies can be found when Chimariko is compared to distant neighbors to the east.

Table 7: Characteristics of Chimariko and its distant neighbors to the east

Language	Chimariko	Yana[1]	Achumawi[2]	Maidu[3]
Language Family	isolate	Hokan	Hokan: Karuk-Shasta:Palaihninan	Penutian: Maiduan
Consonants	33	22	17	18
Stop series	pl, asp, glott	pl, glott	pl	pl, glott
Obstruent voicing	no	yes	yes (only affricate, not contrastive)	yes
Back velar *q*	yes	no	yes	no
Voiceless lateral	no	no	no	no
Retroflex *ṭ*	yes	no	no	no
Gemination	no	no	no	no
Labialized cons.	no	no	no	no
Vowels	5	5	6	6
Vowel length	no	yes	yes	no

pl = plain; asp = aspirated; glott = glottalized; cons. = consonants

[1] see Sapir and Swadesh 1960:2-7

[2] see Olmsted1966:9-10

[3] see Shipley 1964:6-15

All the distant neighbors to the east have small consonant inventories as compared to Chimariko, all lacking aspirated stops, voiceless laterals, retroflex apicals, and labialized consonants. Contrary to Chimariko, all have voiced obstruents.

Overall, the comparison of phoneme inventories and several areal characteristics shows, not surprisingly, that close neighbors share more traits than distant ones. While Chimariko, Wintu, and Hupa all have large consonant inventories with three series of stops, the languages to the east, Yana, Achumawi, and Maidu have smaller inventories. Shasta, a direct neighbor of Achumawi, also shows a smaller consonant inventory. A similar distribution can be observed for back velars. Whereas the immediate neighbors Chimariko, Wintu, and Hupa all include a back velar in their inventories, the languages to the west, as well as Shasta, lack a back velar. Shasta behaves very much like its direct neighbor Karuk in that it lacks back velars, voiceless laterals, and labialized consonants, but it has geminates. A similar observation can be made for Hupa and Yurok, both with voiceless laterals and labialized consonants. The only trait unique to Chimariko in this area is the presence of retroflex apicals.

The syllable structures and restrictions to syllable types found in Northern California are very similar. All languages have open syllables, and the smallest word is always CV. Most languages do not allow onsetless syllables. In Chimariko and Hupa they occur only as the result of initial consonant elision, usually /h/ or /ˀ/. Complex onsets are rare in Chimariko and do not occur in two of its direct neighbors: Wintu and Hupa. They are found in Shasta, the languages to the west of the Chimariko territory, and in Achumawi. Similarly as with the phonological traits compared, Shasta behaves more like the languages to the west than like Chimariko and its other two immediate neighbors. The same occurs with complex codas which are very rare in Chimariko and absent in its direct neighbors, except for Shasta. Complex codas are found in some languages to the west and to the east of Chimariko. The main characteristics of syllable structure in Northern California are summarized in the following table.

Table 8: Characteristics of Northern California syllable structures[1]

Language	Open syllables	Onsetless syllables	Complex onsets	Complex codas	Minimal word
Chimariko and its immediate neighbors					
Chimariko	yes	no/restricted	yes (restrict.)	yes (restrict.)	CV
Wintu	yes	no	no	no	CV
Hupa	yes	yes/restricted	no	yes (restrict.)	CV
Shasta	yes	no	yes	yes	CV
Distant neighbors to the west					
Karuk	yes	no	yes (restrict.)	no	CV
Yurok	yes	no	yes	yes	CV
Wiyot	yes	no	yes	yes	CV
Distant neighbors to the east					
Yana	yes	no	no	yes	CV
Achumawi	yes	yes	yes	yes	CV
Maidu	yes	no	no	no	CV

[1] For sources see Tables 5-7

Phonotactic restrictions are not always described in great detail in the grammars consulted. Therefore, the comparison of the languages spoken in Northern California in this regard is only tentative. However, some generalizations can be made. The phoneme /r/ does not occur word-initially except in loanwords. Aspirated sounds and for the most part glottalized sounds are not found in syllable-final position. Consonant clusters in onset and coda position are either absent or very restricted. Coda clusters often include a glide as one of their segments. For Achumawi are there no major restrictions described for clusters. Nevertheless, the sources are limited. Table 8 illustrates these restrictions. Overall, syllable structure and phonotactic restrictions are very similar in languages of Northern California.

Stress systems are often described in detail in the grammars consulted. However, the phonetic correlates of stress are not always mentioned. In general, stress patterns show many similarities in Northern California. Immediate neighbors of Chimariko, Hupa, Shasta, and Wintu, all show weight-sensitive stress systems. While their weight hierarchies are slightly different, all have CVV as their heaviest syllable. Root stress, as well as penultimate stress and leftward attraction of stress, are also very common in the area. Shasta, for example, has penultimate stress, but moves the stress in longer sequences to the first preceding heavy syllable. Acoustic correlates of stress include pitch and intensity for Hupa. For Shasta, a high-low pitch tonal accent has been described. Hence the acoustic correlate of stress in Chimariko, which is pitch, is also attested in other languages of the area. Given that stress is easily transferred through language contact, it is likely that the languages in Northern California have shifted their stress patterns as a result of multilingualism in the area. For Chimariko it can be speculated that vowel length on stressed syllables was developing as a contact phenomenon given the weight-sensitive stress systems of neighboring languages with CVV as the heaviest syllable type.

To conclude, many of the phonological traits found in Chimariko also occur in other languages of the area, in particular in its close neighbors. The phoneme inventories are largest in and around Chimariko and smaller to the west and east of its territory. In general, traits are concentrated in contiguous areas. While certain Chimariko traits are not shared with Shasta, these are shared with its direct neighbors to the west, hence still forming a contiguous area. Syllable structure and phonotactic restrictions are shared by most languages of the area. Equally, stress systems show similar patterns. Interestingly, these shared traits occur in genetically unrelated languages. In fact, the languages compared belong to four major language families and stocks: Penutian, Athabaskan, Algic, and Hokan. Therefore, the traits can be described as areal phenomena due to language contact rather than genetic relationship.

3. MORPHOPHONEMIC ALTERNATIONS

This chapter describes phonological alternation operations that are specific to certain domains of the morphology, such as different verb stem categories yielding different shapes in the pronominal affixes, as well as the processes determining the shapes of the negative affixes and others. Many of these processes affect the vowels of morphemes (backing, assimilation, elision). Some also affect the consonants (elision, metathesis).

3.1 Pronominal alternations

Pronominal affixes show a C or CV structure with vowel elision in certain environments. The position of the pronominal affix, i.e. prefixed or suffixed, depends on the verb stem class. Pronominal affixes are suffixed only in one verb stem class.

Harrington (020-1109, 020-1110) and Grekoff (1950-1999) suggest that most predicates have an initial underlying thematic vowel that defines the shapes of the verbal affixes. A similar analysis is adopted here. Chimariko has six different verb stem classes, five having an initial vowel *a, e, i, o,* or *u*, and one without an initial vowel. While the pronominal markers are prefixed in the first five classes, they are suffixed in the latter. A summary and examples are in Table 1.

Table 1: Verb stem classes

Verb stem class	Pronouns	Examples
a-stems	prefixes	*ama* 'to eat', $ak^{h}o$ 'to kill', *awu* 'to give', $ap^{h}a$ 'to marry', *asu* 'to be'
e-stems	prefixes	*exači* 'to steal', *epat* 'to stay', *eṭahes* 'to run away'
i-stems	prefixes	*ik'o* 'to talk', *imiči* 'to kick', $i\check{c}^{h}eski$ 'to cook', *ima* 'to see', *iwo* 'to stay'
o-stems	prefixes	*oko* 'to tattoo', *onu* 'to growl at', *ohu* 'to whistle', *op'u* 'to work'
u-stems	prefixes	*uwa* 'to go', *usim* 'to follow'
Ø-stems	suffixes	*q'e* 'to die', *ṭewu* 'be big', *kow* 'to holler', *lul* 'to drop'

The shapes of the pronominal affixes for all verb stems are summarized in Table 2.

Table 2: Pronominal affixes for all verb stems

Verbal prefixes	Set I :		Set II :	
	Singular Agent	Plural Agent	Singular Patient	Plural Patient
First person	*y-*, $^{?}$-	*ya-*	$\check{c}^{h}$-	$\check{c}^{h}a$-
Second person	*me-, m-*	$q^{h}o$-, q^{h}-	*m-*	$q^{h}a$-
Third person	*h-/Ø*	*h-/Ø*	*h-/Ø*	*h-/Ø*
Verbal suffixes	Set I:		Set II:	
	Singular Agent	Plural Agent	Singular Patient	Plural Patient
First person	-$^{?}$(*i*)	?	- $\check{c}^{h}V$,- $\check{c}^{h}u$	- $\check{c}^{h}a$
Second person	*-m(V)*	-$q^{h}V$	*-m(V)*	-$q^{h}V$
Third person	*-h/Ø*	*-h/Ø*	*-h/Ø*	*-h/Ø*

Table 3: Pronominal affix by verb stem class (following Harrington 020-1109)

Person/Number	i-stem	a-stem	e-stem	o-stem	u-stem
1SG Agent	*ʔi-*	*ye-*	*ye-*	*yo-*	*yu-*
1SG Patient	*čʰu-*	*čʰa-*	*čʰu-*	*čʰo-*	*čʰu-*
1PL Agent	*ya-*	*ya-*	*ya-*	*ya-*	*ya-*
1PL Patient	*čʰa-*	*čʰa-*	*čʰa-*	*čʰa-*	*čʰa-*
2SG	*me-, mi-*	*me-, ma-*	*me-*	*me-, mi-*	*me-, mi-*
2PL	*qʰo-, qʰu-*	*qʰo-, qʰu-*	*qʰo-, qʰu-*	*qʰo-, qʰu-*	*qʰo-, qʰu-*
3	*hi-*	*ha-*	*he-*	*ho-*	*hu-*

Harrington's table includes some unclear cases and has several mistakes in the first and second person forms. The revised table is shown below. Boldfaced forms are the actual pronominal prefixes.

Table 4: Pronominal affixes including initial stem vowel by verb stem class

Person	i-stem	a-stem	e-stem	o-stem	u-stem
1SG Agent	***ʔ**i-*	***y**e-*	***y**e-*	***y**o-*	***y**u-*
1SG Patient	***čʰ**u-*	***čʰ**a-*	***čʰ**o-*	***čʰ**o-*	***čʰ**u-*
1PL Agent	***ya-***	***ya-***	***ya-***	***ya-***	***ya-***
1PL Patient	***čʰa-***	***čʰa-***	***čʰa-***	***čʰa-***	***čʰa-***
2SG	***me-**, mi-*	***me-**, ma-*	***me-**, me-*	***me-**, mo-*	***me-**, mu-*
2PL Agent	***qʰo-**, qʰu-*	***qʰo-**, qʰa-*	***qʰo-**, qʰo-*	***qʰo-**, qʰo-*	***qʰo-**, qʰu-*
2PL Patient[1]	***qʰa-***	***qʰa-***	***qʰa-***	***qʰa-***	***qʰa-***
3	***h**i-*	***h**a-*	***h**e-*	***h**o-*	***h**u-*

[1]For a discussion of the status of 2PL Patient forms see 8.1.1

Several patterns are apparent in Table 4:

1) The first person singular agent has a different shape for the i-stem class. This can be explained by the fact that the sequence *y-i* (palato-alveolar glide - high front vowel) is avoided due to the similarity of the two sounds. This is summarized in the following rule: y -> ʔ /___i .
2) The initial stem vowel surfaces in the first person singular agent except for the a-stems where it would result in the same form as for the plural, i.e. *ya-*, hence eliminating the contrast in number.
3) First person plural forms always contain the vowel /a/ marking number.
4) The initial stem vowel always surfaces in the third person pronouns.
5) In general, no front vowels /e, i/ occur after /qʰ/ and /čʰ/.

The vowel alternations for the second person are explained in 8.1.4. In the first person singular patient forms and the second person plural agent forms the stem-initial front vowels are backed, hence e -> o and i -> u. This is illustrated in the following phonological rule: [-back] -> [+back] / q^h, $\check{c}^h$_______ .

Some deviations from the forms in Table 4 are found in the data, as the following example shows.

1. *ik'o* 'to say' (i-stem): ***hek'o*** instead of ***hik'o*** (from 'Fugitives at Burnt Ranch')

hek'omatta, hak^{h}ode$^?$, č'imarop, xawiyop hak^{h}ode$^?$n
h-ek'*o-ma-tta h-ak^{h}o-de$^?$ č'imar-op xawiy-op h-ak^{h}o-de$^?$-n*
3-say-?-DER 3-kill-DER person-DEF Redwood.Indian-DEF 3-kill-DER-ASP
'The boy told it, they killed the boy, the people, the Indians killed him'

In example 1, the stem-initial vowel /e/ surfaces with the third person marker *h-* rather than /i/ as expected with i-stem verbs. Given the nature of the data collection and the fluency of the speakers at the time of data collection, some deviations from the system described in Table 4 can be expected.

In some instances partial deletion of a pronominal affix occurs. This is the case with the third person prefix *h-*, which is phonologically weak, as illustrated below. Deletion of /h/ is found after consonants and vowels.

2. 'Fugitives at Burnt Ranch'
č'imar xotai heṭaheskut uwatkut
č'imar xotai h-eṭahe-sku-t ***ø****-uwa-tku-t*
man three 3-run.away-DIR-ASP 3-come-DIR-ASP
'Three men came as fugitives'
. . . .
hetaxawi uwatkukon
heta-xawi ***ø****-uwa-tku-kon*
many-Redwood.Indians 3-come-DIR-FUT
'Lots of Redwood Indians will come'

3. 'Fugitives at Burnt Ranch'
kimot $^?$u$^?$ir asunda
kimot $^?$u$^?$ir ***ø****-asu-nda*
these stranger 3-be-ASP
'These are strangers'

The patterns in the suffixed pronouns are less clear. Vowel alternations can be observed for the second persons. However, it is unclear whether they are conditioned by the verb stem or the following suffix. The vowel in the first person agent and the second person suffixes is sometimes lost, as can be seen below.

4. 'Woman wanders'
q'e^{ʔ}xanan
q'e-^{ʔ}-xana-n
die-1SG.A-FUT-ASP
'I am going to die'

5. Harrington 020-1103
q'emkunat
*q'e-**m**-kuna-t*
die-2SG-NEG-ASP
'You did not die'

The rules and examples in the following sections are largely based on notes of an unfinished chapter on morphophonemics by George Grekoff (008.012).

3.2 Negation and imperatives

3.2.1 Negation

There are two negative affixes: the suffix *-k'una* and the circumfix *x-V. . -na*, where V stands for /a, e, o, u/ and represents the stem-initial vowel. Both affixes have allomorphs. While *-k'una* has only two allomorphs: *-k'una* and *-^{ʔ}na*, *x-V. . -na* has many different forms alternating the vowel according to the verb stem class and the preceding prefix. Several other morphophonemic processes can also be observed.

3.2.1.1 Deletion of pronominal affix with x-. . -na. In the presence of the negative circumfix *x-. . -na* the first person singular agent pronouns and the third person pronouns are deleted in the prefixed verb stem classes, as in the examples below.

6. 6a. Third person pronouns

'Woman wanders'
xukeenan
***Ø-x**-ukee-**na**-n*
3-NEG-know-NEG-ASP
'She did not know'

'Mrs Bussell'
xowonat
***Ø-x**-owo-**na**-t*
3-NEG-stay-NEG-ASP
'She does not stay (at home)'

6b. First person agent pronouns

'Mrs Bussell'
xewunan
***Ø-x**-ewu-**na**-n*
1SG.A-NEG-give-NEG-ASP
'I did not give her (food)'

'Mrs Bussell'
xok'o^{ʔ}nanan
***Ø-x**-ok'o-^{ʔ}na-**na**-n*
1SG.A-NEG-speak-APPL-NEG-ASP
'I did not speak to her'

But: 6c. *q^{h}a* + NEG = *q^{h}axa- . . -na*

Grekoff 008-012
q^{h}axaweynat
*q^{h}a-**x**-awey-**na**-t*
2PL-NEG-mad-NEG-ASP
'You are not mad'

6d. *ya* + NEG = *yaxa-. . -na*

'Fugitives at Burnt Ranch'
yaxak^{h}onaxan^{ʔ}i
*ya-**x**-ak^{h}o-**na**-xan-^{ʔ}i*
1PL.A-NEG-kill-NEG-FUT-ASP
'We won't kill them'

3.2.1.2 Vowel backing and vowel assimilation with x-. .-na. The front vowels /e, i/ that surface in the e-stem and i-stem verbs respectively are backed in the presence of the negative circumfix *x-. . -na*. This is illustrated below.

7. 7a. i-stem verbs

xuk'onan
***x-uk'o-na**-n*
NEG-say-NEG-ASP
'He didn't say'

7b. e-stem verbs

noxoxačina
*no-**x-oxači-na***
IMP.SG-NEG-steal-NEG
'Don't steal it!'

This process can be summarized as follows: [-back] -> [+back] /x___ . This rule does not apply if the pronominal affix for the second person singular *m-*, the imperative singular prefix *n-*, or the first person patient form *-e-* are present, as in the following example.

8. *nexesiman* (*usim* 'to follow'; also: metathesis: -na -> -an)
*n-e-**x-esim-an***
IMP.SG-1P-NEG-follow-NEG
'Don't follow me!'

Example 8 also shows the assimilation of the vowel immediately following the *x-* of the negative circumfix to the vowel in the preceding prefix. This is illustrated below.

9. 9a. *č^{h}a-* + NEG = *č^{h}axa-. . -na* (regardless of verb stem class)

č^{h}axamičitnam (i-stem)
*č^{h}a-**x-amičit-na**-m*
1PL.P-NEG-kick-NEG-ASP
'He didn't kick us'

č^{h}axanunan (u-stem)
*č^{h}a-**x-anu-na**-n*
1PL.P-NEG-scold-NEG-ASP
'He didn't scold us'

9b. *q^{h}a* + NEG = *q^{h}axa-. . -na*

q^{h}axaweynat (a-stem)
*q^{h}a-**x-awey-na**-t*
2PL-NEG-mad-NEG-ASP
'You are not mad'

9c. *ya* + NEG = *yaxa. . -na*

yaxaxotanat (i-stem)
*ya-**x-axota-na**-t*

1PL.A-NEG-look.at-NEG-ASP
'We are not looking at him'

9d. . . *wa* + NEG = . . *waxa-*. . *-na*

čʰowaxap'umiyna (o-stem)
*čʰo-wa-**x-ap**'u-miy-**na***
IMP.PL-COLL-NEG-work-CAUS-NEG
'Don't you work for me!'

newaxap'umiyna (o-stem)
*n-e-wa-**x-ap**'u-miy-**na***
IMP.SG-1P-COLL-NEG-work-APPL-NEG
'Don't you work for me!'

9e. *čʰo* + NEG = *čʰoxo-*. . *-na*

čʰoxoxotana (i-stem)
*čʰo-**x-o**xota-**na***
IMP.PL-NEG-look.at-NEG
'Don't you look at me!'

9f. *ne* + NEG = *nexe-*. . *-na*

nexexotana (i-stem)
*n-e-**x-e**xota-**na***
IMP.SG-1P-NEG-look.at-NEG
'Don't look at me'

nexesiman (u-stem) (metathesis: -na -> -an)
*n-e-**x-e**sim-**an***
IMP.SG-1P-NEG-follow-NEG
'Don't follow me!'

The last example also illustrates metathesis in the second part of the circumfix. After consonants *-na* becomes *-an*.

The negative *-k'una* does not show many alternations. It has two allomorphs: *-k'una* and *-ˀna*. The short form sometimes occurs after vowels (see 3.3.7).

10.	V_________	But also:	V________
	*ˀaˀa-**ˀna**-tinta*		*ˀanoˀa-**k'una**-t*
	*ˀaˀa-**ˀna**-tinta*		*ˀanoˀa-**k'una**-t*
	meat-NEG-ASP		pitchwood-NEG-ASP
	'It isn't meat'		'It wasn't pitchwood'.

3.2.2 Imperatives

Similar to the process found in the negative circumfix, vowel backing also occurs in the imperative plural prefixes, i.e. after /čʰ/. This is shown below.

11. i-stem verbs | e-stem verbs

i-stem verbs	e-stem verbs
čʰuxota	*čʰopat*
čʰ-uxota	***čʰ-opat***
IMP.PL-look.at	IMP.PL-settle.down
'Look at him!' (pl)	'Settle down!' (pl)

3.3 Other alternations

Many morphophonemic processes are based on vowel or consonant elision at morpheme edges, and they depend on the preceding or following sound. In general, sequences of two vowels or three consonants are avoided.

3.3.1 Stem shapes: Deletion of final vowel

A number of verbal and nominal stems delete their final vowel when followed by certain affixes, such as the nominalizer *-ew* or the definite markers *-op* or *-ot*. This is shown in the following examples.

12. With nominalizer *-ew*

h-ama-ew -> *hamew*
3-eat-NOM
'What one eats, food'

h-ik'o-ew -> *hik'ew*
3-talk-NOM
'One's talk, manner of talking'

13. With definite marker *-op*

ʔuleyta-op -> *uleytop*
small.one-DEF
'The small one'

3.3.1 Aspectual suffixes

The aspectual suffix *-ta* has two allomorphs: *-ta* and *-t*, depending on the preceding sound. After a consonant *-ta* is found, while after vowels *-t* occurs.

14.

V_____	C______
hiwot	*huwamta*
*h-iwo-**t***	*h-uwa-m-**ta***
3-sit-ASP	3-go-DIR-ASP
'He sat'	'He went forth'
huwumna^{ʔ}čit	*^{ʔ}iwinq^{h}utta*
*h-uwu-m-na^{ʔ}či-**t***	*^{ʔ}-iwin-q^{h}ut-**ta***
3-go-DIR-all-ASP	1SG.A-dump-into.water-ASP
'All went home'	'I dumped them in water'
ye^{ʔ}aqtut	*wihičanta*
*y-e^{ʔ}a-qtu-**t***	*wi-hi-čan-**ta***
1SG.A-get-into.water-ASP	burn-3-APPL-ASP
'I get in the water'	'It burned on'

It is unclear which allomorph is basic as two rules are possible and plausible:
Rule 1: ta -> t /C_____# (final vowel deletion is a common process)
Rule 2: t -> ta /V_____# (vowel insertion to avoid final consonant clusters)

Rule 1 is plausible since word-final vowel deletion is a common process in Chimariko. Rule 2 is plausible given that final consonant clusters are very limited (see 2.2.3).

The aspectual suffix *-inta* has the following two allomorphs *-inta* and *-nta*, depending on the preceding sound. While *-inta* surfaces after consonants, *-nta* is found after vowels, given that two consecutive vowels are generally avoided.

15.

V_____	C______
he^{ʔ}anta	*hič^{h}ininta*
*he^{ʔ}a-**nta***	*hič^{h}in-**inta***
good.ones-ASP	big.ones-ASP
'They are good ones'	'They are big ones'
č^{h}uk'o^{ʔ}nanta	*hikeyinta*
*č^{h}-uk'o-^{ʔ}na-**nta***	*h-ikey-**inta***
1SG.P-talk-APPL-ASP	3-understand-ASP
'They talk to me'	'She understood now'

This vowel deletion can be summarized with the following rule: inta -> nta /V_____.

3.3.3 Locative and directional affixes

Grekoff (008.012) notes vowel syncope in locative-directional affixes: *č'ana* 'to, toward, onto', *č'ama* 'in, into', *xunok* 'in, into, through', *q^{h}a* 'along a steep slope', *q^{h}utu* 'into water', *ku* 'hither', *mu* 'forth, thither', and *pa* 'off away'. Some examples are below.

16. *q^{h}utu -> q^{h}ut*

^{ʔ}iwinq^{h}utta
*^{ʔ}-iwin-**q^{h}ut**-ta*
1SG.A-dump-into.water-ASP
'I dumped them in water'

17. *mu -> m*

huwamta
*h-uwa-**m**-ta*
3-go-DIR-ASP
'He went forth'

Consonant elision is found with *-wu* 'backwards'. The following examples illustrate this.

18.

V_____	C_____
h-iwo-wu-k-ta -> *hiwo**wu**kta*	*h-iman-wu-k-ta ->* *himan**u**kta*
3-fall.over-DIR-DIR-ASP	3-fall.down-DIR-DIR-ASP
'He fell over backwards'	'He fell down backwards'

3.3.4 Metathesis

Some affixes show metathesis conditioned by the immediately preceding sound, i.e. depending on whether it is a consonant or a vowel, as in the following examples.

19. *na^{ʔ}ači* 'all'

-> *na^{ʔ}či* /C____
huwumna^{ʔ}čit
*h-uwu-m-**na^{ʔ}či**-t*
3-go-DIR-all-ASP
'All went home'

-> *n^{ʔ}ači* /V____
haman^{ʔ}ačit
*h-ama-**n^{ʔ}ači**-t*
3-eat-all-ASP
'They all ate'

20. *q^{h}utu* 'into water'

-> *q^{h}ut* /C____
^{ʔ}iwinq^{h}utta
*^{ʔ}-iwin-**q^{h}ut**-ta*
1SG.A-dump-into.water-ASP
'I dumped them in water'

-> *qtu* /V____
(with de-aspiration of q^{h})
ye^{ʔ}aqtut
*y-e^{ʔ}a-**qtu**-t*
1SG.A-get-into.water-ASP
'I get in the water'

In *-naˀači* 'all', the second /a/ is deleted, and the affix shows two different shapes switching the remaining /a/ and the glottal stop in position depending on the sound preceding the suffix. The same process occurs with the suffix *-qʰutu* 'into water'.

In several verbal suffixes the glottal stop can change its position depending on the sound that precedes the affix. This results in the following allomorphs: *-ˀya/-yaˀ* 'again, some more', *-ˀyew/-yeˀw* 'reflexive', and *-ˀna/-naˀ* 'plant'.

21.

V_______	C_______
hišehetkuˀyat *h-išehe-tku-**ˀya**-t* 3-lead-DIR-again-ASP 'She brought some more (dogs)'	*himamyaˀt* *h-imam-**yaˀ**-t* 3-see-again-ASP 'He sees him again'
hisumtaˀyakon *h-isumta-**ˀya**-kon* 3-look.at-again-FUT 'He is going to look at it again'	*haˀatokyaˀkon* *h-aˀatok-**yaˀ**-kon* 3-return.hither-again-FUT 'He is going to come back'
hakʰoˀyewtaˀnta *h-akʰo-**ˀyew**-taˀn-ta* 3-kill-REFL-PST-ASP 'He has killed himself'	*hok'imyeˀwta* *h-ok'im-**yeˀw**-ta* 3-hang-REFL-ASP 'He hanged himself'
muneˀna *mune-**ˀna*** acorn.of.black.oak-plant 'Black oak'	*hak'ewnaˀ* *hak'ew-**naˀ*** nut.of.sugar.pine-plant 'Sugar pine'

Other affixes undergoing the same process include *-saˀs* 'inferential modal', *-taˀ* 'perfective', and *-teˀw* 'indefinite third person plural actor'.

3.3.5 Affixes with initial consonant clusters

Affixes with initial consonant clusters drop the initial consonant when preceded by another consonant to avoid sequences of three consonants. Such affixes include: *-lle* 'determinative used with numerals', *-nni* 'locative', *-tta* 'indefinite actor', and *-ˀtamhu* 'turning motion, change in direction'.

22.

V_____			C_____		
qʰoqʰu-lle	->	*qʰoqʰu**lle***	*x̣utay-lle*	->	*x̣utay**le***
two-DET			three-DET		
'The two of them'			'The three of them'		

ˀasoti-nni -> *ˀasoti**nni***
winter-LOC
'In the winter'

himaˀ-nni -> *himaˀ**ni***
head-LOC
'At the head'

h-ičxe-tta-ta -> *hičxe**ttat***
3-be.inside-DER-ASP
'It is in there'

h-imam-tta-xanata -> *himam**ta**xanat*
3-see-DER-FUT-ASP
'He will be seen'

h-iṭu-ˀtamhu-ta -> *hiṭu**ˀtamhut***
3-act.with.hand-DIR-ASP
'She turned it around'

ya-tukluš-ˀtamhu-ta -> *yatukluš**tamhut***
1PL.A-act.with.hand-DIR-ASP
'We turned him over'

3.3.6 Suffixes with the initial vowel /a/

Many suffixes with an initial vowel /a/ drop that vowel when preceded by a vowel. Following Grekoff (008.012), these include: *-a* intensive, *-aˀ* interrogative, *-ah* 'endowed with', *-aiku* 'exclusively, only', *-akon* 'future', *-aqle* 'dubitative', *-al* 'speculative', *-apo* 'diminutive, pejorative', *-apʰuˀ* 'perfective interrogative', *-asun* 'stative', *-aš* 'adversative', and *-ašku* 'privative'. Some examples are given below.

23. V_____ C______

m-uwa-tku-aˀ -> *muwatku**ˀ***
2SG-go-DIR-Q
'Do you come?'

m-akut-aˀ -> *makut**aˀ***
2SG-cut-Q
'Did you cut it?'

y-ama-akon -> *yema**kon***
1SG.A-eat-FUT
'I am going to eat'

y-amam-akon -> *yamam**akon***
1SG.A-see-FUT
'I am going to see'

naˀi-aš -> *naˀi**š***
'But as for me'

čʰutiy-aš -> *čʰutiy**aš***
'As for my body'

This process can be summarized with the following rule: a -> Ø / V_____.

3.3.7 Suffixes with initial glottalized obstruents /k', c', č'/ or with /č/

Four suffixes of the shape CVCV with initial k', c', č', or č reduce the first syllable to a glottal stop after vowels: *-k'una/-ˀna* 'negative, *-c'ama/-ˀma* 'in, into', the applicative *-č'ana/-ˀna* 'to, onto', and the completive *-čaxa/-xa* 'all'. Some also drop the final vowel.

24. V________ C_______

n-ic'a-č'ana -> *nic'a**ˀna***
IMP.SG-act.with.teeth-APPL
'Bite (the meat) off (the bone)'

n-ataˀ-č'ana -> *nataˀ**č'an***
IMP.SG-chop-APPL
'Chop on it'

ˀ-ic'a-ˀna-čaxa-xana-t -> *ˀ-ic'aˀna**ˀxa**xanat*	*y-ok'im-č'an-čaxa-n* -> *yok'imč'an**čaxan***
1SG.A-act.with.teeth-APPL-all-FUT-ASP	1SG.A-hang-APPL-all-ASP
'I am going to gnaw it all off clean'	'I have hung them all up'

For the negative, this rule is optional (see also 3.2).

25. V_______ But also: V______

ˀaˀa-k'una-tinta ->	*ˀaˀa**ˀna**tinta*	*ˀanoˀa-k'una-t* ->	*ˀanoˀ**ak'una**t*
meat-NEG-ASP		pitchwood-NEG-ASP	
'It isn't meat'		'It wasn't pitchwood'	

3.3.8 Possessive markers

The vowel in some possessive markers is deleted before certain affixes, such as *-owa* and *-oq*.

26. /e,i/ deleted before *-owa*:

ˀuwela-ˀi-owa -> *ˀuwelaˀowa*
boy-POSS-ACCOMP
'Together with my boy'

pʰunsal-ye-owa -> *pʰunsalyowa*
woman-POSS-ACCOMP
'With his wife'

27. /e/ deleted before before *-oq*:

pʰunsal-ye-oq -> *pʰunsalyoq*
woman-POSS-former
'His former wife'

When the first person possessive marker *-ˀi* is suffixed, i.e. in alienable possession, and followed by the definite marker *-op*, the vowel is dropped and the preceding vowel occasionally assimilates to /o/.

28.

šunuhulla + ˀi + op	=	*šunuhullo̲ˀo̲p̲*	'My old woman'
čitxa + ˀi + op	=	*čitxoˀop*	'My blanket'
šinčela + ˀi + op	=	*šinčela̲ˀo̲p̲*	'My dog'
ˀiṭi + ˀi + op	=	*ˀiṭiˀop*	'My man'

3.3.9 The derivative -Vˀ

The derivative suffix -Vˀ, where V stands for /a, e, i, o, u/ assimilates the vowel to the vowel of the stem.

29.	*pq'il* + Vˀ + *hita*	=	*pq'iliˀit*	'it is crooked'
	wil + Vˀ	=	*wiliˀ*	'red'
	tul + Vˀ	=	*tuluˀ*	'stiff'
	pʰoṭ + Vˀ	=	*pʰoṭoˀ*	'dusty'
	t'an + Vˀ	=	*t'anaˀ*	'thick' (in consistency)

3.4 Morphophonemics in areal-typological perspective

Morphophonemic processes are often very language-specific. Therefore, no areal features have been identified. However, similar processes to the ones described in this chapter, though differing in their details, are also found in neighboring languages. In particular, vowel elision due to VV sequences at morpheme boundaries and consonant loss to avoid impermissible consonant clusters are frequent. Such processes have been described for Shasta, Wintu, Karuk, and Wiyot. Vowel and consonant elision at morpheme boundaries and word edges, especially for the phonologically weak /h/, are very common cross-linguistically.

Vowel alternations and vowel assimilation across affixes, similar to the process occurring with the negative circumfix in Chimariko, can also be seen in Shasta, Wintu, Yurok, Karuk. While in Chimariko vowels assimilate with regard to backness, in Wintu harmonic assimilations are based on vowel height.

Different pronominal shapes based on verb stem classes do not occur in the neighboring languages. Only Yurok shows a similar phenomenon having /e/ and /o/ stems with the corresponding vowel surfacing in the suffixes.

Overall, the morphophonemic processes found in Chimariko are common cross-linguistically but are not areal features.

4. WORD CLASSES

This chapter describes lexical categories and the criteria used for their distinction, i.e. their particular morphological and syntactic behavior. Chimariko distinguishes nouns, pronouns, adjectives, numerals, quantifiers, verbs, adverbs, copulas, particles, adpositions, and interjections. The status of adpositions is not clear.

4.1 Nouns

Nominal stems differ from verbal stems in that they can take possessive, privative, locative, and definite affixes, as well as case suffixes marking instruments or companions. It is unclear whether the locative is an affix or a postposition (see 5.5.1). Nominal stems may occur without any affixes, while verbal stems do not.

1. With possessive affix (from ‘Cutting finger when cleaning salmon’)

kima^{ʔ}ase ^{ʔ}uluyta^{ʔ}i huwatkun, č^{h}uxotayetkut

kima^{ʔ}ase	***^{ʔ}uluyta-^{ʔ}i***	*h-uwa-tku-n*	*č^{h}-uxota-ye-tku-t*
today	**sister-POSS**	3-go-DIR-ASP	1SG.P-look.at-?-DIR-ASP

‘My sister came over today, she came to visit me’

2. With privative affix (from ‘Crawfish’)

^{ʔ}aq^{h}a ye^{ʔ}aq^{h}tut čitxayamulla

^{ʔ}aq^{h}a	*ye-^{ʔ}aq^{h}tu-t*	***čitxa-yamu-lla***
water	1SG.A-into.water-ASP	blanket-without-DEP

‘I went immersingly into the water being naked’

3. With instrumental case suffix (from ‘Cutting finger when cleaning salmon’)

č^{h}uṭa ṭeyta yek^{h}utni č^{h}iselimtu, ^{ʔ}umul yek^{h}uta^{ʔ}če,

č^{h}u-ṭa	*ṭe-yta*	*y-ek^{h}ut-ni*	***č^{h}iseli-mtu***	*^{ʔ}umul*	*y-ek^{h}u-ta^{ʔ}če*
POSS-hand	?-POSS	1SG.A-cut-ASP	knife-INST	salmon	1SG.A-cut-ASP

‘I cut my thumb with a knife, when I was cleaning a salmon’

4. With locative and definite affix (from ‘Woman wanders’)

na^{ʔ}ahunmu ^{ʔ}awakunoi, ha^{ʔ}atpimda ^{ʔ}iṭirop

n-a^{ʔ}a-hun-mu	***^{ʔ}awa-kunoi***	*h-a^{ʔ}a-tpi-m-da*	***^{ʔ}iṭir-op***
IMP.SG-?-CONT-DIR	house-inside	3-?-DIR-DIR-ASP	man-DEF

‘Take her in the house, the man came out (and found her)’

5. With case suffix marking companions

5a. Harrington 020-0532
p^{h}unsalyowa

5b. Harrington 021-019
^{ʔ}uwela^{ʔ}owa

*pʰunsal-y-**owa***	*ˀuwela-ˀ-**owa***
woman-POSS-ACOMP	boy-POSS-ACOMP
'With his wife'	'Together with my boy'

Affixes termed 'instrumental' also occur with verbal stems. However, they are different in shape and function from the one found with nominal stems, as they also encode the instrument itself, such as for example *-mitei* 'with the foot' (see 8.2.6).

Nominal stems resemble verbal stems in that they can take the same inferential affix, as in the following example (see also 4.6). Nevertheless, the inferential could also be a clitic (see 4.8.7). Certain verbal affixes may occur with nominal stems in cases of verbalization (see 5.2.4).

6. With inferential affix (from 'Hollering at New River')

ˀapu xošektanat, himisamdudaˀn sideˀw

ˀapu	*x-ošekta-na-t*	***himisamdu-daˀn***	*si-deˀw*
fire	NEG-make-NEG-ASP	devil-INF	say-DER

'He made no fire, it must have been the devil, they said'

Nouns occur in noun phrases, either on their own or together with adjectives, numerals, quantifiers and/or adpositions. However, there is no evidence for a cohesive noun phrase, since there is no linking morphology between the potential parts (see 9.6). The examples below illustrate the co-occurrence of nouns with other lexical categories.

7. Co-occurrence with adjectives (from 'Woman wanders')

pʰuncar isik ˀimatni

pʰuncar	***isik***	*ˀ-imat-ni*
woman	pretty	1SG.A-find-ASP

'I found a pretty woman'

8. Co-occurrence with numerals (from 'Fugitives at Burnt Ranch')

č'imar xotai heṭaheskut uwatkut,

č'imar	***xotai***	*h-eṭahe-sku-t*	*uwa-tku-t*
man	three	3-run.away-DIR-ASP	go-DIR-ASP

'Three men came as fugitives'

9. Co-occurrence with quantifiers (from 'Woman wanders')

kumičin č'imar isiˀtinta, ˀimikot sumusut

kumičin	***č'imar***	*isiˀ-tinta*	*ˀimikot*	*sumu-su-t*
all	person	good-ASP	friend	like-be-ASP

'All people are good, they were like my friends'

10. Co-occurrence with adpositions (from Dixon 1910:335)

> *awa xunoi yeaxuʔnmoxanan*
> **awa   xunoi   ye-axuʔnmo-xana-n**
> house inside   1SG.A-?-FUT-ASP
> 'I shall go into the house'

Nouns function mostly as arguments, except in predicate nominal clauses where they combine with the copula to form predicates (see 9.3.3).

11. Predicate nominal (from 'Fugitives at Burnt Ranch')

> *kimot ʔuʔir asunda, čʰakʰo,   heṭaheshutaʔa sunda*
> **kimot   ʔuʔir   asu-nda   čʰ-akʰo   h-eṭahe-shu-taʔa   su-nda**
> these   stranger   be-ASP   IMP.PL-kill   3-run.away-DIR-?   be-ASP
> 'These are strangers, kill them, they are running away'

4.1.1 Common nouns and proper nouns

Common nouns do not differ significantly from proper nouns. Nevertheless, while common nouns occur with and without any morphology attached, proper nouns, for the most part, have either derivational morphology attached or are the result of compounding.

12. 12a. Common nouns

ʔama	'land'
čʼimar	'person'
hamew	'food'

ʔiṭir-op	'the man'
man-DEF	

12b. Proper nouns (personal names and placenames)

qʰaʔa-nolle	'round rock'	name of Friday
rock-round		(Chimariko consultant, see 1.3)
sumna-ʔama	'upstream land'	Manzanita Flat
upstream-land		
mayča-lla	'little field'	Underwood place
field-DIM		
himaʔ h-ičʰuk-tače	'head is lying there'	Green or Hennessey place
head 3-lying-LOC		(on the Trinity)

Only very few personal names have been recorded, while many placenames occur in the data (see 4.1.2).

4.1.2 Placenames

There are approximately 250 different placenames in the Harrington data (Bauman 1980:18). While some are transparent in meaning, others are not. Bauman (1980:18) notes that many placenames with corresponding Hupa or Wintu names are calques or loan translations of one another. His study, however, focuses on Chimariko placenames without providing any evidence of loan translations in neighboring languages. To examine the extension of the Chimariko territory Bauman studies placenames in three areas: New River, Big Bar, and Hyampom. These are summarized in the table below.

Table 1: Chimariko placenames (from Bauman 1980)

Name	Translation	Place
New River area		
čutamtače	'waterfalls (in river)'	Burnt Ranch
čalita /čalitasom	?; *-som* 'upstream'	Ironsides Mountain
mayča soˀre	'rough or ragged field'	Thomas or Ladd place (confluence of Quinby Creek with the New River)
himaˀ hičʰuktače	'head is lying there'	Green/Hennessey place (on the Trinity)
hime hakuče	?; *hime* 'night' (?)	Big Creek
ˀamaitace	?; *ˀama* 'land'	Hawkin's Bear or Irving place
ˀcxeposta	'dusty place'	Dyer's Ranch or Bell's Flat
tiˀra ˀapxay	'bird shit'	Bussell place at China Creek
qʰaˀa yawišmuče	'rock goes across place'	Forks of the New River
hissa hadamuče	?; *hissa* 'trail'	Dave Gray's place (on the Trinity)
Big Bar area		
čʰičʰanma	'manzanita place'	Taylor Flat
ˀak'ice	'salt place'	Below North Fork
qʰaˀa hetxattače	?; *qʰaˀa* 'stone'	Way up the Trinity
pʰoč'imi hičimu	?; *pʰoč'imi* 'bearskin'	Chaparral Mountain
sumnaˀama	'upstream land'	Manzanita Flat (upstream of Big Bear)
č'untxapmu	?	Big Flat
hičʰeqʰut	'deerlick at edge of water'	William Patterson place at Big Bar
tiltil ˀacuqʰa	'fishhawk creek'	Big Bar Creek at Big Flat
široki	?	French Creek near Del Loma
Hyampom area		
mayča	'field, flat'	Hyampom
čanqʰoma	?	Hayfork
hak'imtače	?	Spot in the South Fork River
hamuhči	?	Ross Ranch near Hayfork
hexasuče	'milt of a male salmon'	Falls in the Hayfork River
hicu kʰiˀnače	'where water flows	Fishing hole on the South Fork River

	against a rock'	
mayčalla	'little field'	Underwood place (downstream of Hyampom on the South Fork River)
muneriče	?	Where mines used to be located (downstream of Hyampom on the South Fork River)
paẋkʰoče mayča	?; *mayča* 'field'	Grassy Flat
paẋẋanˀače	?	Hinkley's field
p'usur qʰaˀanwa	'mouse rock house'	North of Hyampom on the Trinity trail
sisillače	?	Small hill north of Hayfork – South Fork confluence
čʰurinˀace	?	Oren Treat's place
č'upuqʰutta	'rock dropping in water and making noise'	Bluff on north edge of Hayfork River
waˀwayraˀače	?; *waaˀra* 'crow'	Will Olsen's place at Hyampom
ˀapunˀa txuylala	?; *ˀapunˀa* 'cedar', *txoy* 'scent'	Fishing hole in the South Fork River

The question marks in the table indicate that the original meaning is unclear. For some placenames only parts can be translated. It is apparent from the table above that placenames are frequently the result of compounding. These compounds often contain *ˀama* 'land', *mayča* 'field' or *qʰaˀa* 'rock'. Many of the names in the table end in *-(ta)če* or *-ce*. This could be a locative or derivational suffix meaning 'there, at' or 'the place of'. However, it does not occur with all placenames.

In language contact situations existing placenames are often maintained when a dominant group enters a new territory. This would suggest that Chimariko placenames were in use in places where their territory had been invaded by the Hupa and maybe by the Wintu and Shasta. Nevertheless, Bauman finds widespread placename borrowing in the form of calques and loan translations. Borrowing of the actual forms is rare. Bauman (1980:24) identifies some instances where Wintu has borrowed Chimariko placenames, in particular when local flora or fauna are included in the name. Interestingly, Chimariko placenames rarely indicate a directional orientation implying that the place was named from another location, as is often the case with Hupa or Wintu placenames (Bauman 1980:24).

4.2 Pronouns

Chimariko has personal, interrogative, and demonstrative pronouns. Other kinds of pronouns found in other languages, such as possessive or reflexive pronouns, are affixes in Chimariko.

4.2.1 Personal pronouns

Free personal pronouns are optional, as opposed to bound pronouns (see 8.1.4), and are used in combination with bound pronominal marking. Contrary to the bound pronouns, they seem to signal topic shift and contrast, but they do not index semantic roles, as the same forms are used for agents and patients. The forms in the table below occur most often in the data.

Table 2: Personal pronouns

	Singular	Plural
1	noʔot	načʰitot
2	mamot	mamqʰetot
3	pʰaʔmot	

Only the first and second person pronouns show a number distinction. A contracted form of the first person plural načʰot appears occasionally. The third person pronoun is based on the demonstrative with the same form (see 4.2.2), a common cross-linguistic feature. It has been noted for other languages spoken in the same area, such as Yuki (Mithun 2004a:2). Dixon (1910:322) also identifies two dual pronouns: nōutowa 'we two' and mamutowa 'you two'. The dual meaning is less clear in the Harrington data, as in the following example, and -owa could be the same comitative suffix found on nouns.

13. 13a. Harrington 020-0359   13b. Harrington 020-0359
     mamotowa čʰamaʔ   mamotowa noʔotowa čʰaki mačaʔlda
     mamot-owa čʰa-maʔ   mamot-owa noʔot-owa čʰa-ki   mačaʔlda
     2SG-DUAL POSS-head   2SG-DUAL 1SG-DUAL POSS-throat dry
     'Your and my head(s)'   'Our throats are dry'

The personal pronouns in Table 2 all end in the suffix -ot, which marks definiteness; it is also found on nouns. Dixon (1910:320) lists it as a 'suffix with an intensive, or emphatic meaning, such as indeed, really, in truth' and affirms that it can go on all stem classes. Grekoff (015.011) suggests that -ot has a "definitve" meaning. Given the presence of -ot in the personal pronouns, it can be inferred that their function may be primarily emphatic or topical in nature. This would be consistent with their optional presence and lack of a semantic role distinction. The optional presence of personal pronouns and their role in discourse is illustrated below.

14. Optional personal pronoun noʔot 'I' (from 'Woman wanders')

(1) xawi čʰušehektasun, sinda
     xawi   čʰ-ušehe-k-tasun   si-nda
     Redwood.Indians   1SG.P-take.along-DIR-PST   say-ASP
     'The bad Indians took me to this country, (the woman) said'

(2) čʼimar it akʰoteʔn, noʔot čʰušehemdeʔwšur
     čʼimar it   akʰo-teʔ-n   noʔot   čʰ-ušehe-m-deʔw-šur
     person many kill-DER-ASP 1SG   1SG.P-take.along-DIR-DER-formerly
     'They killed lots of people, they took me off my folks,'

(3) hit akʰodeʔw čʼimara, noʔot čušehemdeʔw kʼoṭihut
     hit   akʰo-deʔw   čʼimar-a   noʔot č-ušehe-m-deʔw   kʼoṭihu-t

many kill-DER person-? 1SG 1SG.P-take.along-DIR-DER run.away-ASP
'They killed many people, they took me off, I fled'

(4) *ˀawa hida imamda ˀamaq'eˀta*
ˀawa hida i-mam-da ˀama-q'e-ˀ-ta
house lots 1SG.A-see-ASP country-die-1SG.A-ASP
'I saw lots of houses, I will die in this country'

. . .

(5) *č'imariko ˀiko'tinda, noˀot xukeenadinda,*
č'imariko ˀi-ko'-tinda ***noˀot*** *x-ukee-na-dinda*
Chimariko 1SG.A-talk-ASP 1SG NEG-know-NEG-ASP
'I talk Chimariko, I don't understand'

(6) *ˀikeedinda, ˀiwoxandinda*
ˀi-kee-dinda ˀ-iwo-xan-dinda
1SG.A-hear-ASP 1SG.A-sit.down-FUT-ASP
'I understand that I will stay here'

In the example above the personal pronoun *noˀot* 'I' occurs in lines (2), (3), and (5) in addition to the bound pronominal affix, while only the bound pronominal affix occurs in lines (1), (4), and (6). Whereas in (2) and (3) *noˀot* 'I' functions as a patient, as can be seen in the form of the bound pronominal affix, in (5) it is an agent. The woman is the main topic of the narrative, and the personal pronoun helps to keep track of that topic.

Other forms of the personal pronouns occur with a contrastive affix instead of *-ot*. These pronouns contrast one person to another.

Table 3: Topical and contrastive pronouns

'Topical': suffix *-ot*	*noˀ-ot* 'I, me'	*mam-ot* 'you'	*način-ot* 'we, us'
'Contrastive': suffix *-iš/-uš*	*naˀ-iš* 'but I, as for me'	*mam-uš* 'but you, as for you'	*način-uš* 'but we, as for us'

In the data examined, the contrastive pronouns are far less common than the topical ones. While free personal pronouns are rare in the oral narratives analyzed, in what seems to be elicited data they appear almost exclusively with the topical suffix. It is unclear whether both types of pronouns can be used in combination in a clause. The examples below illustrate the use of pronouns.

15. 15.a. Harrington 020-1125
mamqʰetot qʰuk'oˀnat č'imarot
mamqʰetot *qʰ-uk'o-ˀna-t č'imar-ot*
2PL 2PL-talk-APPL-ASP person-DEF
'Did you fellows talk to him?'

15b. Harrington 020-1125
himow, yak'oˀnan pʰaˀmot

himow ya-k'o-ˀna-n ***pʰaˀmot***
yes 1PL.A-talk.APPL-ASP 3
'Yes, we talked to him'.

16. Harrington 020-0362
mamuš qʰosixanaˀ
mamuš *qʰosi-xana-ˀ*
2SG what-FUT-Q
'What are you going to do?'

4.2.2 Interrogative pronouns

Interrogative pronouns are used in question-word-questions (see 10.2). They occur clause-initially. There are no similarities in the shapes of the different interrogative pronouns, except for the suffix *-lla* of unclear meaning. It occurs in *qʰomalla* 'where' and *ˀawilla* 'who'.

17. 'On grandmother getting the hiccups'
pačʰaˀ qʰosumsiˀ, pačʰi misekmuˀ
pačʰaˀ *qʰ-osumsi-ˀ* ***pačʰi*** *m-isekmu-ˀ*
what 2PL-do-Q what 2SG-swallow-Q
'What did you all do, what did you swallow?'

18. 'Fugitives at Burnt Ranch'
qʰoqʰ uwadokta, č'imara, qʰomall akʰodeˀ
qʰoqʰ uwa-do-kta č'imar-a ***qʰomall*** *akʰo-de-ˀ*
two go-?-DIR man-? where kill-DER-Q
'Two got back here home, where did they kill him?'
...
qʰomalla qʰuktaˀ
qʰomalla *qʰu-kta-ˀ*
where 2PL-DIR-Q
'Where have you been?'

19. Harrington 020-1124
ˀawilla hawuˀ
ˀawilla *h-awu-ˀ*
who 3-give-Q
'To whom did he give it?

Dixon (1910:322) lists eight different interrogative pronouns. They all derived from a single stem *qo-* or *qa-*, according to him. The forms are very similar to the ones recorded by Harrington, as can be seen below.

Table 4: Interrogative pronouns (Dixon, 1910:322 and Harrington)

Dixon	Harrington	
qomas or *awilla*	*ˀawilla*	who
qâtci or *pātci*	*pačʰaˀ, pačʰi*	what
qomalla	*qʰomalla*	where
qosidadji	*qʰositaˀče*	why
	pačʰaˀaqʰositaˀče	what for (what-why)
qâsuk	*qʰosuk*	when
qâtala		how many
qâtcu		how far
qâtramdu		how often

4.2.3 Demonstrative pronouns

Demonstrative pronouns differ from demonstrative determiners in that the noun, if present, does not have a focal marker suffixed (see 4.3), as in the following example.

20. 'Fugitives at Burnt Ranch'
kimot ˀuˀir asunda, čʰakʰo, heṭaheshutaˀa sunda
kimot *ˀuˀir asu-nda čʰ-akʰo h-eṭahe-shu-taˀa su-nda*
these stranger be-ASP IMP.PL-kill 3-run.away-DIR-? be-ASP
'These are strangers, kill them, they are running away'

Dixon (1910:322) describes two kinds of demonstrative pronouns, those indicating 'near the speaker, here' and those indicating 'at a distance, there'. The form in the example above resembles Dixon's *qewot* 'this'. The other form Dixon describes, *pamut* 'that', resembles the third person personal pronoun. The same forms are used for the demonstrative pronouns and determiners (see 4.3).

4.3 Demonstrative determiners

Demonstrative determiners have the same forms as demonstrative pronouns. Contrary to demonstrative pronouns they co-occur with a noun in the same noun phrase, either preceding or following it. The co-occurring noun always has a definite suffix *-ot*.

21. Closer to the speaker 'this' (from 'Woman wanders')
kimot č'imarot niwo sudadinda hisik ik'onda ˀawami sumusudinda
kimot č'imar-ot *n-iwo su-da-dinda hisik ik'o-nda*
this person-DEF IMP.SG-stay be-ASP-ASP good talk-ASP
'This man told her to stay there, he talked nice'

22. Closer to the speaker 'this' (from 'Woman wanders')
kimot ˀiṭirot č'imar hit, ˀimikot č'imara, ˀiṭixaˀideˀw sumusut
kimot ˀiṭir-ot *č'imar hit ˀimikot č'imar-a ˀiṭixaˀi-deˀw sumu-su-t*
this man-DEF person lots friend person-? chief-DER like-be-ASP
'This man, lots of people, a friend of the people, he was like a chief'

23. Further away from the speaker 'that' (from 'Mrs Bussell')

huwaktat masunu šunuhullot pʰaˀmot

h-uwa-kta-t	*masunu*	***šunuhull-ot***	***pʰaˀmot***
3-go-DIR-ASP	always	old.woman-DEF	that.one

'She always goes around, that old woman'

There are two demonstrative determiners: *kimot* 'this' and *pʰaˀmot* 'that'. Their exact functions are unclear due to the closed corpus. It can be speculated that *kimot* indicates that something is closer to the speaker while *pʰaˀmot* indicates that something is further away from the speaker.

4.4 Adjectives

Adjectival stems are identical to the verb stem class taking pronominal suffixes. They can take pronominal, tense, aspect, and modal suffixes. Corresponding stative verbs and adjectives are based on the same root, such as *ṭewu* 'be big, big'.

Adjectives can have two syntactic functions: they are either attributive or predicative. Attributive adjectives differ from both verbs and nouns in two ways: (1) they do not take any affixes and (2) they always co-occur with a noun. Adjectives in predicative function do not differ from verbs morphologically or syntactically. This is shown in the examples below.

24. Attributive adjective (from 'Woman wanders')

hiwanda, čitx isiˀ isiˀdaˀn ˀičinšoll isiˀ yoxaˀidaˀn

h-iwa-nda	***čitx***	***isiˀ***	*isiˀ-daˀn*	***ˀičinšoll***	***isiˀ***	*y-oxaˀi-daˀn*
3-go-PROG	blanket	good	good-INF	dress	good	1SG.A-make-INF

'She was coming, good blanket, it must have been good, I will make a good dress'

25. Attributive adjective (from 'Dailey chased by the bull')

ˀisiyakutni haˀačʰakinta mušmuš ṭewu,

ˀi-siyakut-ni	*haˀa-čʰa-k-inta*	***mušmuš***	***ṭewu***
1SG.A-?-ASP	?-1SG.P-DIR-PROG	bull	big

'I looked back, the big bull was taking after me'

26. Predicative adjective (from 'Fugitives at Burnt Ranch')

hisiˀmedaˀ, maik isiˀmedaˀ, ˀama xoliˀxanan

hisiˀ-me-daˀ	*maik*	***isiˀ-me-daˀ***	*ˀama*	***xoliˀ-xana-n***
good-?-PST	?	good-?-PST	country	bad-FUT-ASP

'All is good down there now, it will be good, the country will be all bad'

27. Predicative adjective = stative verb (from Harrington 020-1113)

mamq^hedot ṭewuq^hoxanat
mamq^hedot ***ṭewu-q^ho-xana-t***
2PL big-2PL-FUT-ASP
'You are going to be big'

While predicate nominals are accompanied by a copula *su* 'to be' that takes verbal affixes, predicate adjectives are not, since they do not differ from verbs (see 4.8.1).

4.5 Numerals and quantifiers

Chimariko has several numerals and a set of other quantifiers that co-occur with nouns. Numerals and other quantifiers can take determinative or verbal suffixes when not co-occurring with nouns.

4.5.1 Numerals

Chimariko combines a quinary and a decimal system of numerals. The numbers from 6 to 8 are based on 5 + X, where X is 1, 2, or 3. Similarly, the numbers from 16 to 18 are based on 10 + 5 + X, where X is 1, 2, or 3. The number 5 is different from the base 5 in the compounds, *ṭanehe* '5' and *čipom/špom* '5 plus something' respectively. The number 10 translates to 'one arrow'. The numbers from 11 to 15 are based on 10 + X, where X stands for 1, 2, 3, 4, or 5. The same as for 5, the number 10 and the base 10 in the compounds have different shapes, *p'unčipom* '10' and *rasut/sut* '10 plus something' respectively. Two different shapes have been recorded for 20: (1) *šanpunasut* combining the number 10 and the base 10 and (2) *xok^humdunšanpun* meaning 'two times ten'. The same pattern as in (2) occurs with 40: *q^huygundunsanpun* 'four times ten'. Dixon also records 30 as *xodamtun sa^ʔanpun* 'three times ten' and 100 as *pucua pun* 'one wood'. The numerals recorded by Harrington and Sapir are summarized in the table below.

Table 5: Chimariko numerals

Number	Harrington 020-0005 (Sally Noble)	Harrington 022-005 (Lucy Montgomery)	Sapir
1	*p'un*	*p'un*	*p'un*
2	*q^hoq^hu*	*xokk^hu*	*xok^hu*
3	*xotai*	*xutoy*	*xut'ay*
4	*k^hulgu*	*quytu / quygu*	*xoko*
5	*čranehe*	*ṭanehe*	*č^hanehe*
6	*p'un-čipom*	*p'un čipom / p'un čibom*	*p'un-sip^hom*
7	*kok^hu-špom*	*xok^hišpom*	*xok^hu-sp^hom*
8	*xota-čipom*	*xutayčibom*	*xut'ay-č^hip^hom*
9	*p'un-čuku*	*p'un čiku/ p'un čigu*	*p'un-p'em*
10	*san-pun*	*šan bun*	*sa^ʔan-p'un*
11		*p'unrasut*	
12		*xok^husut*	

13		*xutasut*	
14		*qʰuygusut*	
15		*ṭanehesut*	
16		*p'unčibomasut*	
17		*xokʰuspumasut*	
18		*xutayčibomasut*	
19		*p'unčigusut*	
20	*kokum tun san-pun*	*šanpunasut / šanbunasut* *xokʰumdunšanpun*	
40		*qʰuygundunsanpun/* *qʰuygundunsanbun*	

Numerals occur together with nouns in noun phrases, either preceding or following the noun. They do not take any affixes when co-occurring with nouns.

28a. 'Fugitives at Burnt Ranch'
č'imar xotai heṭaheskut uwatkut
č'imar ***xotai*** *h-eṭahe-sku-t* *uwa-tku-t*
man three 3-run.away-DIR-ASP go-DIR-ASP
'Three men came as fugitives'
. . .
yaxamamnan, p'un ˀiṭilla ˀuleeda himamda
ya-x-amam-na-n ***p'un*** ***ˀiṭi-lla*** *ˀuleeda* *h-imam-da*
1PL.A-NEG-see-NEG-ASP one man-DIM sibling 3-see-ASP
'We didn't see it, a boy saw it'

28b. 'Hollering at New River'
himedašur ˀapu pačʰigut, ˀawa qʰoqʰ huhooidat
himedašur *ˀapu* *pačʰigut* ***ˀawa*** ***qʰoqʰ*** *h-uhooida-t*
next.morning fire no.more house two 3-?-ASP
'The next morning there was no fire, there were two houses here too'

Numerals can also occur without an accompanying noun, as in the following examples.

29a. 'Fugitives at Burnt Ranch'
qʰoqʰ uwadokta, č'imara, qʰomall akʰodeˀ
qʰoqʰ *uwa-do-kta* *č'imar-a* *qʰomall* *akʰo-de-ˀ*
two go-?-DIR man-? where kill-DER-Q
'Two got back here home, where did they kill him?'

29b. Harrington 020-1132
p'un himičitta šičela
p'un *h-imičit-ta* *šičela*
one 3-kick-ASP dog
'One kicks the dog all the time'

Following Grekoff (008.012) numerals can have a determinative suffix *-lle* attached.

30. *q^h^oq^h^u-lle* 'the two of them' (Harrington 020-0466)
x̣utay-lle 'the three of them'

Numerals can be verbalized by taking verbal suffixes, as in the following examples.

31. 31a. Harrington 020-0406
qʰoqʰuxanat
qʰoqʰu-xana-t
two-FUT-ASP
'There are going to be two'

31b. Harrington 020-0406
šuur qʰoqʰuneq
šuur qʰoqʰu-neq
formerly two-PST
'There used to be two'

Haas (1976) found that several languages in Northern California have changed their numeral systems as a result of language contact. Following Haas (1976:355), the numeral systems in Northern California are decimal, quinary, senary, or quaternary. While Athabaskan languages have decimal systems, Algonquian languages are generally quinary. The Algonquian Yurok and Wiyot, two distant neighbors of Chimariko to the west, developed decimal systems due to contact with Athabaskan Hupa. Close neighbors of Chimariko have either a quinary or a decimal system. Shasta and Wintu are quinary, though the system is less clear in Wintu, and Hupa is decimal. Given that Chimariko has both, it may have adapted part of its quinary system to decimal due to the close contact with Hupa. However, numbers higher than 10 are sometimes poorly recorded or simply not used very often. A summary of the numeral systems in Northern California based on the numbers from five to ten is given in the following table. No other language has the exact same system as Chimariko.

Table 6: Numeral systems in Northern California (from Haas 1976)

Language	Numbers 5-10					
Chimariko	5	+1	+2	+3	-1	10
Close neighbors						
Hupa	5	6	7	8	9	10
Shasta	5	+1	+2	+3	+4	5x2
Wintu	5	2x3	7	2x4	-1	10
Distant neighbors to the west						
Karuk	5	+1	+2	+3	?	10
Yurok	5	6	7	8	9	10
Wiyot	5	6	7	8	9	10
Distant neighbors to the east						
Yana	5	+1	+2	+3	+4	10
Achumawi	5	6	+2	4x2	-1	10
Maidu (two systems)	5	3x2	3x2+1	-	-	5x2
	5	+1	+2	-	-	5x2

4.5.2 Quantifiers

In addition to numerals, Chimariko has a set of quantifiers used to specify the amount or quantity of an entity. The quantifiers occur with or without accompanying nouns. With accompanying nouns they immediately follow the noun for the most part.

32. Without accompanying noun (from 'Woman wanders')

č'imar hey^{ʔ}ewinda, kumičin č^{h}uk'o^{ʔ}nan
č'imar h-ey^{ʔ}ew-inda ***kumičin*** *č^{h}-uk'o-^{ʔ}na-n*
person 3-?-ASP all 1SG.P-talk-APPL-ASP
'The people are good,they all talk to me good'

33. Without accompanying noun (from 'Hopping game')

lawinta weč^{h}up himantamut, lawinta hup^{h}u hice^{ʔ}p^{h}emtu
law-inta ***weč^{h}up*** *h-iman-tamu-t law-inta hup^{h}u h-ice^{ʔ}p^{h}e-mtu*
?-ASP some 3-fall-DIR-ASP ?-ASP foot 3-?-INST
'Some of them give out and fall down, with one foot they couldn't stand it'

34. Without accompanying noun (from 'On grandmother getting the hiccups')

hisekmut, hisi^{ʔ}ta hatru. hita hisekmuta^{ʔ}
h-isekmu-t hisi^{ʔ}-ta haṭu ***hita*** *h-isekmu-ta^{ʔ}*
3-swallow-ASP good-ASP then lots 3-swallow-INF
'She swallowed, and then she was all right. I guess she took a little too much.'
. . .
^{ʔ}isekmu čisit, xakimnan, xotalla hipuhunmate^{ʔ}q^{h}, sit.
^{ʔ}-isekmu či-si-t x-akim-na-n ***xotalla*** *h-ipu-hunma-te^{ʔ}q^{h} si-t*
1SG.A-swallow ?-say-ASP NEG-?-NEG-ASP a.little 3-work-DIR-ADM say-ASP
'I tried to swallow it, but it wouldn't go down, a little one should put (in the mouth), she said'

35. With accompanying noun (from 'Fugitives at Burnt Ranch')

xoli^{ʔ}ta^{ʔ}n, q^{h}ak^{h}ot, hetaxawi uwatkukon
xoli^{ʔ}-ta^{ʔ}n q^{h}-ak^{h}o-t ***heta-xawi*** *uwa-tku-kon*
bad-INF 2PL-kill-ASP many-Redwood.Indians go-DIR-FUT
'It is not right, you killed him, lots of Redwood Indians will come'

36. With accompanying noun (from 'Woman wanders')

hisi^{ʔ}ta p^{h}uncarop, hamew it exa^{ʔ}ita, hisi^{ʔ}ta,
hisi^{ʔ}ta p^{h}uncar-op ***hamew it*** *exa^{ʔ}i-ta hisi^{ʔ}ta*
good woman-DEF food lots make-DER good
'The new (good) woman, (she) cooked lots of (good) food'

37. With accompanying noun (from 'Woman wanders')

č'imar it ak^{h}ote^{ʔ}n
č'imar ***it*** *ak^{h}o-te^{ʔ}-n*
person lots kill-DER-ASP
'(The bad Indians) killed lots of people'

no^{ʔ}ot č^{h}ušehemde^{ʔ}wšur hit ak^{h}ode^{ʔ}w č'imara
no^{ʔ}ot č^{h}-ušehe-m-de^{ʔ}w-šur ***hit*** *ak^{h}o-de^{ʔ}w* ***č'imar-a***
1SG 1SG.P-take.along-DIR-DER-formerly many kill-DER person-?
'They took me off my folks, they killed many people'

38. With accompanying noun (from 'Woman wanders')

^{ʔ}awa hida imamda ^{ʔ}amaq'e^{ʔ}ta,
^{ʔ}awa ***hida*** *imam-da ^{ʔ}ama-q'e-^{ʔ}-ta*
house lots see-ASP country-die-1SG.A-ASP
'I saw lots of houses, I will die in this country'

39. With accompanying noun (from 'Woman wanders')

hamew ita yeman, hopew
hamew ***ita*** *y-ema-n hopew*
food lots 1SG.A-eat-ASP acorn.soup
'I eat lots, lots of acorn-soup'

In example 35 the quantifier is prefixed to the noun. This is the only example of this nature, and it may be that these are separate words. There is no distinction between quantifiers that go with count nouns or mass nouns, as examples 35-39 show, since there is no evidence for a formal distinction between count and mass nouns. Semantically, examples 35, 37, and 38 have count nouns while in examples 36 and 39 there are mass nouns, all occurring with *it/ita/hida* 'lots'.

Quantifiers can occur with what appears to be pronominal suffixes. However, the pronominal forms do not coincide in shape with verbal pronominal markers (see 8.1.1).

40. Harrington 020-0406

kumičinče	*kumičinq^{h}e*	*p^{h}a^{ʔ}mot kumičinča*
kumičin-če	*kumičin-q^{h}e*	*p^{h}a^{ʔ}mot kumičin-ča*
all-1PL	all-2PL	3 all-?
'all of us'	'all of you (plural)'	'all of them'

4.6 Verbs

Verbal stems differ from nominal stems in that they take pronominal, tense, aspect, and modal affixes, among others (see chapter 8). Verbs are the only word class that can take pronominal prefixes. They never occur without any affixes.

41. With pronominal and tense affix (from 'Crawfish')

pʰiˀa yehatat, hiničxeˀkut, ˀičiˀta, puqʰela ˀitxaˀmat

pʰiˀa	***y-ehata-t***	***h-iničxeˀku-t***	***ˀ-ičiˀ-ta***	*puqʰela*	***ˀ-itxaˀma-t***
grease	1SG.A-have-ASP	3-smell-ASP	1SG.A-catch-ASP	basket	1SG.A-put-ASP

'I had grease, they smelled it, I caught them, I put them in a basket'

42. With pronominal and aspectual affix (from 'Hollering at New River')

č'imar hepatta čeminčan

č'imar	***h-epat-ta***	*čeminčani*
people	3-sit-ASP	across.the.river

'The people were living on the other side of the river'

43. With pronominal and modal affix (Harrington 020-1103)

q'ehkunatiˀarhini
q'e-h-kuna-tiˀarhini
die-3-NEG-MOD
'I guess he didn't die'

Verbs can also take negative and interrogative affixes, as in the following examples.

44. With negative and modal affix (from 'Fugitives at Burnt Ranch')

čʰaxakʰona, wečʰup čʰaxakʰona, ˀama xoliˀyu

čʰa-x-akʰo-na	*wečʰup*	***čʰa-x-akʰo-na***	*ˀama*	*xoliˀ-yu*
IMP.PL-NEG-kill-NEG	some	IMP.PL-NEG-kill-NEG	country	bad-ADM

'Don't kill them, some said don't kill them, lest it spoil the country'

45. With interrogative affix (from 'On grandmother getting the hiccups')

pačʰaˀ qʰosumsiˀ, pačʰi misekmuˀ

pačʰaˀ	***qʰ-osumsi-ˀ***	*pačʰi*	***m-isekmu-ˀ***
what	2PL-do-Q	what	2SG-swallow-Q

'What did you all do, what did you swallow'

Many other affixes occur with verbal stems (see chapter 8), but they are not summarized here.

Verbs function as predicates and can form clauses by themselves. They can take one, two, or three arguments. Adjectival/stative stems, in contrast, can take only one argument, and they cannot occur with the entire set of verbal affixes. For example, only verbal stems can take the detransitivizing *-teˀw* suffix or the reflexive suffix.

46. 'Fugitives at Burnt Ranch' (3 clauses)

yaxak^{h}onaxan$^?$i, mak^{h}otaxantinda, k'otnihu,

[ya-x-ak^{h}o-na-xan-$^?$i]	***[m-ak^{h}o-ta-xan-tinda]***	***[k'ot-ni-hu]***
1PL.A-NEG-kill-NEG-FUT-ASP	2SG-kill-DER-FUT-ASP	run.away.IMP.SG-CONT

'We won't kill them, he is going to kill you, run away'

47. 'Woman wanders' (with detransitivizing *-te$^?$w*)

hišehekte$^?$w, hexačide$^?$w, hišehet, k'oṭihut,

*h-išehek-**te$^?$w***	*h-exači-**de$^?$w***	*h-išehe-t*	*k'oṭi-hu-t*
3-take.along-DER	3-steal-DER	3-take.along-ASP	run.away-CONT-ASP

'Bad Indians took her along, they stole her, they took her along, she ran away'

4.7 Adverbs

Adverbs function as specifiers for verbs, adjectives, entire clauses, and other adverbs. Most adverbs in Chimariko specify verbs, i.e. the time, place, or manner of an action or state.

48. Adverb specifying the time of a state (from 'Hollering at New River')

himedašur $^?$apu pač^{h}igut

himedašur	*$^?$apu*	*pač^{h}igut*
next.morning	fire	no.more

'The next morning there was no fire'

49. Adverb specifying the time of a state (from 'Crawfish')

šur txol hetat

šur	*txol*	*hetat*
formerly	crawfish	they.were.many

'Formerly there were many crawfish'

50. Adverb specifying the time of an action (from 'Mrs Bussell')

masunu huwaktanhut šunuhullot

masunu	*h-uwa-kta-nhu-t*	*šunuhull-ot*
always	3-go-DIR-CONT-ASP	old.woman-DEF

'The old woman (Mrs. Bussell) goes around all the time'

. . .

kimass uwatkun, huwomni welmu

kimass	*uwa-tku-n*	*h-uwo-m-ni*	*welmu*
today	go-DIR-ASP	3-go-DIR-ASP	quickly

'Today she came, she went back home at once'

51. Adverb specifying the time of an action/state
(from 'Cutting finger when cleaning salmon')

kimaˀase ˀuluytaˀi huwatkun, čʰuxotayetkut, hiwonta xanim
kimaˀase *ˀuluyta-ˀi h-uwa-tku-n čʰ-uxota-ye-tku-t h-iwo-nta* ***xanim***
today sister-POSS 3-go-DIR-ASP 1SG.P-look.at-?-DIR-ASP 3-stay-PROG still
'My sister (Martha) came over today, she came to visit me, she is still here'

52. Adverb specifying the time of an action
(from 'On grandmother getting the hiccups')

puneš ṭamma hiput
puneš *ṭamma h-ipu-t*
once salmon.meal 3-work-ASP
'Once (my grandmother) took a mouthful of salmon-meal'

53. Adverb specifying the place of an action (from 'Fugitives at Burnt Ranch')

wisseeda čʰumčaxa
wisseeda *čʰ-um-čaxa*
downstream IMP.PL-DIR-COMP
'You all move down (to Billy Noble's place)'

54. Adverb specifying the place of a state (from 'Hollering at New River')

č'imar hepatta čeminčani, ˀakʰa ṭewut
č'imar h-epat-ta ***čeminčani*** *ˀakʰa ṭewu-t*
people 3-sit-ASP across.the.river water big-ASP
'The people were living on the other side of the river, the water was high.'

55. Adverb specifying the manner of an action (from 'Mrs Bussell')

welmu uwomni
welmu *uwo-m-ni*
quickly go-DIR-ASP
'At once she returned'

56. Adverb specifying the manner of an action (from 'Cutting navel')

keˀčʰulala, malla nakʰohoshu, xočʰulla xoliˀtinta, hičʰu nexaˀy
keˀčʰulala malla n-akʰohoshu ***xočʰulla*** *xoliˀ-tinta* ***hičʰu*** *n-exaˀy*
this.long there IMP.SG-cut short bad-ASP long IMP.SG-make
'This long (gesture), there you cut it off, it is bad short, make it long'

57. Adverb specifying the manner of an action/state (from 'Postnatal seclusion')

^{ʔ}elohq^{h}ut lu^{ʔ}it, ^{ʔ}ešoh xamanat

^{ʔ}eloh-q^{h}ut	*lu^{ʔ}-it*	***^{ʔ}ešoh***	*x-ama-na-t*
hot-liquid	drink-ASP	cold	NEG-eat-NEG-ASP

'She drinks the hot liquid, she does not eat cold'

^{ʔ}elohaikulla hamat, ^{ʔ}alla p'un, sumusut hiwot, p'olalla

^{ʔ}eloh-aikulla	*h-ama-t*	*^{ʔ}alla*	*p'un*	*sumu-su-t*	*h-iwo-t*	***p'olalla***
hot-only	3-eat-ASP	month	one	like-be-ASP	3-stay-ASP	alone

'She only eats hot, for one month, she lives like this, alone'

58. Adverb specifying the manner of an action (from 'Crawfish')

memat txolop ^{ʔ}iwinq^{h}utta

memat	*txol-op*	*^{ʔ}-iwin-q^{h}ut-ta*
alive	crawfish-DEF	1SG.A-dump-into.water-ASP

'I dumped them alive, the crawfish, immersingly'

Certain adverbs may be analyzed as compounds, such as *hime-da-šur* 'night-?-formerly' meaning 'the next morning', *kim-a^{ʔ}ase/kim-ass* 'this-day', or *^{ʔ}eloh-aikulla* 'hot-only'. In others, the meaning of potential parts is no longer transparent, as in *čeminčani* 'across the river'.

Adverbs do not have any identifiable affixes attached, except for *xoč^{h}ulla* 'short', *p'olalla* 'alone', and *^{ʔ}elohaikulla* 'hot only' all ending in *-lla* of uncertain meaning. Therefore, it is difficult to define them as a morphosyntactic category. They are found in clauses with verbs only or in clauses with verbs and nouns or pronouns. Most often they occur clause-initially.

The same stems can function as adjectives, stative verbs (see 7.1), or adverbs, such as *eloh* 'hot, be hot' or *ešoh* 'cold, be cold' (see examples 57 and 59).

59. *ešoh* 'cold, be cold' as adjective and stative verb (Harrington 020-0009 and 0494)

^{ʔ}ešoq'ehta	*q'a^{ʔ}a ^{ʔ}ešohta*	
***^{ʔ}ešoq'e**-h-ta*	*q^{h}a^{ʔ}a*	***^{ʔ}ešohta***
cold-3-ASP	stone	cold
'He is cold'	'cold stone'	

4.8 Closed small classes of words

There are sets of words in Chimariko that do not belong to any of the word classes described above in terms of their morphological or syntactic behavior. Some occur as both separate words and affixes. In some cases, the limited number of examples precludes a conclusive analysis.

4.8.1 Copula

The copula *su* 'to be' combines with noun phrases to form predicates. It behaves like a verb in that it appears with tense and aspect markers. However, it cannot form a clause by itself.

60a. 'Fugitives at Burnt Ranch'

kimot ˀuˀir asunda, čʰakʰo, heṭaheshutaˀa sunda
[*kimot ˀuˀir* ***asu-nda***] *čʰ-akʰo h-eṭahe-shu-taˀa su-nda*
these stranger be-ASP IMP.PL-kill 3-run.away-DIR-? be-ASP
'These are strangers, kill them, they are running away'
. . .
č'imarop, ˀuˀir asunda, xukeenanda
[*č'imar-op ˀuˀir* ***asu-nda***] *x-ukee-na-nda*
person-DEF stranger be-ASP NEG-understand-NEG-ASP
'He is a stranger, he doesn't understand'

60b. Harrington 020-0491

č'imarot map'un asudaˀ
č'imar-ot map'un asu-da-ˀ
person-DEF that.one be-ASP-Q
'Is that him?'

Copulas are not used with adjectives, since adjectival stems can take verbal affixes to form predicate adjectives. Predicate adjectives are themselves verbs.

61. *ˀamaq'eˀni, hisiˀta č'imara*
ˀama-q'e-ˀ-ni [***hisiˀ-ta*** *č'imar-a*]
country-die-1SG.A-ASP good-ASP person-?
'I will die in this country, the people are good'

4.8.2 Adpositions

Dixon identifies two locative postpositions *xunoi* 'inside' and *tcūmū* 'under'.

62. Locative postpositions (Dixon 1910:335)

a. *āwa xunoi yeaxu'nmoxanan*
āwa ***xunoi*** *ye-axu'nmo-xana-n*
house inside 1SG.A-?-FUT-ASP
'I shall go into the house'

b. *pusua hiya'talot tcūmū*
pusua h-iya'ta-lot ***tcūmū***
board 3-lie-NOM under
'It lies under a board'

In example 62b, the postposition follows the nominalized verb. According to the Harrington data, *kunoi* 'inside' is a suffix, rather than a postposition, as seen below.

63. 'Woman wanders'
naˀahunmu ˀawakunoi
n-aˀahun-mu ***ˀawa-kunoi***
IMP.SG-take-DIR house-inside
'Take her in the house'

It is unclear whether Chimariko has locative suffixes on nouns or locative postpositions due to the limited amount of examples.

4.8.3 Particles

The negative marker *kuna/k'una* can occur as a separate word or as a suffix. It does not take any affixes when occurring as a separate word.

64. Negative particle *k'una* (from 'Cutting navel')

nakʰohoshu k'una
n-akʰohoshu ***k'una***
IMP.SG-cut NEG
'Don't cut it'

65. Negative suffix *-kuna* (Harrington 020-1103 and 1105)

qʰehkunacoˈol	*yemakunaxanat*
*qʰe-h-**kuna**-coˈol*	*y-ema-**kuna**-xana-t*
die-3-NEG-MOD	1SG.A-eat-NEG-FUT-ASP
'Maybe he doesn't die'	'I am not going to eat'

In example 64, *kuna* is identified as a separate word. However, it could also be a negative suffix, since the negative is the last suffix in imperatives, as shown below.

66. Harrington 020-1132
nunuˀ nemičitkuna
*nunuˀ n-e-mičit-**kuna***
? IMP.SG-1P-kick-NEG
'Don't you kick me!'

Similarly, the word *maš* 'but' occurs as a separate word or fused with personal pronouns. As a separate word, it immediately follows the personal pronoun.

67. Particle *maš* 'but' (from 'On grandmother getting the hiccups')

mamot maš mipuhunmat hita, mamuš hita mipuhunmuˀ,
mamot ***maš*** *m-ipu-hunma-t* *hita* ***mamuš*** *hita m-ipu-hunmu-ˀ*
2SG but 2SG-work-DIR-ASP lots but.you lots 2SG-work-DIR-Q
'But you took lots, but did you take lots'

The word *maš* 'but' could also be interpreted as a clitic occurring here in full free form and syntactically attached to an initial topic *mamot* 'you' (addressing the grandmother, who is the main participant of the narrative, directly). Following that analysis the reduced form of the clitic *-š* occurs in *mamu-š* 'but you'. There are not enough examples for a full analysis of this issue.

4.8.4 Evidentials and discourse markers

Another set of words may be analyzed as evidential or discourse markers. They include *pʰaˀyit* 'he/she thus said', *sit* 'he/she said', and *sideˀw* 'it was said, they said'. Direct speech segments are not always introduced by an utterance predicate in the narratives.

68. 'Dailey chased by the bull'
moxowetnan, pʰaˀyit pʰuncarye
mo-x-owet-na-n ***pʰaˀyit*** *pʰuncar-ye*
2SG-NEG-hook-NEG-ASP thus.say woman-POSS
'He didn't hook you, thus said his wife'
. . .
hawitomta, čʰuwetni sit, hawitomta
h-awi-tom-ta *čʰu-wet-ni* ***si-t*** *h-awi-tom-ta*
3-afraid-?-ASP 1SG.P-hook-ASP say-ASP 3-afraid-?-ASP
'He was scared, he hooked me he said, he was scared'

xowetnat, hek'omatta, pʰaˀyit čʰuwetni sit
x-owet-na-t *h-ek'o-ma-tta* ***pʰaˀyit*** *čʰu-wet-ni* ***si-t***
NEG-hook-NEG-ASP 3-say-?-DER thus.say 1SG.P-hook-ASP say-ASP
'But he did not hook him, he told, thus he said, he hooked me, he said'

69. 'Hollering at New River'
ˀapu xošektanat, himisamdudaˀn sideˀw
ˀapu x-ošekta-na-t *himisamdu-daˀn* ***si-deˀw***
fire NEG-make-NEG-ASP devil-INF say-DER
'He made no fire, it must have been the devil, they said'

70. 'On grandmother getting the hiccups'
ˀisekmu čisit, xakimnan, xotalla hipuhunmateˀqʰ, sit.
ˀi-sekmu ***či-si-t*** *x-akim-na-n* *xotalla* *h-ipu-hunma-teˀqʰ* ***si-t***
1SG.A-swallow ?-say-ASP NEG-?-NEG-ASP a.little 3-work-DIR-ADM say-ASP
'I tried to swallow it, but it wouldn't go down, a little one should put, she said'

While these words show some verbal morphology, such as tense, aspectual, and derivational suffixes, they do not have any pronominal markers, and they cannot form clauses by themselves. Hence, they are different from verbs and considered a separate lexical category. They indicate that something was said, and they immediately follow the quoted speech segment.

4.8.5 Connectives

Chimariko does not have a conjunction with the meaning 'and'. Other words, however, may be analyzed as connectives (see also 12.1). The word *haṭu* 'then' could be either an adverb or a conjunction. No morphological or syntactic criteria point to one or the other. However, adverbs occur most often clause-initially, while *haṭu* 'then' occurs post-verbally.

71a. 'On grandmother getting the hiccups'
luˀni, ˀaqʰa luˀit haṭu
luˀ-ni *ˀaqʰa* *luˀ-it* ***haṭu***
drink-IMP.SG water drink-ASP then
'Drink, she drank then [water]'

hisekmut, hisiˀta haṭu. hita hisekmutaˀ
h-isekmu-t *hisiˀ-ta* ***haṭu*** *hita* *h-isekmu-taˀ*
3-swallow-ASP good-ASP then lots 3-swallow-INF
'She swallowed, and then she was all right. I guess she took a little too much.'

71b. 'Cutting navel'
nunuˀ, ˀaweye hinoˀylala hatu, nihuy, nataqmu honapu,
nunuˀ *ˀaweye* *h-inoˀy-lala* ***hatu*** *n-ihuy* *n-ataqmu* *honapu*
? sac 3-bear-? thereupon IMP.SG-wash IMP.SG-tie.up navel
'Let it be, she bears the sac thereupon, wash him, tie the navel'

4.8.6 Interjections

Only one interjection has been found in the data. The word *himow* 'yes' does not show any identifiable morphology.

72. 'On grandmother getting the hiccups'
himow, hita ˀipuhunmut.
himow *hita* *ˀ-ipu-hunmu-t*
yes lots 1SG.A-work-DIR-ASP
'Yes, I took lots.'

4.8.7 Clitics

There are several clitics in Chimariko. While some, such as the conditional *=soˀop* can never occur as separate words, others, such as the modal *=tiˀarhiniˀ* 'I guess', occur as separate words or attached to a constituent. Some suffixes that occur with verbal and nominal stems, such as the inferential *-taˀn* and other modal markers, may in fact be clitics, in particular when they have a clausal scope. However, the status of clitics is unclear due to the lack of phonological evidence, such as stress assignment, and due to the limited amount of data.

73. Conditional clitic =*soˀop* (from 'Hollering at New River')

kowmilot himisamtu hapukʰeˀxanat, himisamdu k'unoˀop

kow-mi-lot	*himisamtu*	*h-apukʰeˀ-xana-t*	*himisamdu*	*k'un=oˀop*
holler-POSS-NOM	devil	3-steal-FUT-ASP	devil	NEG=COND

'The devil will steal your voice, if it is not a devil'

ˀap hišektakon, č'imarsoˀop, xošektanakon

ˀap	*h-išekta-kon*	*č'imar=soˀop*	*x-ošekta-na-kon*
fire	3-make-FUT	person=COND	NEG-make-NEG-FUT

'He will make a fire, if a person, he does not make a fire'

Example 73 illustrates that =*soˀop* is a clitic since it is attached to the negative particle *k'una*. While particles cannot take any suffixes, they can take clitics, given that clitics are attached to clausal constituents and not to particular word classes.

4.8.8 Other word classes

The word *pʰaˀaasinni* 'that.way' could be viewed as an adverb or as a demonstrative pronoun. Due to the limited number of examples with demonstrative pronouns it is not possible to determine whether *pʰaˀaasinni* 'that way' functions as an adverb or a demonstrative pronoun.

74. 'Hopping game'

hiceˀpʰ upʰo hucumṭuket čimar xačile hapimtat pʰaˀaasinni

hiceˀpʰ	*upʰo*	*h-ucu-m-ṭuket*	*čimar*	*xačile*	*h-apim-ta-t*	***pʰaˀaasinni***
?	foot	3-hop-DIR-?	Indian	children	3-play-DER-ASP	that.way

'They hop on foot, the Indian children play that way'

4.9 Word classes in areal-typological perspective

The languages of Northern California have a category of noun or nominal stems and a category of verbs or verbal stems, each taking a different set of affixes and having different syntactic functions with some overlap. Adjectives or adjectival stems generally share morphological and syntactic properties with both nouns and verbs. In addition, most languages have a separate word category of pronouns. Furthermore, all languages have one or more category of words that do not take any affixes. Most often, this category is labelled adverbs or particles, and it is not uniform in its syntactic function. Overall, the word classes found in Chimariko are very similar to those found in neighboring languages.

5. NOUN MORPHOLOGY

This chapter describes the internal structure of nouns, as well as word formation processes such as compounding. It is divided into inflectional and derivational morphology.

5.1 Inflectional morphology

Chimariko has few inflectional morphemes on nominal stems: possessives, definite markers, and locative affixes, as well as case suffixes marking instruments and companions. Inflectional morphemes are either prefixed or suffixed.

5.1.1 Possession

Possession is marked on the possessed. Possessive affixes have for the most part the same forms as verbal pronominal affixes, and they are equally either prefixed or suffixed. The difference in the affixing pattern shows a contrast between alienable and inalienable possession.

Table 1: Possessive affixes

	Prefixed (body parts)	Suffixed (objects, kinship)
1SG 'my'	*č^{h}-*	*-^{ʔ}e/-^{ʔ}i*
2SG 'your'	*m-*	*-mi*
3SG 'his, her'	*h-*	*-ita/-ye*
1PL 'our'	*č^{h}a-*	*-č^{h}e*
2PL 'your'	*q^{h}-*	*-q^{h}*
3PL 'their'	*h-*	*-ita*

Except for the third person suffixed forms, the markers coincide with the bound pronominal forms. The position of the possessive pronouns, prefixed or suffixed, can be related to alienability, as the following examples show. Inalienable possessions, such as body parts, are prefixed. Alienable possessions, such as objects and kinship terms, are suffixed. The contrast is illustrated in example 5.

1. Harrington 020-1135

č^{h}-uṭa	'my hand'
m-iṭa	'your hand'
h-iṭa	'his/her hand'
č^{h}a-ṭa	'our hand',
q^{h}-uṭa	'your hand'
h-iṭa	'their hand'

2.

č^{h}-usot	'my eye'
m-usot	'your eye'
h-usot	'his, her eye'

čʰa-sot	'our eye'
qʰ-usot	'your eye'
h-usot	'their eye'

3.

ˀawa-ˀe	'my house'
ˀawa-mi	'your house'
ˀawa-ita	'his, her house'

4. Harrington 020-1157

ˀuluita-ˀe	'my sister'
ˀuluita-mi	'your sister'
ˀuluita-ita	'his sister'
ˀuluita-čʰe	'our sister'
ˀuluita-ita	'their sister'

5. Harrington 020-1135

čʰ-uweš	'my horn' (deer says)
noˀot huweš-ˀi	'my horn' (Frank says)

6a. 'Dailey chased by the bull'

moxowetnan, pʰaˀyit pʰuncarye

mo-x-owet-na-n	*pʰaˀyit*	*pʰuncar-ye*
2SG-NEG-hook-NEG-ASP	thus.say	woman-POSS

'He didn't hook you, thus said his wife'

6b. Harrington 020-0172

Dailey ˀamaye

Dailey	*ˀama-ye*
	land-POSS

'Dailey's ranch'

6c. Harrington 020-0665

Dailey ˀawaida

Daiely	*ˀawa-ida*
	house-POSS

'Dailey's house'

Possessive affixes are closer to the root than affixes marking nominal syntactic relations, such as the case suffix *-owa*:

7.

7a. Harrington 021-019	7b. Harrington 020-0532
ˀuwelaiowa	*pʰunsalyowa*
ˀuwela-i-owa	*pʰunsal-y-owa*
boy-POSS-ACCOMP	woman-POSS-ACCOMP
'together with my boy'	'with his wife'

5.1.2 Definite suffix

The nominal suffix *-ot/-op/-ut* marks definiteness. In general, it refers to known information that has previously been introduced in the discourse (see 9.1). It does not occur with proper nouns, but it is also present in independent pronouns (see 4.2.1 and 4.2.3) and the demonstrative determiner (see 4.3). For *-ot, -ut,* and *-op* Dixon (1910:320) says the following: 'a suffix apparently with an intensive, or emphatic meaning, such as *indeed, really, in truth*' and affirms that it is used with nominal, pronominal, verbal, adjectival, and adverbial stems. However, there is no support for such meanings in any of the translations, as the following examples illustrate.

8. Definite suffix -*ot* with animals (from Harrington 020-1093)

šičelot čʰawin, čʰutpai, čʰawin
šičel-ot *čʰ-awi-n* *čʰ-utpa-i* *čʰ-awi-n*
dog-DEF 1SG.P-afraid-ASP 1SG.P-bite-MOD 1SG.P-afraid-ASP
'I am afraid of the dog, he might bite, I am afraid'.

9. Definite suffix -*ot* with humans (from Harrington 020-1120)

ˀiṭinot hičiyat
ˀiṭin-ot *h-ičiya-t*
man-DEF 3-have.sores-ASP
'The man had sores on him'.

10. Definite suffix -*op* with humans (from 'Fugitives at Burnt Ranch')

hek'omatta, hakʰoteˀ č'imarop, xawiyop hakʰoteˀn
h-ek'o-ma-tta h-akʰo-teˀ ***č'imar-op*** ***xawiy-op*** *h-akʰo-teˀ-n*
3-say-?-DER 3-kill-DER person-DEF Indian-DEF 3-kill-DER-ASP
'He (the boy) told (it), they killed the boy, the people, the Indians killed him'.

11. Definite suffix -*op* with animals (from 'Fugitives at Burnt Ranch')

memat txolop ˀiwinqʰutta
memat ***txol-op*** *ˀ-iwin-qʰut-ta*
alive crawfish-DEF 1SG.A-dump.liquid-ASP
'I dumped them alive, the crawfish, immersingly'

12. Definite suffix -*op* with inanimates (from 'Crawfish')

hiničxeˀkut, pʰiˀalop, hiničxeˀkut
h-iničxeˀku-t ***pʰiˀal-op*** *h-iničxeˀku-t*
3-smell-ASP bacon-DEF 3-smell-ASP
'They smelled it, that bacon, they smelled it'

The suffix occurs with animate and inanimate participants, and it is invariant for number or semantic role.

5.1.3 Locative suffixes

Independent nominals describing a place do not bear any special marking. Nevertheless, Dixon (1910:335) points to two locative postpositions: *xunoi* 'into' and *čumu* 'under'. In the Harrington data examined *kunoi* 'inside' occurs as a suffix.

13. Locative suffix -*kunoi* (from 'Woman wanders')

naʔahunmu ˀawakunoi
n-aˀa-hun-mu ***ˀawa-kunoi***
IMP.SG-?-CONT-DIR house-inside
'Take her in the house'

The same as in the only example offered by Dixon (1910:335), *kunoi* 'inside' occurs with *ˀawa* 'house' in 13. In addition, a directional affix -*mu* appears in the verb stem. It remains unclear whether the directional verbal affix, the nominal affix, or both describe the location. Therefore, the function of the affix (-)*kunoi*, or postposition as suggested by Dixon, can not be clearly identified as marking a locative relation.

Another suffix indicating a location is -*če* 'there, the place of'. The same suffix is also found on many placenames, most likely due to lexicalisation (see 5.4).

14. Locative suffix -*če*

14.a 'Mrs Bussell'
ˀawaidače xowonat, šičel hiwontat
ˀawa-ida-če *x-owo-na-t* *šičel* *h-iwon-ta-t*
house-POSS-LOC NEG-stay-NEG-ASP horse 3-ride-DER-ASP
'She does not stay at home, she goes around on horseback'

14b. Grekoff 020.006
č'imal huwatkun ˀawamiče
č'imal *h-uwa-tku-n* ***ˀawa-mi-če***
person 3-go-DIR-ASP house-POSS-LOC
'Someone has come to your house'

In example 14b, as in example 13, a directional affix -*tku* occurs with the verb stem. Given that -*če* follows the inflectional possessive affix, it cannot be considered a derivational affix. However, there are no locative case suffixes on nouns in Chimariko. The ending on the noun is probably not relational; it just creates a nominal that specifies a place.

Grekoff also identifies a locative suffix -*(n)ni*. It can be used for locative and temporal expressions, as in the following example.

15. 15a. Harrington 020-0579

himaˀni
himaˀ-ni
head-LOC
'at the tip end, at the head'

15b. Grekoff 008.012

ˀasotinni
ˀasoti-nni
winter-LOC
'in the winter'

5.1.4 Nominal syntactic relations

Core arguments are unmarked for case. Only two kinds of arguments are marked for case in Chimariko: instruments and companions.

5.1.4.1 Instrumental suffix -mtu. When an independent nominal describes an instrument, an instrumental case suffix *-mtu* is added to the noun stem.

16a. 'Cutting finger when cleaning salmon'

čʰuṭa ṭeyta yekʰutni čʰiselimtu, ˀumul yekʰutaˀče

čʰ-uṭa	*ṭe-yta*	*y-ekʰut-ni*	***čʰiseli-mtu***	*ˀumul*	*y-ekʰu-taˀče*
POSS-hand	?-POSS	1SG.A-cut-ASP	knife-INST	salmon	1SG.A-cut-ASP

'I cut my thumb with a knife, when I was cleaning a salmon'

16b. Harrington 020-0420

noˀot ˀaquyemtu čʰuput

noˀot	***ˀaqu-ye-mtu***	*čʰ-upu-t*
1SG	tail-POSS-INST	1SG.P-sting-ASP

'He stung me with his tail.'

16c. Grekoff 020.006

kumičin č'imal kimalla qʰalwemtu hopew hopit

kumičin	*č'imal*	*kimalla*	***qʰalwe-mtu***	*hopew*	*h-opi-t*
all	person	here	spoon-INST	acorn.soup	3-eat-ASP

'People around here eat mush with a spoon'

5.1.4.2 Comitative suffix -owa. When an independent nominal describes a companion, a comitative case suffix *-owa* is added to the noun stem.

17. Harrington 021-0197

ˀuwela-ˀi-owa
boy-POSS-ACCOMP
'Together with my boy'

18. Harrington 020-0532

pʰunsal-ye-owa
woman-POSS-ACCOMP
'With his wife'

5.1.5 Modal suffixes

Certain modal affixes, such as the inferential, occur with verbal and nominal stems.

19. Inferential *-taˀn* (from 'Hollering at New River')

ˀapu xošektanat, himisamduda ˀn sideˀw
ˀapu x-ošekta-na-t ***himisamdu-daˀn*** *si-deˀw*
fire NEG-make-NEG-ASP devil-INF say-DER
'He made no fire, it must have been the devil, they said'

In other instances these affixes are recorded as separate words.

20. Modals as separate words (from 'Hollering at New River')

himisamdu tiˀakon, č'imalsoˀop hišektakon
himisamdu ***tiˀa-kon*** *č'imal=soˀop h-išekta-kon*
devil MOD-FUT Indian=COND 3-make-FUT
'It is a devil, if it is an Indian he will make a fire'

The future tense marker *-kon* often occurs with modal affixes or in clauses following or preceding verbs with modal markers. It is different form the future tense marker *-xana.*

5.1.6 Other nominal affixes

Other nominal affixes are of uncertain meaning or cannot be fully analyzed due to the limited amount of examples, but they seem to be inflectional rather than derivational, as there is no change in meaning.

5.1.6.1 -a of uncertain meaning. The suffix *-a* is only found with *č'imar* 'person'. Though its exact meaning is unclear, it seems to function much like the definite suffix (see 5.1.2) in that the noun with the attached suffix refers to known information.

21. Suffix *-a* with humans ('Fugitives at Burnt Ranch')

qʰoqʰ uwadokta, č'imara, qʰomall akʰodeˀ
qʰoqʰ uwa-do-kta ***č'imar-a*** *qʰomall akʰo-de-ˀ*
two go-?-DIR person-? where kill-DER-Q
'Two got back here home, where did they kill him?'

. .
č'imarot hisikinda, hisikni č'imara nunuˀ
č'imar-ot hisik-inda hisik-ni ***č'imar-a*** *nunuˀ*
person-DEF good-ASP good-ASP person-? ?
'Good folks, the people are good'

5.1.6.2 -ita of uncertain meaning. According to its translation, the suffix *-ita* seems to create a cleft construction. However, there are not enough examples to determine its exact meaning.

22. Grekoff 008.012

p^hunsal^ʔiyta	*^ʔawillita*
*p^hunsal-^ʔi-**yta***	*^ʔawill-**ita***
woman-POSS-?	who-?
'It was my wife who . . '	'Who is the one who . . '

5.1.6.3 -oq 'former, formerly' with temporal meaning. The suffix *-oq* seems to indicate that something happened in the past. However, it is attached to nouns or nominalized clauses instead of verbs. There are not enough examples to fully analyze its meaning and use.

23. Grekoff 008.012
p^hunsalyoq
p^hunsal-y-oq
woman-POSS-formerly
'His former wife'

24. Grekoff 020.009
čhilintosa p^ha^ʔiloq

čhilintosa	*p^ha^ʔil-oq*
coyote	this.say-formerly

'What Coyote had said (formerly)'

5.2 Derivational morphology

While Chimariko has only very limited inflectional nominal morphology, derivational morphology is more elaborate including derivational suffixes, reduplication, and compounding.

5.2.1 Derivational suffixes

Chimariko has several derivational suffixes on nominal stems that are used to form new lexical items. Some are also used with adjectival and other stems.

5.2.1.1 Privative and exclusive suffixes. There are two suffixes with privative meaning occurring on nominal stems: *-yamu* and *-(a)šku/-ckut/-ckun* 'without'. A possible difference in use between *-yamu* and *-(a)šku/-ckut/-ckun* is that the former occurs with attributive nominals while the latter occurs with predicative nominals. However, there is not enough context given in the examples to confirm this analysis. *-(a)šku/-ckut/-ckun* 'without' occurs after the possessive suffix, as in examples 26 and 27 below. It is unclear whether *-yamu* 'without' also occurs in the same position.

25. Privative suffix *-yamu* (from 'Crawfish')

ˀaqʰa yeˀaqʰtut čitxayamulla
ˀaqʰa ye-ˀaqʰtu-t ***čitxa-yamu-lla***
water 1SG.A-into.water-ASP blanket-without-DEP
'I went immersingly into the water being naked'

26. Privative suffix *-(a)šku* (from Grekoff 012.001)

26a. *husotaškut*
*husot-**ašku**-t*
eye-PRIV-ASP
'It has no eyes' (lit. 'being eyeless')

26b. *ˀiṭiˀiškut*
*ˀiṭi-ˀi-**šku**-t*
man-POSS-PRIV-ASP
'I have no husband' (lit. 'without my husband')

27. Privative suffix *-ckut* (from Dixon 1910:316)

*apuye-**ckut***	'tail-less'
*itra-**ckut***	'hand-less'
*hupo-**ckun***	'foot-less'

*puntsar-ie-**ckut*** 'bachelor' (lit. 'without my wife')
woman-POSS-PRIV

Dixon and Grekoff have slightly different shapes for the privative *-(a)šku/-ckut/-ckun*. While Dixon defines the last consonant as being part of the suffix, Grekoff views it as an aspectual marker. The analysis offered by Grekoff fits the data better if the following example is considered.

28. Grekoff 012.001
ˀaṭaškuxanat
*ˀaṭa-**šku**-xana-t*
tree-PRIV-FUT-ASP
'it will have no trees'

The suffix *-(a)šku/-ckut/-ckun* is derivational in that it changes the meaning of the word, and it precedes any tense/aspect marking, i.e. inflectional marking. However, it follows possessive markers, generally regarded as being inflectional. Nevertheless, it is best viewed as derivational due to its semantic impact.

A suffix *-aikulla* with an exclusive meaning is also found on certain nominal and adjectival stems (see also 7.1).

29. Harrington 020-0653
čatxanaykullat
čatxan-aykulla-t
bone-EXCL-ASP
'it is all bone'

5.2.1.2 Diminutive suffix -lla. The derivational suffix *-lla* has sometimes a diminutive function with regard to age or size.

30. Diminutive *-lla* with regard to age

30a. 'Fugitives at Burnt Ranch'
p'un ˀiṭilla ˀuleeda himamda
*p'un ˀiṭi-**lla** ˀuleeda h-imam-da*
one man-DIM sibling 3-see-ASP
'A boy saw it'

30b. Harrington 020-0403
pačʰi mišexanaˀ xalalla
*pačʰi mišexanaˀ xala**lla***
what 2SG-call-FUT-Q baby
'What are you going to call your baby?'

31. Diminutive *-lla* with regard to size (from Bauman 1984)

*mayča-**lla*** 'little field' (Underwood place)
field-DIM

However, the same suffix is found on many other nominal and other stems without a diminutive meaning. In fact, it also occurs with words meaning the opposite: 'old'.

32. *šunuhu-**lla*** 'old woman' (from 'Mrs Bussell')

The same suffix occurs with many different word classes: nouns, pronouns, quantifiers, and adjectives. Examples include: *qʰomalla* 'where', *ˀičinšolla* 'dress', *xotalla* 'a little', *xočʰulla* 'short', and *ˀalla* 'month', among others. Grekoff also finds a set of locative and temporal expressions with the suffix *-lla* (see also 12.4.1).

33. Locative expressions with *-lla* (Grekoff 014.012)

*kima**lla***	'here'
*ma**lla***	'there'
*čirhače**lla***	'in the middle'
*wesa**lla***	'at the door'
*hisa**lla***	'on the road, in the road'
*ˀaxamu**lla***	'behind'

34. Temporal expressions with *-lla* (Grekoff 014.012)

himella	'in the evening'	(*hime* 'night')
nomačilla	'in the fall'	
p'uneš ˀasotilla	'in one year'	(*p'un* 'one', *ˀasoti* 'year')
ˀamanilla	'soon after, then'	

Although there seems to be some variation in the meaning and use of this suffix, *-lla* occurs exclusively word-finally. In addition to the lack of consistency in meaning, it is sometimes recorded as *-la* in the data having the same shape as a different derivational suffix co-occurring with *-lla* occasionally (see 5.2.1.3).

5.2.1.3 Derivational suffixes -la, -lla, -lala. Many words that are not verbs end in *-la* or *-lla*. While some of these words belong to the same semantic category, there are many others as well. In most cases, the suffix can be interpreted as a diminutive expressing affection or descending generation, such as with people and animals. These are common uses of diminutives.

35. Words ending in *-lla* (from Grekoff 014.011)

Kinship terms and people	
himolla	'niece, nephew, grandchild'
ˀičʰilla	'father'
mak'olla	'maternal uncle'
mačolla	'grandmother'
ˀuwella	'young man'
pʰunsalla	'young woman'
xaralla	'baby'
Things	
ˀičinšolla	'dress'
Animals	
hepučinamalla	'duck'
pusuwamalla	'woodworm' (literally 'eats wood')
papilla	'pine squirrel'
ˀapxanč'olla	'fox'

36. Word ending in *-la* (from Grekoff 014.011)

Kinship terms and people	
ˀuwela	'son'
masola	'daughter'
ˀanxala	'nephew'
mutala	'paternal aunt'
mala	'maternal aunt'

xawila	'grandfather'
Things	
puq^hela	'basket'
Animals	
šičela	'dog'
misila	'chipmunk'
imexola	'rabbit'
Placenames	
mayṭala	'little prairie'

Grekoff (014.011) notes that there is a variety of words ending in *-la, -lla, -lala, -lalla,* and *-llalla,* where the main problem is that of 'duration of the various *l*'s'. He concludes that 'it does not seem possible to come to any firm conclusion as to whether a given form has an l or a cluster ll'. As a result, *-la* and *-lla* are in fact the same suffix as *-lala, -lalla,* and *-llalla.*

5.2.1.4 Other derivational affixes. Dixon (1910) identifies several derivational suffixes according to semantic class. These include *-na* on plants, *-tcei* on birds and other animals, and *-matci* on names for seasons.

37. *-na* on plants (from Dixon 1910:314)

*tseli-**na***	'goosberry bush'
*mututma-**na***	'redwood'
*tcitca-**na***	'manzanita'
*qapu-**na***	'deer brush'

38. *-tcei* on birds and other animals (from Dixon 1910:316)

*tcukuku-**tcēi***	'owl'
*konana-**tcēi***	'woodpecker'
*ēxoi-**tcei***	'otter'
*qērek-**tcei***	'humming bird'

39. *-matci* on names for seasons (from Dixon 1910:316)

*ahan-**matci***	'summer'
*kicu-**matci***	'spring'

Dixon (1910:319) identifies several additional suffixes with nominal stems, but does not include any examples. They are: *-hni* 'many', *-tan* 'many', *-rotpin* 'only a, just a', *-gulan* 'merely, only', *-abo* 'also, too'. For *-hni* and *-tan*, both meaning 'many', it is unclear whether they are derivational or inflectional suffixes.

5.2.2 Compounding

Chimariko has Noun-Noun and Noun-Adjective compounds, among others. Dixon (1910:312) lists several compounds in his grammatical sketch. Examples from Dixon and from Harrington are shown below.

40. Compounds with *aq*^{h}*a* 'water' (from Dixon 1910:312)

*tcitci-**aqa**-i*	'cider'	(literally 'manzanita-water')
***aqa**-tceta*	'ocean'	(literally 'water-large')
*apu-n-**aqa***	'whiskey'	(literally 'fire-water')

Compounds with *aq*^{h}*a* 'water' (from 'Crawfish')

***aq*^{h}*a**-q*^{h}*ut*	'river'	(literally 'water-liquid')

Compounds with *q*^{h}*ut* 'liquid' (from 'Postnatal seclusion')

^{ʔ}*eloh-**q*^{h}*ut***	'soup'	(literally 'hot-liquid')

41. Compounds with *alla* 'sun' (from Dixon 1910:312)

*asi-n-**alla***	'sun'	(literally 'day-sun')
*himi-n-**alla***	'moon'	(literally 'night-sun')

42. Compounds with *teni* 'hand' (from Dixon 1910:312)

*xuli-**teni***	'left hand'	(literally 'bad-hand')
*hisi-**deni***	'right hand'	(literally 'good-hand')

43. Compounds with *hime, himi* 'night' (from Dixon 1910:313)

***himi**-n-alla*	'moon'	(literally 'night-sun')
***himi**-santo*	'devil'	(literally 'night-saint')

5.2.3 Reduplication

Nominal stems with two identical consecutive syllables are not attributed to the same word formation process as verbal stems (see 8.2.6), as no semantic function is apparent. This is illustrated in the examples below.

44.

^{ʔ}*ir*^{ʔ}*ir*	'stranger'
mušmuš	'bull'
^{ʔ}*a*^{ʔ}*a*	'deer'
yekyek	'hawk' (Dixon, 1910:311)
čeičei	'red salmon' (Dixon, 1910:311)

Nevertheless, roots or stems with two identical consecutive syllables denoting animals are also found in Shasta. The word for 'bull', *mušmuš,* most likely comes from Chinook Jargon and has entered the language through other languages of the area, given that the same word occurs in several neighboring languages, as shown in Table 2.

Table 2: The word for 'bull, cow'

Chinook Jargon	*moosmoos* 'cow, buffalo'
Chimariko	*mušmuš* 'bull'
Shasta	*musmus* 'cow'
Wintu	*musmus* 'cow, cattle'
Yurok	*musmus* 'cow, bull'
Karuk	*musmus* 'cow'

The words for 'hawk' and for 'buzzard', *yekyek* and *čeičei* respectively, are most likely based on onomatopoeia.

5.2.4 Verbalization

Nominal stems can be verbalized by adding inflectional verbal suffixes, such as pronominal, tense, and aspect markers. It is unclear if there are any restrictions to this process since the data are very limited, and there are multiple examples with the same translation.

45. Verbalized nominals

Harrington 020-0470

a) *mamot č'imar-mi-t*
2SG person-2SG-ASP
'You are an Indian'

b) *mamot č'imar-tida^ʔ*
2SG person-Q
'Are you an Indian?'

himow, no^{ʔ}ot č'imar-če
yes 1SG person-1SG.P
'Yes, I am an Indian'

Grekoff 012.001

c) *no^{ʔ}ot č'imar-su-nda*
1SG person-be-ASP
'I am a person'

or: *no^{ʔ}ot č'imar-č^{h}u-su-nda*
1SG person-1SG.P-be-ASP
'I am a person'

d) *mamot č'imar-mi-su-da-^{ʔ}*
2SG person-2SG-be-ASP-Q
'Are you a person'

e) *č^{h}isamra-m-ta*
bear-2SG-ASP
'You are a bear'

The examples above illustrate how personal and aspectual suffixes are added to *č'imar* 'person' and *čʰisamra* 'bear'. In some instances *su* 'to be' is added, and it is unclear whether it is a suffix or a separate word, as in the following example.

46. Predicate nominal with copula (from 'Fugitives at Burnt Ranch')

kimot ˀuˀir asunda
kimot ˀuˀir asu-nda
these stranger be-ASP
'These are strangers'

While predicate nominals generally occur with the copula *su* 'to be', in some instances the copula is omitted. Most examples are based on *č'imar* 'person', and some may be lexicalized expressions where the copula has been dropped. The limited data do not allow a complete analysis of this issue.

Grekoff suggests that the suffix *-a* derives verbal stems from nominal stems. However, it is possible that the vowel *a* is added for phonological rather than for morphological purposes.

47. Verbalized nominals (Grekoff 012.001)

47a. *č'imar-**a**-nta*
person-DER-ASP
'It's a person'

47b. *map'un-**a**-t*
that.one-DER-ASP
'That's the one'

47c. *čʰisaml**a**-n*
bear-ASP
'That's a bear'

There is no clear evidence of derivational suffixes that form verbal stems from nominal stems. However, nominal stems can take a limited set of verbal affixes to form verbs. The restrictions of this process are unclear due to the nature of the data.

5.3 Kinship terms

Many kinship terms end in the diminutive suffix *-lla* or *-la* expressing affection or descending generation. The same suffix also occurs with many other semantic classes (see 5.2.1.3).

A derivational morpheme that seems to encode an in-law relationship is *ču(ma)-*. It is found with *čumaku* 'father-in-law', *čumakosa* 'mother-in-law, *ičumta* 'son-in-law', and *čusimta* 'daughter-in-law'.

The expressions *šitoˀi* 'mother', *ˀuluita* 'sibling', and *maṭita* 'stepfather' may have the first person -*ˀi* and third person -*ita* possessive pronouns suffixed in lexicalized forms.

48. Kinship terms

ˀičʰilla	'father'
šitoˀi	'mother'
ˀuwela	'son'
masola	'daughter'
xačile	'children'
mačolla	'grandmother'
xawila	'paternal grandfather'
himolla	'grandchild'
ˀuluita	'brother, sister, sibling'
makolla	'uncle' (pat. uncle)
mutala	'paternal aunt'
mala	'maternal aunt'
ˀanxala	'nephew'
maṭita	'stepfather'
puncar	'spouse' 'woman' 'wife'
<u>čuma</u>ku	'father-in-law'
<u>čuma</u>kosa	'mother-in-law'
i<u>čum</u>ta	'son-in-law'
<u>č</u>usimta	'daughter-in-law'
meku	'brother-in-law'
maka	'sister-in-law'

5.4 Placenames

Placenames are often compounds containing *ˀama* 'land', *mayča* 'field', or *qʰaˀa* 'rock', as shown below.

49a. Compounds with *ˀama* 'land'

*sumnaˀ**ama***	'Manzanita Flat'	(literally 'upstream land')

49b. Compounds with *mayča* 'field'

***mayča** soˀre*	'Thomas or Ladd Place'	(literally 'rough field')
*paẋkʰoče **mayča***	'Grassy Flat'	

49c. Compounds with *qʰaˀa* 'rock'

*p'usur **qʰaˀ**anwa*	'North of Hyampom'	(literally 'mouse rock house')

Other placenames are simply descriptions of a place. These are clauses with the locative suffix *-(ta)če*, as shown below.

50a. *himaˀ hičʰuktače*
*himaˀ h-ičʰuk-**tače***
head 3-lie-LOC
'Head is lying there' => Green/Hennessey place (on the Trinity)

50b. *qʰaˀa yawišmuče*
*qʰaˀa yawiš-mu-**če***
rock go.across-DIR-LOC
'Rock goes across the place' => 'Forks of the New River'

In some placenames the derivational morphology is no longer transparent. Nevertheless, many placenames end in *-(ta)če*, most likely meaning 'there, at' or 'the place of'.

51. Placenames wit locative suffix *-(ta)če* (from Bauman 1980)

*čutam**tače***	Burnt Ranch
*hissa hadamu**če***	Dave Gray's place (on the Trinity)
*ˀamai**tace***	Hawkin's Bear or Irving place
*hak'im**tače***	Spot in the South Fork River
*qʰaˀa hetxat**tače***	Way up the Trinity
*sisill**ače***	Small hill north of Hayfork
*waˀwayraˀ**ače***	Will Olsen's place at Hyampom
*čʰurinˀ**ace***	Oren Treat's place

The locative suffix does not occur with all placenames. It is lacking in some of the compounds, for example.

5.8 Noun morphology in areal-typological perspective

In this section the internal structure of nouns in Chimariko is compared to that of its immediate neighbors: Wintu, Shasta, and Hupa. The following topics are examined: possession, definite articles and focal/emphatic affixes, locative and instrumental marking, and derivational affixes, as well as the more general pattern of prefixing versus suffixing.

Case systems are found in many Californian languages, in particular in Central California (Sherzer 1976b:116). Of Chimariko's close neighbors only Wintu has a nominal case system. As a result, possession in Wintu is marked on the possessor with a genitive suffix. Although Shasta does not have a case system as Wintu does, possession is marked in a very similar way in both languages: a suffix on the possessor and independent pronouns. The independent pronouns are formed by adding the genitive or possessive suffix to the basic pronominal roots. In terms of locus of marking (Dryer et al. 2004), possession is marked on the dependent, i.e. the possessor, for Shasta and

Wintu and on the head, i.e. the possessed, for Chimariko and Hupa. Chimariko has possessive affixes on the possessed and an alienable/inalienable distinction. The system is very similar to that of neighboring Hupa, except that in Hupa all body parts and kinship terms occur only in possessed form. In general, head-marking for possession is more common in the Americas than dependent-marking (Dryer et al. 2004).

The distinction between alienable and inalienable possession is very common in California (Sherzer 1976b:118-9). It occurs in Chimariko, Wintu, and Hupa; no evidence has been found for such a distinction in Shasta. While in Chimariko only body parts are marked as inalienable possession and in Wintu only kinship terms, in Hupa both body parts and kinship terms are inalienable. Possession marking for Chimariko and its immediate neighbors is summarized in the table below.

Table 3: Possession in areal perspective

	alienable/ inalienable	inalienable possession	suffixing/ prefixing	shapes of personal pr.	marking
Chimariko	yes	body parts	prefixes and suffixes	identical	possessed/ head
Shasta[1]	?	?	independent pr. suffix	similar (pr. + possessive suffix)	possessor/ dependent
Wintu[2]	yes	kinship	independent pr. genitive suffix	similar (pr. + genitive suffix)	possessor/ dependent
Hupa[3]	yes	body parts, kinship	prefixes	identical	possessed/ head

pr. = pronoun
[1]Silver 1966:183-4 and 201-2
[2]Pitkin 1984:219-234
[3]Golla 1970:210-235

Definite or indefinite articles do not occur in Chimariko or its neighbors. However, Chimariko has a definite suffix *-ot/-ut/-op* that occurs with nouns, pronouns, and determiners. Similar affixes occur in Wintu and Shasta. In Wintu nouns are marked for generic or particular aspect (Dorothy Lee 1944, Pitkin 1984). According to Pitkin (1984:202), 'the generic category is associated with plurality, inanimateness, a mass of parts or individuals; while the particular is specific in force, indicating singularity, animateness, personification, or individuation'. Following Pitkin (1984), the particular suffix *-t* is derived from an original 'topicalizing/foregrounding suffix'. While Chimariko does not mark general or particular aspect in nouns, *-ot/-ut/-op* sometimes functions as a topicalizing/foregrounding suffix. The same suffix occurs with independent personal pronouns in Chimariko marking emphasis or topicality. In Wintu personal pronouns may have the emphatic inflectional suffix *-o*. Semantically, 'it emphasizes the form to which it is suffixed', while syntactically 'it marks that form as an independent pronoun' (Pitkin 1984:250-1). It is interesting to note that the shapes of the Wintu suffixes are similar to the Chimariko suffixes. Shasta has a definite marker that can occur on nouns or pronouns (Silver 1966). However, its shape is very different. There is no indication of marking for definiteness or emphasis/topicality on nouns or pronouns in Hupa.

Locative and instrumental suffixes are very common in Northern California. Chimariko and all its immediate neighbors have locative suffixes on nouns. This is not surprising for Wintu which has a nominal case system. Shasta has two locative suffixes: a temporal and a spatial locative (Silver 1966). In Hupa there are different locative suffixes on nouns, indicating 'in', 'under', 'at the back of' and 'inside of', among others (Golla 1970). Instrumental suffixes occur in Wintu and Shasta. In Wintu instruments are marked with the genitive case, the same as possessors. Shasta has an instrumental suffix with the meaning 'by means of'. The different locative and instrumental suffixes in Chimariko and its neighboring languages vary in form and function, and it is unclear whether one system has had an impact on another in the past.

Derivational affixes on nouns are not described in great detail for Chimariko's close neighbors. They seem to be limited to diminutives and a small set of other affixes. Diminutive suffixes or postclitics are reported for Wintu and Shasta, but not for Hupa. This makes sense, since Hupa has diminutive consonant symbolism.

Overall, while there are some similarities in the internal structure of nouns between Chimariko and its close neighbors, each language has a different set of affixes and categories. But all four languages have one thing in common: suffixing is far more frequent than prefixing. This is not surprising since it is a general pattern found in the world's languages (Mithun 2003).

6. PRONOUN MORPHOLOGY

This chapter describes the internal structure of pronouns. Pronouns have a limited set of suffixes that are mainly derivational.

6.1 Morphological structure of personal pronouns

Personal pronouns show a number distinction for first and second person, in addition to a distinction between first, second, and third person. The root for first person is *na-*, and the root for second person is *mam-*. In the first person plural pronoun a segment *-čʰi* is added to the root, similar in shape to the bound pronominal affix *čʰa-* encoding first person plural patient forms. In the second person plural form a segment *-qʰe* is added, similar in shape to the bound pronominal affix *qʰo/qʰa* encoding second person plural.

1. *noˀ-ot* 1SG
   *na-**čʰi**-t-ot* 1PL
   mam-ot 2SG
   *mam-**qʰe**-t-ot* 2PL
   pʰaˀm-ot 3

The pronouns all end in *-ot*, a definite marker (see 6.2). A contracted form of the first person plural *načʰot* appears occasionally. The third person pronoun is based on the demonstrative with the same form (see 4.2.2), a common cross-linguistic feature.

In addition to the basic forms, there is a set of personal pronouns with a contrastive meaning. These pronouns contrast one person to another and have a suffix *-iš/-uš* instead of *-ot*, as illustrated in the table. *-iš/-uš* 'but' could also be interpreted as a clitic (see 4.8.3).

Table 1: Definite and contrastive pronouns

Definite suffix *-ot*	*noˀ-ot* 'I, me'	*mam-ot* 'you'	*na-čʰit-ot* 'we, us'
Contrastive suffix *-iš/-uš*	*naˀ-iš* 'but I, as for me'	*mam-uš* 'but you, as for you'	*na-čʰit-uš* 'but we, as for us'

In the data examined, the contrastive pronouns are far less common than the definite ones.

2. 'Fugitives at Burnt Ranch'
   ˀirˀir musunda mamot, k'otnihu
   ˀirˀir *m-usu-nda* ***mamot*** *k'ot-ni-hu*
   stranger 2SG-to.be-ASP 2SG run-IMP.SG-CONT
   'You are a stranger, run away'

3. 'On grandmother getting the hiccups'
mamuš hita mipuhunmuˀ
mamuš *hita m-ipu-hunmu-ˀ*
but.you lots 2SG-work-DIR-Q
'But did you take lots'

Dixon (1910:322) also identifies two dual pronouns: *nōutowa* 'we two' and *mamutowa* 'you two', both with the dual suffix *-owa* attached to the singular pronoun, *noˀot* 'I' and *mamot* 'you' respectively. An example is given below.

4.

4a. Harrington 020-1128	4b. Harrington 020-0359
yakʰoyew mamotowa	*mamotowa noˀotowa čʰaki mačaˀlda*
y-akʰo-yew ***mamot-owa***	***mamot-owa noˀot-owa*** *čʰa-ki mačaˀlda*
1SG-kill-REFL 2Sg-DUAL	2SG-DUAL 1SG-DUAL POSS-throat dry
'Let's you and me kill each other.'	'Our throats are dry'

6.2 Definite *-ot* with personal and demonstrative pronouns

Personal and demonstrative pronouns end in *-ot*, which marks definiteness on nouns (see 5.1.2).

5. Personal and demonstrative pronouns

*noˀ**ot***	1SG	*kim**ot***	'this'
*način̓ʰit**ot***	1PL	*pʰaˀm**ot***	'that'
*mam**ot***	2SG		
*mamqʰet**ot***	2PL		
*pʰaˀm**ot***	3		

Dixon (1910:320) lists *-ot* as a 'suffix with an intensive, or emphatic meaning, such as indeed, really, in truth' and affirms that it can occur with all stem classes. Grekoff (015.011) suggests that *-ot* has a 'definitive' meaning. Given its presence in the personal pronouns, it can be inferred that their function may be primarily emphatic or topical in nature. This would be consistent with their optional presence and lack of a semantic role distinction. Demonstrative pronouns are often used to refer back to the topic.

6. 'Fugitives at Burnt Ranch'
č'imar xotai heṭaheskut uwatkut, heṭaheskut č'utamdače
č'imar xotai h-eṭahe-sku-t wa-tku-t h-eṭahe-sku-t č'utamdače
man three 3-run.away-DIR-ASP go-DIR-ASP 3-run.away-DIR-ASP Burnt Ranch
'Three men came as fugitives, they ran away to Burnt Ranch'

kimot ˀuˀir asunda, čʰakʰo, heṭaheshutaˀa sunda
kimot *ˀuˀir asu-nda čʰ-akʰo h-eṭahe-shu-taˀa su-nda*
these stranger be-ASP IMP.PL-kill 3-run.away-DIR-? be-ASP
'These are strangers, kill them, they are running away'

6.3 Roots and affixes in demonstrative and interrogative pronouns

Certain demonstrative and interrogative pronouns occur with a derivational suffix *-lla* of unclear meaning.

7. *q^homalla* 'where'
   malla 'there'
   $^?$awilla 'who, to whom'
   q^hoč^{h}u$^?$mulla 'how far'
   kella 'here, hither
   kimalla 'here'

Other suffixes, except for *-ot* (see 6.2), are not apparent in demonstrative and interrogative pronouns. However, there are some similarities in the word-initial shapes, most likely the original roots or stems. Many interrogative pronouns begin with *q^ho-* or *q^ha-*. Dixon (1910:322) lists eight different interrogative pronouns and asserts that they are all derived from a single stem *qo-* or *qa-*. The forms are very similar to the ones recorded by Harrington, as can be seen below.

Table 2: Interrogative pronouns (Dixon, 1910:322; Harrington)

Dixon	Harrington	
qomas or *awilla*	*$^?$awilla*	who
qâtci or *pātci*	*pač^{h}a$^?$*, *pač^{h}i*	what
qomalla	*q^homalla*	where
qosidadji	*q^hosita$^?$če*	why
	pač^{h}a$^?$aq^hosita$^?$če	what for (what-why)
qâsuk	*q^hosuk*	when
qâtala		how many
qâtcu		how far
qâtramdu		how often

The interrogative marker *q^ho-/q^ha-* could also be analyzed as a prefix:

8. *q^ho-malla* 'where'
   malla 'there'

Prefixes are rare in Chimariko. There are pronominal prefixes on verbs and possessive prefixes on nouns. No derivational prefixes have been identified. Hence, *q^ho-/q^ha-* is best analyzed as a root or stem of question markers.

Demonstrative pronouns show a deictic distinction between *ki-* 'here, close to the speaker' and *p^ha-* or *ma-* 'there, further away from the speaker'.

9. Demonstratives with *ki-* 'here, closer to the speaker'

   kimalla 'here'
   kimot 'these'

10. Demonstratives with *pʰa-* 'there, further away from speaker'

pʰaˀmot 'that one'

11. Demonstratives with *ma-* 'there, further away from speaker'

malla 'there'
map'un 'that one'

The distinction can be seen clearly with pairs such as *kimalla* 'here'/*malla* 'there' and *pʰaˀmot* 'that, those'/*kimot* 'this, these'.

12. 'Cutting navel'
malla nakʰohoshu, xočʰulla xoliˀtinta, hičʰu nexaˀy
malla *n-akʰohoshu xočʰulla xoliˀ-tinta hičʰu n-exaˀy*
there IMP.SG-cut short bad-ASP long IMP.SG-make
'There you cut it off, it is bad short, make it long'

6.4 Verbalization

Certain pronouns, such as *ˀawilla* 'who' and *map'un* 'that one', can occur together with *asu* 'to be' to form clauses. In the Harrington data *asu* 'to be' sometimes appears as a suffix rather than as a separate word.

13. Harrington 020-0703
ˀawillamasudaˀ
ˀawilla-m-asu-da-ˀ
who-2SG-be-ASP-Q
'Who are you?'

14. Harrington 020-0703
noˀot map'unčusunda
noˀot map'un-č-usu-nda
1SG that.one-1SG.P-be-ASP
'That's me'

However, the pronouns occur also with *asu* 'to be' as a separate word.

15. Harrington 020-0467
qʰomas musuda
qʰomas m-usu-da
who 2SG_be-ASP
'Who are you?'

16. Harrington 020-0467
ˀawilla sudaˀ

ˀawilla su-da-ˀ
who be-ASP-Q
'Who is he?'

When *asu* 'to be' is added to a pronoun it is unclear whether it is a suffix or a separate word. If it is one word, it is better analyzed as a compound.

6.5 Pronoun morphology in areal-typological perspective

In this section the internal structure of pronouns in Chimariko is compared to that of its immediate neighbors: Wintu, Shasta, and Hupa, as well as to that of other languages in California. According to Sherzer (1976b) all languages in California distinguish singular and plural forms in personal pronouns. In addition, some languages, such as Chimariko, Wintu, Maidu, Yurok, and Atsugewi, among others, have a dual. Chimariko only has a number distinction for first and second persons, the same as Wintu, but unlike Shasta and Hupa which also distinguish number for third persons.

The shapes of the personal pronouns show certain similarities. It has been noted in the past (Nichols 1983) that many first person pronouns in the Americas tend to have an initial *n-* while second person pronouns begin with *m-*. This is true for Chimariko and for Wintu, and in part for Shasta and Hupa. The personal pronouns in Shasta show some additional similarities to the bound pronominal affixes in Chimariko. The first person singular and the first person plural have the same or a very similar initial consonant. This is illustrated in the following table.

Table 3: Pronoun shapes in Shasta and Chimariko

Chimariko	1SG.A *y-*	1PL.P *čʰa-*	2SG *m-*	2PL *qʰ-*
Shasta[1]	1SG *ya·ˀa*	1PL *ča·k'a*	2SG *ma·ˀi*	2PL *ma·ˀik'a*

[1]Silver 1966:201

The pronouns in Wintu and Shasta differ from the ones in Chimariko and Hupa in that they can take inflectional affixes marking case in Wintu and possession in both. Independent possessive pronouns do not occur in Chimariko or Hupa.

Demonstrative pronouns and third person pronouns have the same or similar shapes in all four languages. This is a very common trait in California and along the entire Pacific Coast (Dryer et al. 2004). In Wintu and in Chimariko demonstrative and third person personal pronouns are identical in shape.

Other kinds of pronouns are described in less detail. Hupa has a set of interrogative pronouns, whereby the initial morpheme has a very similar shape in the entire set, the same as in Chimariko. Given the limited description or lack of other types of pronouns, no complete comparative analysis is possible. To conclude, many similarities are found in the shapes and number and person distinctions of personal pronouns. However, in some languages pronouns allow a greater variety of affixes than in others.

7. ADJECTIVE MORPHOLOGY

This chapter describes the structure of adjectives. Corresponding adjectives and stative verbs are built on the same roots. They can take pronominal, tense, aspect, and modal affixes.

7.1 Verbal morphology with adjectival roots and stems

Adjectives in predicative function can take pronominal, tense, aspect, and modal affixes.

1. 'Fugitives at Burnt Ranch'
čʰaxakʰona, wečʰup čʰaxakʰona, ˀama xoliˀyu
čʰa-x-akʰo-na wečʰup čʰa-x-akʰo-na ˀama ***xoliˀ-yu***
IMP.PL-NEG-kill-NEG some IMP.PL-NEG-kill-NEG country bad-ADM
'Don't kill them, some said don't kill them, lest it spoil the country'
. . .
xoliˀtaˀn hakʰot, xawiy asunda, xukeenat
xoliˀ-taˀn *h-akʰo-t xawiy asu-nda x-ukee-na-t*
bad-INF 3-kill-ASP Redwood.Indian be-ASP NEG-understand-NEG-ASP
'It is not right to kill him, he was a Redwood Indian, he didn't understand'
. . .
hisiˀmedaˀ, maik isiˀmedaˀ, ˀama xoliˀxanan
hisiˀ-me-daˀ *maik isiˀ-me-daˀ ˀama* ***xoliˀ-xana-n***
good-ASP-INF ? good-ASP-INF country bad-FUT-ASP
'Everything is all right there now, it will be all right, the country will be all bad'

2. 'Cutting Navel'
xočʰulla xoliˀtinta, hičʰu nexaˀy
xočʰulla ***xoliˀ-tinta*** *hičʰu n-exaˀy*
short bad-ASP long IMP.SG-make
'It is bad short, make it long'

3. 'Woman wanders'
hiwanda, čitx isiˀ isiˀdaˀn
h-iwa-nda čitx isiˀ ***isiˀ-daˀn***
3-go-ASP blanket good good-INF
'She was coming, good blanket, it must have been good'

4a. Harrington 020-1113
pʰuncalla ṭewunda
pʰunca-lla ***ṭewu-nda***
woman-DIM big-PROG
'The little girl is growing up'

4b. Harrington 020-1113
noˀot ṭewut
noˀot ***ṭewu-t***
1SG big-ASP
'I am big'

4c. Harrington 020-1113
noˀot ṭewčut
noˀot ***ṭew-ču-t***
1SG big -1SG.P-ASP
'I am getting big'

Due to the limited amount of examples it is unclear whether there are any restrictions on the use of verbal affixes with adjectival stems.

7.2 Comparatives and superlatives

Comparatives and superlatives are rare in the collected data. They only occur with a limited number of adjectival roots and stems. The comparative is formed by adding a suffix *-lla* or *-lala* to the root or stem of an adjective. Inflectional affixes that generally occur with adjectival roots may be added to the derived comparative stem.

5. Comparatives

5a. Harrington 020-0610
k'uwanlallaˀni kimaˀase
*k'uwanla-**lla**-ˀ-ni kimaˀase*
?-DER-1SG.A-ASP today
'I am a little better today'

5b. Harrington 020-0610
k'uwanlalamaˀ
*k'uwanla-**la**-ma-ˀ*
?-DER-2SG-Q
'Are you a little better?'

5c. Harringon 020-0518
nuwaˀyamlala
*n-uwa-ˀyam-**lala***
IMP.SG-go-quick-DER
'Walk a bit faster'

5d. Harrington 020-0091
ṭewulla niẋaˀy
*ṭewu-**lla*** *n-iẋaˀy*
big-DER IMP.SG-make
'Make it bigger'

5e. Grekoff 014.012
himitalla tinta
*himita-**lla*** *tinta*
heavy-DER ASP
'It is a little heavier'

5f. Grekoff 014.012
x̣ayellop
*x̣aye-**ll**-op*
young-DER-DEF
'The younger one (wife)'

5g. Grekoff 014.012
hičumlala
*hičum-**lala***
?-DER
'A bit further'

In 5c *n-uwa-ˀyam-lala* 'walk a bit faster', the derived stem *ˀyamlala* 'faster' functions most likely as an adverb and is a separate word, though it is recorded as fused together with the verb *nuwa* 'walk!' in one word. The derivational suffixes *-lla, -lala*, and *-la* occur with many different word classes having different meanings and functions (see 5.2.1.2, 5.2.1.3, and 6.3). It is unclear whether these are different suffixes or the same suffix having different shapes. They also occur with plain adjectives, as in example 6.

6. Harrington 020-0487 and 0406
xučʰu-lla 'short'
hučo-lla 'full'

Superlatives are formed by adding a suffix *-če* to a comparative stem. Like the comparatives, the derived superlative stems can take inflectional affixes that occur with simple adjectival roots.

7. Superlatives (from Grekoff 014.012)

7a. *x̣ayellače*
*x̣aye-lla-**če***
young-DER-DER
'The youngest one (sister)'

7b. *ṭewučullače*
*ṭewu-ču-lla-**če***
big-1SG.P-DER-DER
'I am the oldest'

7c. *č^{h}axayellače*
*č^{h}a-xaye-lla-**če***
1SG.P-young-DER-DER
'I am the youngest'

Comparatives and superlatives are rare in the languages of the Americas. There are no descriptions of similar processes in neighboring languages.

7.3 Other suffixes

The exclusive suffix *-aikulla* 'only' occurs with adjectival stems, as in the following example. It is unclear whether the suffix can also occur with other kinds of stems, and whether any inflectional affixes can be added.

8. 'Postnatal seclusion'
ˀelohaikulla hamat, ˀalla p'un, sumusut hiwot, p'olalla

ˀeloh-aikulla	*h-ama-t*	*ˀalla*	*p'un*	*sumu-su-t*	*h-iwo-t*	*p'olalla*
hot-only	3-eat-ASP	month	one	like-be-ASP	3-stay-ASP	alone

'She only eats hot, for one month, she lives like this, alone'

8. VERB MORPHOLOGY

This chapter describes the internal structure of verbs and certain word formation processes that lead to new verb stems, such as noun incorporation and reduplication, among others. Verbs have prefixes, suffixes, and a circumfix. The chapter is divided into inflectional and derivational morphology.

8.1 Inflectional morphology

Chimariko has inflectional morphemes on verb stems that mark the following: pronominal reference, tense, aspect, and modality. Only pronominal affixes are sometimes prefixed. All other inflectional affixes are suffixes. The verb templates in Table 1 illustrate the sequence of morphemes.

Table 1: Verb templates for inflectional morphology

Person	Root	Negative '*kuna*'	Directional	Tense/Aspect	Mood

Person	Negative '*x-*'	Root	Negative '*-na*'	Directional	Tense/Aspect	Mood

Root	Person	Tense/Aspect	Mood

8.1.1 Pronominal reference

Bound pronouns are obligatory and mark the arguments in a clause. They appear on the verb, whether or not there is also a coreferential noun phrase.

1. Pronominal reference with/without noun phrase ('Dailey chased by the bull')

Dailey hik'ot mušmuš č^{h}uwetni, yečučutapmun

Dailey	*h-ik'o-t*	*mušmuš*	*č^h-uwet-ni*	*y-ečuču-tapmun*
Dailey	3-say-ASP	bull	1SG.P-hook-ASP	1SG.A-?-DIR

'Dailey said: the bull hooked me, I dodged'

In example 1, the third personal pronoun *h-* appears with a coreferential noun *Dailey*, while the first person agent and patient prefixes, *y-* and *č^h-* respectively, occur without.

The pronouns are prefixed or suffixed depending on the verb stem. Prefixing is far more frequent and occurs with five out of six different stem classes (see 3.1). The bound pronominal prefixes including the initial stem vowel are summarized in Table 2 by verb stem class. The entire set of affixes for all stem classes is presented in Table 3.

In Table 3, Set I and Set II correspond to agent and patient forms. Regardless of their position with respect to the verb stem, only first person pronouns show a distinction for agent and patient roles in all instances. Second and third person markers have the same forms for both semantic roles except for the second person plural forms in transitive sentences with third person actors (see 9.2.1). A number distinction is apparent only in first and second person affixes. In general, first person forms show the most distinctions, followed by second and third person markers.

Table 2: Pronominal affixes including initial stem vowel by verb stem class

Person	i-stem	a-stem	e-stem	o-stem	u-stem
1SG Agent	**ʔi-**	**ye-**	**ye-**	**yo-**	**yu-**
1SG Patient	**čʰu-**	**čʰa-**	**čʰo-**	**čʰo-**	**čʰu-**
1PL Agent	**ya-**	**ya-**	**ya-**	**ya-**	**ya-**
1PL Patient	**čʰa-**	**čʰa-**	**čʰa-**	**čʰa-**	**čʰa-**
2SG	**me-**[1], **mi-**	**me-**[1], **ma-**	**me-**[1], **me-**	**me-**[1], **mo-**	**me-**[1], **mu-**
2PL	**qʰo-**[2], **qʰu-**	**qʰo-**[2], **qʰa-**	**qʰo-**[2], **qʰo-**	**qʰo-**[2], **qʰo-**	**qʰo-**[2], **qʰu-**
2PL Patient	**qʰa-**[3]	**qʰa-**[3]	**qʰa-**[3]	**qʰa-**[3]	**qʰa-**[3]
3	**hi-**	**ha-**	**he-**	**ho-**	**hu-**

[1] includes a first person patient reflected in the vowel /e/
[2] includes a first person patient reflected in the vowel /o/
[3] occurs only in transitive sentences with third person actors

In table 2 the actual pronominal affixes are boldfaced, and affixes are shown including the initial stem vowel.

Table 3: Pronominal affixes for all verb stems

Verbal prefixes				
	Set I :		Set II :	
	Singular Agent	Plural Agent	Singular Patient	Plural Patient
First person	*y-, ʔ-*	*ya-*	*čʰ-*	*čʰa-*
Second person	*me-*[1], *m-*	*qʰo-*[2], *qʰ-*	*m-*	*qʰa-*[3]
Third person	*h-*	*h-*	*h-*	*h-*

Verbal suffixes				
	Set I:		Set II:	
	Singular Agent	Plural Agent	Singular Patient	Plural Patient
First person	*-ʔ(i)*	?	*- čʰV,- čʰu*	*- čʰa*
Second person	*-m(V)*	*-qʰV*	*-m(V)*	*-qʰV*
Third person	*-h/Ø*	*-h/Ø*	*-h/Ø*	*-h/Ø*

[1] includes a first person patient reflected in the vowel /e/
[2] includes a first person patient reflected in the vowel /o/
[3] occurs only in transitive sentences with third person actors

Table 4: Distinctions in bound pronominal marking

	Different singular/plural forms	Different agent/patient forms
First person	x	x
Second person	x	x (only 2PL with 3 as actor)
Third person	-	-

Only one pronoun is overtly marked on the verb, according to a hierarchical pattern whereby speech act participants, i.e. first and second persons, are favored over third persons. There is one exception: when a second person acts on a first, a first person patient is marked in addition to the second person agent. The agent-patient distinction for first persons occurs in both transitive and intransitive clauses.

2. Harrington 020-1113
noˀot ṭewčʰuxanat
*noˀot ṭew-**čʰu**-xana-t*
1SG large-1SG.P-FUT-ASP
'I am going to be big'.

3. Harrington 020-1105
yemakunaxanat
***y**-ema-kuna-xana-t*
1SG.A-eat-NEG-FUT-ASP
'I am not going to eat.'

4. 'Fugitives at Burnt Ranch'
pʰaˀasitaˀče yekʰotinda, čʰaxaduˀxakon, wisseeda čʰumčaxa
*pʰaˀasitaˀče **y**-ekʰo-tinda **čʰa**-xaduˀx-akon wisseeda čʰu-m-čaxa*
that.why 1SG.A-kill-PROG 1PL.P-?-FUT downstream IMP.PL-DIR-COMP
'That's why I killed him, they will kill us, you all move down to B. Noble's place.'
[lit. 'you all move downstream']
1>3 => **1** 3>1 => **1**

5. 'Crawfish'
pʰiˀa yehatat, hiničxeˀkut, ˀičiˀta, puqʰela ˀitxaˀmat
*pʰiˀa **y**-ehata-t **h**-iničxeˀku-t **ˀ**-ičiˀta puqʰela **ˀ**-itxaˀ-ma-t*
grease 1SG.A-have-ASP 3-smell-ASP 1SG.A-catch basket 1SG.A-put-?-ASP
'I had grease, they smelled it, I caught them, I put them in a basket'

1 => **1** 3>3 => **3** 1>3 => **1** 1>3 => **1**

6. 'Dailey chased by the bull'
moxowetnan, pʰaˀyit pʰuncarye
***mo**-x-owet-na-n pʰaˀyit pʰuncar-ye*
2SG-NEG-hook-NEG-ASP thus.say woman-POSS
'He didn't hook you, thus said his wife,'

3>2 => **2**

Examples 2 and 3 are intransitive clauses. In 2 there is a first person patient pronoun *čʰu-* 'I' suffixed to the verb stem, while in 3 there is a first person agent pronoun *y-* 'I' prefixed to the verb. Agent and patient pronouns also occur in transitive clauses, as in example 4. Example 4 shows the person hierarchy in pronominal marking. When a first person acts on a third, as in *yekʰotinda* 'I killed him', the first person is marked on the verb. The first person is also marked in *čʰaxaduˀxakon* 'they will kill us', when a third person acts on a first. The person hierarchy is summarized in the following table.

Table 5: Person hierarchy in pronominal marking

Actor > Undergoer	Pronoun on verb
1>1	1 agent
1>2	1 agent
1>3	1 agent
2>1	2 (+ 1)
2>2	2
2>3	2
3>1	1 patient
3>2SG	2
3>2PL	2PL patient
3>3	3

Harrington and Grekoff note a difference in the shape of the second person singular pronouns that reflects the undergoer of the action, i.e. whether it is a first or a third person. They attribute the vowel /e/ or /o/ to a first person undergoer.

7.	2->1	2->3
7a.	Harrington 020-1126 *mamqʰedot qʰok'oˀnakunaxanaˀ* *mamqʰedot* ***qʰ-o****-k'o-ˀna-kuna-xana-ˀ* 2PL 2PL-1P-talk-APPL-NEG-FUT-Q 'Are you not going to talk to me?'	Harrington 020-1126 *mamqʰedot quk'oˀnaxanaˀ* *mamqʰedot* ***qʰ-u****k'o-ˀna-xana-ˀ* 2PL 2PL-talk-APPL-FUT-Q 'Are you going to talk to him?'
7b.	Harrington 020-1128 *mekʰoxanaˀ* ***m-e****-kʰo-xana-ˀ* 2SG-1P-kill-FUT-Q 'Are you going to kill me?'	Harrington 020-1128 *makʰoxanaˀ* ***m-a****kʰo-xana-ˀ* 2SG-kill-FUT-Q 'Are you going to kill him?'
7c.	Harrington 020-1126 *mek'oˀnaˀ* ***m-e****-k'o-ˀna-ˀ* 2SG-1P-talk-APPL-Q 'Are you talking to me?'	Harrington 020-1125 *pačʰi mik'oˀnaˀtitaˀ* *pačʰi* ***m-i****k'o-ˀna-titaˀ* who 2SG-talk-APPL-Q 'Who were you talking to?'
7d.	Harrington 020-1133 *mamot mewanut* *mamot* ***m-e****-wa-nu-t* 2SG 2SG-1P-COLL-growl.at-ASP 'You growled at us'	Harrington 202-1133 *mamot xačile monut* *mamot xačile* ***m-o****nu-t* 2SG children 2SG-gowl.at-ASP 'You growled at the kids'

In addition to these pronominal affixes, there is a collective prefix *wa-*, according to

Grekoff (008.012). It sometimes replaces pronominal marking on the verb, as in 8a and 8d. Its exact meaning and use, however, are unclear due to the limited amount of examples.

8. Collective prefix *wa-*

8a. Harrington 020-0552
waxap'unat
***wa**-xa-p'u-na-t*
COLL-NEG-work-NEG-ASP
'We didn't work'

8b. Grekoff 008.012
č^{h}owaxap'umiyna
*č^{h}o-**wa**-xa-p'u-miy-na*
IMP.PL-COLL-NEG-work-APPL-NEG
'Don't you work for me'

8c. Grekoff 008.012
ṭeyni wap'ut kumičin č'imar
*ṭeyni **wa**-p'u-t kumičin č'imar*
hard COLL-work-ASP all people
'They worked hard together'

8d. Harrington 020-0551
nač^{h}idot waxaṭ'o^{ʔ}nan
*nač^{h}idot **wa**-xa-ṭ'o^{ʔ}na-n*
1PL COLL-NEG-gather.acorn-ASP
'We did not gather acorns'

8.1.2 Tense and aspect

Chimariko has a rich tense and aspect system expressed through verbal suffixes. However, the functions and semantic scope of these suffixes, as well as possible co-occurrence and other restrictions of use, are not fully understood, due to the nature of the data. In addition, it is sometimes unclear whether an affix encodes tense, aspect, or both. The suffixes described in different sources are summarized in Tables 6 and 7.

Table 6: Temporal suffixes

Suffix	Gloss	Function/Meaning	Source
-ak/-k	PST	Past (completed action)	Dixon (1910:319)
-neq	PST	Past (formerly)	Harrington ('to die')
-nip	PST	Past ('already') Completive past	Harrington 020-1098 Harrington ('to die')
-ta^{ʔ}	PST	Ancient past, perfective	Grekoff (013.018)
-ta^{ʔ}sun	PST	Completive past ('already')	Harrington ('to die')
-sun	PRS	Present (from *su* 'to be')	Berman (2001b:1051)
-(i)n/-n *-ni/-n(i)*	ASP	Present (uncompleted action)	Berman (2001b:1051) Dixon (1910:319)
-(a)kon	FUT	Future ('going to') Future ('will')	Harrington ('to eat') Harrington ('to die')
-xan(a)	FUT	Future	Berman (2001b:1051) Dixon (1910:319) Harrington ('to die')

Table 7: Aspectual suffixes

Suffix	Gloss	Function/Meaning	Source
-tinta *-nta/-inta*	PROG	Progressive (durative) Progressive Present participle Present participle	Harrington ('to eat') Harrington 020-1097 Dixon (1910:331) Berman (2001b:1051)
-hun/-nhu	CONT	Continuative	Berman (2001b:1051) Dixon (1910:319)
-wet	CONT	Continuative	Dixon (1910:319)
-ˀya	CONT	Continuative 'again, some more'	Harrington 020-1096 Grekoff (008.012)
-pum *-tapum*	ASP	Iterative 'again'	Dixon (1910:319) Grekoff (013.018)
[*-(yu)wu*	RET	Retornative, reditive	Harrington 020-1096][1]
-ˀi	ASP	'after a while'	Grekoff (013.018)
-(i)n/-n *-ni/-n(i)*	ASP	Present (uncompleted action)	Berman (2001b:1051) Dixon (1910:319)
-ta/-t/-tu	ASP	Stative, resultative	Harrington ('to die')
-taˀče	ASP	Resultative	Grekoff (013.018)
-ˀxa	COMP	Completive ('all')	Harrington ('to eat') Harrington 020-1096
-čaxa	COMP	Completive ('all')	Harrington 020-1096
-naˀači	COMP	Completive ('all')	Grekoff 008.012
-k/-p	ASP	Definite, punctual	Grekoff (013.018)

[1] could be either aspectual or derivational suffix

Tables 6 and 7 illustrate the fact that aspectual marking is much more elaborate in Chimariko than temporal marking. Even among the "tense" markers in Table 6, many may encode aspect rather than tense. The suffix *-ak* is used to denote a completed action in the past, according to Dixon (1910:319). Most likely it corresponds to *-k*, an aspectual suffix identified by Grekoff (013.018). No examples occur in the narratives. The two suffixes *-neq* and *-nip* both encode an event that happened in the past. In addition, both are often accompanied by a temporal adverb, *šur* 'formerly', *šuraku* 'already', or *moˀa* 'yesterday'.

9. *-neq* with and without *šur* 'formerly' (Harrington 020-1102; 020-1103)

9a. *q'ehneq šuur*
*q'e-h-**neq*** *šuur*
die-3-PST formerly
'She died formerly'

9b. *q'ehta ˀikeeneq*
q'e-h-ta *ˀ-ikee-**neq***
die-3-ASP 1.SG.A-hear-PST
'I heard he was dead'

10. *-nip* with *šuraku* 'already' (Harrington 020-1118)

šuraku ˀik'onip
šuraku *ˀ-ik'o-**nip***
already 1.SG.A-talk-PST
'I spoke already'

11. *-nip* with *moˀa* 'yesterday' (Harrington 020-1120)

hokodeˀnip moˀa
*h-oko-deˀ-**nip*** *moˀa*
3-tattoo-DER-PST yesterday
'They tattooed her yesterday'

In addition to indicating past tense, both suffixes also refer to actions or states that are completed. Similarly, the *-taˀ* and *-taˀsun* suffixes encode events in the past that are completed, as shown below. The difference between *-taˀ*, *-taˀsun*, *-neq*, and *-nip* is unclear. In *-taˀsun* the last syllable may have developed from the verb *su* 'to be'.

12. Harrington 020-1102
moˀa q'ehtaˀsun
moˀa *q'e-h-**taˀsun***
yesterday die-3-PST
'She died yesterday'

The suffix *-ni/-in* is most likely an aspectual marker, although it has been identified by Dixon (1910) and Berman (2001b) as encoding an uncompleted event in present tense. It will be treated in the discussion of the aspectual suffixes.

The two future suffixes *-kon* and *-xana* differ in that *-xana* can be followed by aspectual suffixes, while *-kon* cannot. If present, *-kon* is the last suffix of the predicate. Unlike *-xana*, *-kon* occurs with modal affixes and in clauses preceding or following verbs with modal markers. This is illustrated below.

13. *-xana* with aspectual suffix *-t* (from 'Hollering at New River')

kowmilot himisamtu hapukʰeˀxanat
kow-mi-lot *himisamtu* *h-apukʰeˀ-**xana-t***
holler-POSS-NOM devil 3-steal-FUT-ASP
'The devil will steal your voice'

14. *-xana* with aspectual suffix *-n* (from 'Woman wanders')

q'eˀxanan, ˀamaq'eˀni, nunuˀ yuwam
*q'e-ˀ-**xana-n*** *ˀama-q'e-ˀ-ni* *nunuˀ* *y-uwa-m*
die-1SG.A-FUT-ASP country-die-1SG.A-ASP ? 1SG.A-go-DIR
'I am going to die, I will die in this country, I am going to go'

15. *-kon* without additional aspectual suffixes (from 'Hollering at New River')

ˀap hišektakon, č'imarsoˀop, xošektanakon
ˀap *h-išekta-**kon*** *č'imar=soˀop* *x-ošekta-na-**kon***
fire 3-make-FUT person=COND NEG-make-NEG-FUT
'He will make a fire, if a person, he does not make a fire'

16. *-kon* with modal marker *-tiˀa* (from 'Hollering at New River')

himisamdu tiˀakon, č'imalsoˀop hišektakon
himisamdu ***tiˀa-kon*** *č'imal=soˀop* *h-išekta-kon*
devil MOD-FUT Indian=COND 3-make-FUT
'It is a devil, if it is an Indian he will make a fire'

According to Harrington's verb inflection charts for *oko* 'to tattoo' and *q'e* 'to die' (Harrington 020-1094 to 020-1095), *-xana* may be followed by the aspectual suffixes *-n, -t, -ˀi, -nta, -tinta* or the modal suffixes *-ˀ, -taˀ, and -titaˀ*, while *-kon* may be preceded only by the modal suffix *-tiˀa*. This is illustrated in the table below.

Table 8: Co-occurrence of *-xana* and *-kon* with other suffixes

Root	Derivational, (Person), Negative	***-xana***	*-n, -t, -ˀi, -nta, -tinta* *-ˀ, -taˀ, -titaˀ*
Root	Derivational, (Person), Negative	*-tiˀa*	***-kon***

According to Grekoff (012.018), *-kon* is a modal suffix encoding 'future', while *-xana* is a 'future intentive' suffix.

The aspectual suffixes show more distinctions than the tense markers and are overall less clear. The progressive or durative has three different shapes, most likely of the same suffix: *-tinta, -inta, -nta*. It can co-occur with the future *-xana* or with the ancient past *-taˀ*. In the narratives it is most often the only tense-aspect suffix verb-finally.

17. *-tinta* with future suffix *-xana* (from 'Fugitives at Burnt Ranch')

yaxakʰonaxanˀi, makʰotaxantinda, k'otnihu,
ya-x-akʰo-na-xan-ˀi *m-akʰo-ta-xan-**tinda*** *k'ot-ni-hu*
1PL.A-NEG-kill-NEG-FUT-ASP 2SG-kill-?-FUT-PROG run-IMP.SG-CONT
'We won't kill them, he is going to kill you, run away'

18. *-nta* without other tense-aspect markers (from 'Woman wanders')

ˀimikot sumusut čʰuk'oˀnanda
ˀimikot *sumu-su-t* *čʰ-uk'o-ˀna-**nda***
friend like-be-ASP 1SG.P-talk-APPL-PROG
'Like friends, they talk to me'

19. *-nta* without other tense-aspect markers ('Cutting finger when cleaning salmon')

kimaˀase ˀuluytaˀi huwatkun, čʰuxotayetkut, hiwonta xanim

kimaˀase	*ˀuluyta-ˀi*	*h-uwa-tku-n*	*čʰ-uxota-ye-tku-t*	*h-iwo-**nta***	*xanim*
today	sister-POSS	3-go-DIR-ASP	1SG.P-look.at-?-DIR-ASP	3-stay-PROG	still

'My sister (Martha) came over today, she came to visit me, she is still here.'

The progressive *-tinta/-inta/-nta* does not always reflect a progressive meaning in the translations, in particular when it occurs with the verb *su* 'to be'. It is unclear whether this is due to it having multiple functions and meanings or whether this is due to vague translations, or a combination of various factors.

There are three different suffixes identified in the various sources as having a continuative meaning: *-hun/-nhu, -wet*, and *-ˀya*. It is unclear how they differ from each other. The meaning of *-ˀya* is unclear. It does not always have a continuative interpretation (see example 23).

20a. Continuative *-hun/-nhu* (from Mrs. Bussell)

masunu huwaktanhut šunuhullot

masunu	*h-uwa-kta-**nhu**-t*	*šunuhull-ot*
always	3-go-DIR-CONT-ASP	old.woman-DEF

'Mrs. Bussell goes around all the time'

20b. Continuative *-hun/-nhu* (from Harrington 020-1096)

hitakseˀta hop'unhut

h-itak-seˀta	*h-op'u-**nhu**-t*
3-rain-COND	3-work-CONT-ASP

'(Frank) is working while it is raining.'

21. Continuative *-wet* (from Dixon 1910:332)

*imum-**wet***	'I run all the time'
*yema-**wet***	'I eat continually'

22. Continuative *-ˀya* (Harrington 020-1096)

22a. *hidayaˀt masunu*

*h-ida-**yaˀ**-t*	*masunu*
3-rain-CONT-ASP	always

'It kept on raining'

22b. *nitxaˀya*

*n-itxa-**ˀya***

IMP.SG-put-CONT

'Put it (apple sauce) away!'

23. Iterative *-pum/tapum* (Harrington 020-0493 and Harrington 020-0414)

23a. *ničʰeskitpum*

n-ičʰeski-tpum

23b. *yedakmutpum*

y-edakmu-tpum

IMP.SG-warm.up-ASP	1SG.A-splice.together-ASP
'Warm it up again'	'I am going to splice it together'

Harrington terms *-(yu)wu* the 'retornative' or 'reditive' suffix. Since this suffix can be followed by the future *-xana*, as well as by an aspectual suffix, *-(yu)wu* does not seem to be an aspectual suffix, but rather a derivational suffix. However, there are not enough data to reach a conclusion on this issue.

24. 'Retornative/reditive' *-(yu)wu* (Harrington 020-1096)

24a.	*nixodayuwu*	24.b	*ˀixodeyuwux*
	*n-ixoda-**yuwu***		*ˀ-ixode-**yuwu**-x*
	IMP.SG-watch-RET		1SG.A-watch-RET-?
	'Go back and look at him!'		'I am going back home to look at him.'

24c. *ˀihomdewuxanat*
*ˀ-ihomde-**wu**-xana-t*
1SG.A-?-RET-FUT-ASP
'I am going to go back to get some more.'

The suffix *-ˀi* is of unclear meaning. Grekoff (013.018) suggests that it means 'after a while'. Two examples occur in the narratives.

25. *-ˀi* 'after a while' (from 'On Grandmother getting the hiccups')

ˀaqʰa nawum, luˀni, ˀaqʰa luˀit haṭu

ˀaqʰa	*na-wum*	*luˀ-ni*	*ˀaqʰa*	*luˀ-**i**-t*	*haṭu*
water	IMP.SG-give	drink-IMP.SG	water	drink-ASP-ASP	then

'Give her water, drink, she drank then water'

26. *-ˀi* 'after a while' (from 'Postnatal seclusion')

ˀelohqʰut luˀit, hopew, ˀelohqʰut luˀit

ˀeloh-qʰut	*luˀ-**i**-t*	*hopew*	*ˀeloh-qʰut*	*luˀ-**i**-t*
hot-liquid	drink-ASP-ASP	soup	hot-liquid	drink-ASP-ASP

'She drinks a hot liquid, soup, she drinks the hot liquid'

The exact meanings of the two aspect suffixes *-(i)n/-n/-ni/-n(i)* and *-ta/-t/-tu* are unclear. The first one may correspond to an imperfective focusing on a portion of the event, while the latter may correspond to a perfective focusing on the event as a whole. It is also possible that they simply express the fact that an event is uncompleted (*-(i)n/-n/-ni/-n(i)*) or the opposite (*-ta/-t/-tu*). Given the nature of the data, no clear function can be attributed to either of these two suffixes. Both co-occur with the future *-xana* and with other suffixes.

27. *-ta/-t/-tu* (from 'Fugitives at Burnt Ranch')

xoliˀtaˀn hakʰot, xawiy asunda, xukeenat
*xoliˀ-taˀn h-akʰo-**t** xawiy asu-nda x-ukee-na-t*
bad-INF 3-kill-ASP Redwood.Indian be-ASP NEG-understand-NEG-ASP
'It is not right to kill him, he was a Redwood Indian, he didn't understand'

28. *-ta/-t/-tu* and *-(i)n/-n/-ni/-n(i)* (from 'Dailey chased by the bull')

Dailey hik'ot mušmuš čʰuwetni, yečučutapmun
*Dailey h-ik'o-**t** mušmuš čʰu-wet-**ni** ye-čuču-tapmun*
Dailey 3-say-ASP bull 1SG.P-hook-ASP 1SG.A-?-DIR
'Dailey said: the bull hooked me, I dodged'

29. *-(i)n/-n/-ni/-n(i)* (from 'Dailey chased by the bull')

moxowetnan, pʰaˀyit pʰuncarye
*mo-x-owet-na-**n** pʰaˀyit pʰuncar-ye*
2SG-NEG-hook-NEG-ASP thus.say woman-POSS
'He didn't hook you, thus said his wife'

30. *-(i)n/-n/-ni/-n(i)* (from 'Dailey chased by the bull')

ˀisiyakutni haˀačʰakinta mušmuš ṭewu, čʰuwetxanan čisit
*ˀ-isiyakut-**ni** haˀa-čʰa-kinta mušmuš ṭewu čʰ-uwet-xana-**n** či-si-t*
1SG.A-?-ASP ?-1SG.P-PROG bull big 1SG.P-hook-FUT-ASP ?-say-ASP
'I looked back, the bull was taking after me, I said: he is going to hook me'

Only one example with the resultative *-taˀče* occurs in the narratives (see also 12.4.1).

31. Resultative *-taˀče* (from 'Cutting finger when cleaning salmon')

čʰuṭa ṭeyta yekʰutni čʰiselimtu, ˀumul yekʰutaˀče,
*čʰ-uṭa ṭe-yta y-ekʰut-ni čʰiseli-mtu ˀumul y-ekʰu-**taˀče***
POSS-hand ?-POSS 1SG.A-cut-ASP knife-INST salmon 1SG.A-cut-ASP
'I cut my thumb with a knife, when I was cleaning a salmon'

The two completive suffixes *-ˀxa* and *-čaxa* are similar in shape and can co-occur with other aspectual suffixes.

32a. *-čaxa* with aspectual suffix *-t* (from 'Crawfish')

hoputeˀw ˀama, txol makumčaxat q'ehčaxat
*hopu-teˀw ˀama txol makum-**čaxa-t** q'e-h-**čaxa-t***
mine-DER land crawfish perish-COMP-ASP die-3-COMP-ASP
'They mined the land, all crawfish perished all, they died all.'

32b. -*čaxa* with aspectual suffix -*t* (from 'Woman wanders')

čitxa lulihčaxat q'eˀxanan,
čitxa *lul-ih-**čaxa-t*** *q'e-ˀ-xana-n*
blanket drop-1SG.A-COMP-ASP die-1SG.A-FUT-ASP
'I lost all my blankets, I am going to die.'

33. -*čaxa* without other aspectual suffixes (from 'Fugitives at Burnt Ranch')

wisseeda čʰumčaxa
wisseeda *čʰ-um-**čaxa***
downstream IMP.PL-DIR-COMP
'You all move down to Billy Noble's place.'

34. -*ˀxa* with aspectual suffix -*t* (Harrington 020-1096)

ˀamehissaṭoˀmuˀxat
*ˀame-h-issaṭoˀmu-**ˀxa**-t*
hungry-3-?-COMP-ASP
'They all died of hunger.'

The completive suffix -*naˀači* 'all' can equally co-occur with other aspectual suffixes.

35. -*naˀači* with aspectual suffix -*t*

35a.	Harrington 020-1107	35b.	Grekoff 008.012
	huwumnaˀčit		*hamanˀačit*
	h-uwu-m-naˀči-t		*h-ama-nˀači-t*
	3-go-DIR-COMP-ASP		3-eat-COMP-ASP
	'All went home'		'They all ate'

No examples of the definitive or punctual -*k*/-*p* identified by Grekoff occur in the data. Overall, the tense-aspect system is not fully understood due to the nature and limitations of the data.

8.1.3 Mood

Chimariko has a rich mood system including different interrogative suffixes, two types of negative affixes, and many irrealis expressions, such as conditional, dubitative, and inferential and other suffixes and clitics. In general, modal suffixes are the final pieces in the verbal morpheme template. Most do not co-occur with aspectual suffixes. In some cases it is unclear whether the mood morpheme is a suffix or a clitic. Only the ones that are clearly clitics are marked as such. The modals are summarized in Table 9.

Table 9: Modal affixes and clitics

Suffix	Gloss	Function/Meaning	Source
-a	Q	Interrogative	Berman (2001b:1051) Dixon (1910:320)
-(a)ˀ	Q	Interrogative	Harrington ('to die') Grekoff (012.035)
-titaˀ/-itaˀ	Q	Interrogative	Harrington (020)
-pʰuˀ	Q	Interrogative Perfective interrogative	Harrington ('to eat') Dixon (1910:320) Grekoff (012.018)
-ye	Q	Interrogative	Berman (2001b:1051)
x- . . -na	NEG	Negative	Harrington ('to die')
-k'una/-kuna	NEG	Negative	Harrington ('to die') Grekoff (012.018)
-(a)qre/-(a)qle *-(a)qre hin*	MOD	Conjectural, Dubitative	Grekoff (012.035)
-tiˀarhiniˀ	MOD	Dubitative ('I guess')	Harrington ('to die')
-tialhin	MOD	Dubitative	Dixon (1910:319)
-tiˀar	MOD	Speculative ('might')	Grekoff (013.018)
-c'oˀar	MOD	Speculative ('might')	Grekoff (013.018)
-c'oˀl/-c'ol	MOD	'maybe' Speculative ('might')	Harrington ('to die') Grekoff (013.018)
-ar/-al	MOD	Speculative ('might')	Grekoff (012.035)
-(a)l	MOD	'I guess'	Harrington ('to die')
-i	MOD	Speculative ('might')	Harrington 020-0001
-seˀta *-teˀta* *(-seˀta)*	COND	Conditional Emphatic ('I myself...')	Grekoff (012.035) Grekoff (012.035) Harrington 'to eat'
=soop *=soˀop* *=(s)oˀop*	COND	Conditional	Berman (2001b:1051) Dixon (1910:319) Harrington 020-0005 Grekoff (012.035)
-me	MOD	'almost' Potential	Harrington 020-0004 Grekoff (013.018)
-(a)kon	FUT	Potential future	Grekoff (012.035)
-xa(n)	FUT	Purposive future	Grekoff (012.035)
-aˀ	MOD	Optative, intensive, assertive	Grekoff (012.035)
-tcai	MOD	Desiderative	Dixon (1910:319)
n-/ne-	IMP.SG	Imperative	Harrington (020)
čʰ-/čʰa-	IMP.PL	Imperative	Harrington (020)
-yu(y)	ADM	Dubitative, admonitive	Grekoff (012.035)
-teˀq	ADM	Admonitive	Grekoff (013.018)
x . .-itk'i	INT	Asseverative (negative)	Grekoff (012.035)
x . .-itqi	INT	Intensive ('never, not at all')	Grekoff (013.018)
-kutqi	INT	Intensive ('certainly, surely)	Grekoff (013.018)

-marˀi	INT	Adversative Intensive ('regardless')	Grekoff (013.018)
-taˀn	INF	Inferential	Grekoff (012.035)
-taˀče	ASP	Resultative	Grekoff (012.035)
-iˀal	EV	'apparently'	Grekoff (008.012)
-saˀs	EV	Evidential (hearsay)	Grekoff (012.035)

8.1.3.1 Interrogatives. There are three different interrogative suffixes: *-(a)ˀ*, *-titaˀ/-itaˀ*, and *-pʰuˀ*. It is unclear how their meanings and functions differ from one another. All occur in question-word questions, as well as in yes-no questions.

36. *-aˀ* in question-word question (from 'Fugitives at Burnt Ranch')

qʰomal uwamaˀ
*qʰomal uwa-m-**aˀ***
where go-DIR-Q
'Where did that man go to?'

37. *-(a)ˀ* in question–word question (from 'On grandmother getting the hiccups')

pačʰaˀ qʰosumsiˀ, pačʰi misekmuˀ
pačʰaˀ qʰ-osumsi-ˀ pačʰi m-isekmu-ˀ
what 2PL-do-Q what 2SG-swallow-Q
'What did you all do, what did you swallow'

38. *-(a)ˀ* in yes-no question (from 'On grandmother getting the hiccups')

mamuš hita mipuhunmuˀ
mamuš hita m-ipu-hunmu-ˀ
but.you lots 2SG-work-DIR-Q
'But did you take lots?'

39. *-titaˀ* in yes-no question (Harrington 020-1103)

mamot q'emkunatitaˀ
*mamot q'e-m-kuna-**titaˀ***
2SG die-2SG-NEG-Q
'Did you not die?'

40. *-titaˀ* in question-word question (Harrington 020-1133)

pačʰaˀaqʰositaˀče mamqʰedot qʰonutidaˀ
*pačʰaˀaqʰositaˀče mamqʰedot qʰ-onu-**tidaˀ***
what.why 2PL 2PL-growl.at-Q
'What did you (plural) growl at him for?'

41. *-p^{h}u^{ʔ}* in yes-no question Harrington 020-1199

p^{h}a^{ʔ}mot hamap^{h}u^{ʔ}
*p^{h}a^{ʔ}mot h-ama-**p^{h}u^{ʔ}***
3 3-eat-Q
'Did that fellow eat?'

In addition, Berman lists two interrogative suffixes *-a* and *-ye*, based on examples with a final glottal stop. Hence, Berman's *-a* could correspond to *-(a)^{ʔ}* and *-ye* could be a misinterpretation.

42. Interrogatives *-a* and *-ye* (Berman 2001b:1051)

42a. *maweya^{ʔ}*
*m-awey-**a**-^{ʔ}*
2SG-angry-Q-?
'Are you angry?'

42b. *mak^{h}oye^{ʔ}*
*m-ak^{h}o-**ye**-^{ʔ}*
2SG-kill-Q-?
'Are you going to kill me?'

8.1.3.2 Negation. There are two negative affixes: the circumfix *x-. . -na* and the suffix *-k'una/-kuna/-^{ʔ}na* (see chapter 11). The latter can occur as a separate word (see 4.8.3). The circumfix *x-. . -na* occurs only with the same five stem classes that take pronominal prefixes, while *-k'una/-kuna/-^{ʔ}na* occurs with all stem classes. Both may be followed by other modal affixes or by tense-aspect suffixes.

43. *x- . . -na* with tense-aspect suffix (from 'Fugitives at Burnt Ranch')

xukeenatinda
***x**-ukee-**na**-tinda*
NEG-understand-NEG-PROG
'You don't understand'

44. *x- . . -na* with tense-aspect suffix (from 'Mrs Bussell')

^{ʔ}awaidače xowonat
^{ʔ}awa-ida-če ***x**-owo-**na**-t*
home-POSS-LOC NEG-stay-NEG-ASP
'She does not stay at home'

45. *-k'una* as separate word with modal marker (from 'Hollering at New River')

himisamdu k'uno^{ʔ}op ^{ʔ}ap hišektakon
*himisamdu **k'un**=o^{ʔ}op ^{ʔ}ap h-išekta-kon*
devil NEG=COND fire 3-make-FUT
'If it is not a devil, he will make a fire'

46. -*k'una* as suffix with modal suffix (Harrington 020-1103)

q'ehkunac'oˀl
*q'e-h-**kuna**-c'oˀl*
die-3-NEG-MOD
'Maybe he doesn't die'

47. -*k'una* as suffix with tense-aspect suffix (Harrington 020-1103)

noˀot q'eˀkunatinta
*noˀot q'e-ˀ-**kuna**-tinta*
1SG die-1SG.A-NEG-ASP
'I didn't die'

48. -*k'una* and *x-*. . .*-na* with same verb stem (Harrington 020-1105)

48a. *yemakunaxanat*
*y-ema-**kuna**-xana-t*
1SG.A-eat-NEG-FUT-ASP
'I am not going to eat'

48b. *xemanaxanat*
***x**-ema-**na**-xana-t*
NEG-eat-NEG-FUT-ASP
'I am not going to eat'

8.1.3.3 Irrealis mood. There are several modal suffixes encoding doubt, conjecture, or speculation. They can be summarized in four groups: (1) *-(a)qre/-(a)qle, -(a)qre hin,* (2) *-tiˀarhiniˀ, -tialhin, -tiˀa(r),* (3) *-c'oˀar, -c'oˀl/-c'ol,* (4) *-ar/-al, -(a)l.* The suffixes in each group are morphophonemic or other variants of the same suffix. Examples with different suffixes are sometimes translated in a similar way with 'I guess' or 'might'. It is unclear whether the suffixes in the different groups vary in meaning and/or use. In the verb morpheme template they occupy the last slot, i.e. they occur verb-finally. *-(a)qre/-(a)qle* may be followed by *tiˀar(hiniˀ)* as a separate word or by *(-)hin* of unclear meaning. *(-)hin* occurs as a suffix or as a separate word. Comparing the shapes of the suffixes in all four groups, it becomes apparent that the suffixes in group (4) may have played a role in the formation process of the suffixes in groups (2) and (3).

49a. Grekoff 013.018
hakʰoteˀqre tiyˀarhin
*h-akʰo-teˀ-**qre*** *tiyˀarhin*
3-kill-DER-MOD MOD
'Maybe he (devil) gets killed'

49b. Grekoff 013.018
hexatumhuqrehin
*h-exatumhu-**qre-hin***
3-?-MOD-MOD
'They boil them, I suppose'

49c. Harrington 020-1105
hamaqle
*h-ama-**qle***
3-eat-MOD
'It looks like he's been eating'

50. Examples with *-tiˀarhiniˀ*

50a. Harrington 020-1103
q'ehkunatiˀarhiniˀ
*q'e-h-kuna-**tiˀarhiniˀ***
die-3-NEG-MOD
'I guess he didn't die'

50b. Harrington 020-1103
q'ehxantiˀarhini
*q'e-h-xan-**tiˀarhini***
die-3-FUT-MOD
'I guess he is going to die'

50c. Harrington 020-1107
hakʰodeˀwtiˀarhin
*h-akʰo-deˀw-**tiˀarhin***
3-kill-DER-MOD
'Must be he got killed'

51. Example with *-tiˀa(r)* (from 'Hollering at New River')

himisamdu tiˀakon, č'imalsoˀop hišektakon

himisamdu	***tiˀa**-kon*	*č'imal=soˀop*	*h-išekta-kon*
devil	MOD-FUT	Indian=COND	3-make-FUT

'It is a devil (it will be a devil, I guess), if it is an Indian he will make a fire'

In example 51, the modal *(-)tiˀa* is a separate word taking the future suffix *-kon*. Given that only one such example occurs in the data, this will not be discussed further. In general, except for the negatives, modal suffixes occur verb-finally, and they are not followed by tense-aspect suffixes.

52. Examples with *-c'oˀar* or *-c'oˀl/-c'ol*

52a. Harrington 020-1103
q'ehkunac'oˀl
*q'e-h-kuna-**c'oˀl***
die-3-NEG-MOD
'Maybe he doesn't die'

52b. Harrington 020-1103
q'ehc'oˀol
*q'e-h-**c'oˀol***
die-3-MOD
'Maybe he died'

52c. Harrington 020-1099
hokottac'oˀol
*h-oko-tta-**c'oˀol***
3-tattoo-DER-MOD
'Maybe she got tattooed'

52d. Harrington 020-1099
hokoc'oˀol
*h-oko-**c'oˀol***
3-tattoo-MOD
'Maybe she tattooed her'

53. Example with *-ar/-al, -(a)l* (Harrington 020-1103)

q'ehkunal
*q'e-h-kuna-**l***
die-3-NEG-MOD
'I guess he doesn't die'

Harrington also lists a suffix *-i* with a speculative meaning. Only one example occurs in the data.

54. Example with *-i* modal suffix (Harrington 020-1093)

šičelot čʰawin, čutpai, čʰawin

šičel-ot	*čʰ-awi-n*	*čutpa-**i***	*čʰ-awi-n*
dog-DEF	1SG.P-afraid-ASP	bite-MOD	1SG.P-afraid-ASP

'I am afraid of the dog, he might bite, I am afraid.'

Another set of suffixes indicates a conditional meaning. There are three different conditional markers: (1) *-teˀta*, (2) *-seˀta*, and (3) *=soˀop*. While (1) describes conditions that cannot be fulfilled because they refer to events in the past, i.e. hypothetical conditions, (2) and (3) refer to conditions that may be fulfilled, i.e. real conditions. It is unclear how (2) and (3) differ in use and meaning, since only one example occurs with (2). While (3) *=soˀop* is a clitic, there is not enough evidence to define all three markers as clitics, though it seems likely that they are all clitics.

55. Examples with *-teˀta*

55a. 'Hollering at New River'

muwetteˀta makʰomet

*m-uwet-**teˀta***	*m-akʰo-me-t*
2SG-hook-COND	2SG-kill-MOD-ASP

'If he had hooked you, he would have killed you right.'

55b. Harrington 020-1107

mallak'uwamnateˀta xakʰottametaˀ

*mallak'-uwa-m-na-**teˀta***	*x-akʰo-tta-me-taˀ*
there-go-DIR-NEG-COND	NEG-kill-DER-MOD-PST

'If he hadn't gone there, they wouldn't have killed him.'

55c. Harrington 020-1106

malla huwamteˀta	*xakʰottatqi*
*malla h-uwa-m-**teˀta***	*x-akʰo-tta-tqi*
there 3-go-DIR-COND	NEG-kill-DER-INT

'If he had gone there, he would not have got killed'

55d. Harrington 020-1106

malla huwamteˀta	*hakʰoteˀtiˀarhin*
*malla h-uwa-m-**teˀta***	*h-akʰo-teˀ-tiˀarhin*
there 3-go-DIR-COND	3-kill-DER-MOD

'If he had gone there, they might have killed him'

56. Example with *-seˀta* (Grekoff 020.009)

hamew č'imal huwatkuseˀta hawut
*hamew č'imal h-uwa-tku-**seˀta** h-awu-t*
food person 3-go-DIR-COND 3-give-ASP
'If someone comes, one offers them food'

57. Examples with *=soˀop*

57a. Harrington 020-1106
mamasoˀop yenuwešxanˀi
*m-ama=**soˀop*** *y-enuweš-xan-ˀi*
2SG-eat=COND 1SG.A-whip-FUT-ASP
'If you eat that thing, I'm going to whip you.'

57b. Harrington 020-1132
nemičisoˀop pusuwamdu yetxanan
*nemi-či=**soˀop*** *pusuwa-mdu y-et-xana-n*
kick-1SP.P=COND stick-INST 1SG.A-hit-FUT-ASP
'If you kick me, I'll hit you with a stick'

As can be seen in the examples above, the verb in the main clause contains a potential suffix *-me* or some other modal suffix in hypothetical conditions. In real conditions, the verb in the main clause occurs with a future suffix *-xana* or *-(a)kon* or with an aspectual suffix *-t*. While Grekoff lists the future suffixes as modals, they are treated as tense markers here. The structures of the conditional clauses are summarized in Table 10.

Table 10: Conditional clauses

	Main clause	Conditional clause
Hypothetical condition	Potential *-me* Modal *-tiˀarhin* Intensive modal *-(i)tqi*	*-teˀta*
Real condition	Aspect *-t*	*-seˀta*
Real condition	Future *-xana/-kon*	*=soˀop*

Given that the conditional marker *=soˀop* can also be attached to other types of words, such as nouns or the negative particle *k'una*, it can be classified as a clitic attached to the clause it marks as a condition.

58. *=soˀop* attached to other kinds of words (from 'Hollering at New River')

kowmilot himisamtu hapukʰeˀxanat, himisamdu k'unoˀop
*kow-mi-lot himisamtu h-apukʰeˀ-xana-t himisamdu k'un=**oˀop***
holler-POSS-NOM devil 3-steal-FUT-ASP devil NEG=COND
'The devil will steal your voice, if it is not a devil'
. .

ˀap hišektakon, č'imarsoˀop, xošektanakon
*ˀap h-išekta-kon č'imar=**soˀop** x-ošekta-na-kon*
fire 3-make-FUT person=COND NEG-make-NEG-FUT
'He will make a fire, if a person, he does not make a fire'

No examples of the optative/intensive *-aˀ* identified by Grekoff or the desiderative *-tcai* mentioned in Dixon (1910:319) occur in the data.

8.1.3.4 Imperative and admonitive. Chimariko has two sets of imperative affixes: *n-*, *ne-* for commands given to a single person and *čʰ-*, *čʰa-* for commands given to more than one person. The vowels in the affixes, *e* and *a* respectively, indicate a first person patient, i.e. that the undergoer of the action of the command is a first person. Similar to the personal affixes (see 8.1.4), the imperative affixes are either prefixed or suffixed depending on the verb stem.

59. Commands given to one person: *n-*, *ne-*

59a. 'Fugitives at Burnt Ranch'
yaxakʰonaxanˀi, makʰotaxantinda, k'otnihu
*ya-x-akʰo-na-xan-ˀi m-akʰo-ta-xan-tinda k'ot-**ni**-hu*
1PL.A-NEG-kill-NEG-FUT-ASP 2SG-kill-?-FUT-PROG run-IMP.SG-CONT
'We won't kill them, he is going to kill you, run away'
. .
ˀirˀir musunda mamot, k'otnihu, nuwawum
*ˀirˀir m-usu-nda mamot k'ot-**ni**-hu **n**-uwa-wu-m*
stranger 2SG-be-ASP 2SG run-IMP.SG-CONT IMP.SG-go-RET-DIR
'You are a stranger, run away, go home'

59b. 'Woman wanders'
ˀuluidaˀe nahak ˀičinšolla, pʰuncar ˀimatni, hamew nawu
*ˀuluida-ˀe **n**-ahak ˀičinšolla pʰuncar ˀ-imat-ni hamew **n**-awu*
sister-1SG IMP.SG-bring dress woman 1SG.A-find-ASP food IMP.SG-give
'My sister, bring me a dress, I have found a woman, give her food'

59c. 'Postnatal seclusion'
keˀčʰulala, malla nakʰohoshu, xočʰulla xoliˀtinta, hičʰu nexaˀy
*keˀčʰulala malla **n**-akʰohoshu xočʰulla xoliˀ-tinta hičʰu **n**-exaˀy*
this.long there IMP.SG-cut short bad-PROG long IMP.SG-make
'This long (gesture), there you cut it off, it is bad short, make it long'

59d. Harrington 020-1124
newu *nawu*
***n-e**-wu* ***n**-awu*
IMP.SG-1P-give IMP.SG-give
Give it to me! Give it to him!

60. Commands given to more than one person: *č^{h}-*, *č^{h}a-*

60a. 'Fugitives at Burnt Ranch'
kimot ^{ʔ}u^{ʔ}ir asunda, č^{h}ak^{h}o
kimot ^{ʔ}u^{ʔ}ir asu-nda ***č^{h}**-ak^{h}o*
these stranger be-ASP IMP.PL-kill
'These are strangers, kill them'
. .
wisseeda č^{h}umčaxa
wisseeda ***č^{h}**-um-čaxa*
downstream IMP.PL-DIR-COMP
'You all move down to Billy Noble's place' [lit. 'you all move downstream']

60b. Harrington 020-1126

č^{h}ak'o^{ʔ}na	*č^{h}uk'o^{ʔ}na*
***č^{h}**-a-k'o-^{ʔ}na*	***č^{h}**-uk'o-^{ʔ}na*
IMP.PL-1P-talk-APPL	IMP.PL-talk-APPL
'Talk to us!'	'Talk to him!'

Examples of negative imperatives (prohibitives) are given below. They add the negative circumfix *x-...na* or the suffix *k'una* to the verb stem. The imperative affixes appear in the same slot in the verb template as the person affixes in negative clauses.

61. Negative imperatives (prohibitives)

61a. 'Fugitives at Burnt Ranch'
weč^{h}up č^{h}axak^{h}ona
weč^{h}up ***č^{h}a**-x-ak^{h}o-**na***
some IMP.PL-NEG-kill-NEG
'Some said, don't kill them.'

61b. 'Cutting navel'
hisuma nitix, xalallop, nak^{h}ohoshu k'una
hi-suma ***n**-itix xalall-op* ***n**-ak^{h}ohoshu* ***k'una***
POSS-face IMP.SG-wipe baby-DEF IMP.SG-cut NEG
'Wipe his face, (of) that baby, don't cut it (the navel)'

Chimariko also has two suffixes that encode admonition: *-yu(y)* and *-te^{ʔ}q*. It is unclear how they differ in meaning or use. A distinction between a positive admonitive *-yu(y)* and a negative admonitive *-te^{ʔ}q* is possible, but it cannot be conclusively demonstrated due to the limited amount of data. Both suffixes occur verb-finally.

62. Admonitive *-yu(y)*

62a. 'Fugitives at Burnt Ranch'
č^{h}axak^{h}ona, weč^{h}up č^{h}axak^{h}ona, ^{ʔ}ama xoli^{ʔ}yu

čʰa-x-akʰo-na *wečʰup* *čʰa-x-akʰo-na* *ˀama* *xoliˀ-**yu***
IMP.PL-NEG-kill-NEG some IMP.PL-NEG-kill-NEG country bad-ADM
'Don't kill them, some said don't kill them, lest it spoil the country'

62b. Harrington 020-1104
muwetyu mušmuš
*m-uwet-**yu*** *mušmuš*
2SG-hook-ADM bull
'You better look out or the bull will take after you'

63. Admonitive *-teˀq* (Grekoff 012.018)

xačile hik'omuda exaˀixanat, xoxačiteˀq, pačʰaˀa xahaˀdeˀq
xačile *h-ik'o-mu-da* *exaˀi-xana-t* *x-oxači-**teˀq*** *pačʰaˀa* *x-ahaˀ-**deˀq***
children 3-talk-?-ASP make-FUT-ASP NEG-steal-ADManything NEG-pick.up-ADM
'He praises the children, never steal, don't pick up anything'

xahaˀdeq pačʰaˀa, hitxattakon, qʰapʰamahk'uteˀq
*x-ahaˀ-**deq*** *pačʰaˀa* *h-itxa-tta-kon* *qʰapʰamah-k'u-**teˀq***
NEG-pick.up-ADM anything 3-put-DER-FUT lie-NEG-ADM
'Let it lie there and don't pick it up, never lie'

8.1.3.5 Evidentials. Chimariko does not have an elaborate system of marking evidentiality. Grekoff (012.018) identifies an evidential suffix *-saˀs* marking hearsay. He does not list any examples, however. In addition, there is an inferential suffix *-taˀn* and a suffix *-iˀal* 'apparently'.

64. Inferential suffix *-taˀn*

64a. 'Hollering at New River'
ˀapu xošektanat, himisamdudaˀn sideˀw
ˀapu *x-ošekta-na-t* *himisamdu-**daˀn*** *si-deˀw*
fire NEG-make-NEG-ASP devil-INF say-DER
'He made no fire, it must have been the devil, they said'

64b. 'Woman wanders'
čitx isiˀ isiˀdaˀn, ˀičinšoll isiˀ yoxaˀidaˀn
čitx *isiˀ* *isiˀ-**daˀn*** *ˀičinšoll* *isiˀ* *y-oxaˀi-**daˀn***
blanket good good-INF dress good 1SG.A-make-INF
'Good blanket, it must have been good, I am going to make a good dress'

65. *-iˀal* 'apparently' (Grekoff 008.012)

hakʰoteˀwiˀal
h-akʰo-teˀw-iˀal
3-kill-DER-EV
'They killed him apparently'

8.1.3.6 Other modal suffixes. There are three suffixes marking an intensive meaning, according to Grekoff: (1) the negative intensive *x-. . -itk'i/x-. . -itqi* 'never, not at all', (2) the positive intensive *-kutqi* 'certainly, surely', and (3) the adversative intensive *-marʔi* 'regardless, even if'. Grekoff does not list any examples.

Following Grekoff, the resultative *-taʔče* is a modal affix. It is regarded as an aspectual suffix here that occurs in dependent adverbial clauses (see 12.4.1).

8.2 Derivational morphology

Chimariko has many derivational suffixes on verb roots deriving new verb stems. The derivational morphemes are attached directly to the verb roots. They include reflexives, reciprocals, applicatives, causatives, detransitivizing suffixes, nominalizers, instrumentals, and directionals. Chimariko also has noun incorporation, a special form of compounding whereby a nominal and verbal stem together form a new verb stem. Dixon (1910:329) lists instrumental prefixes deriving new verb stems. It is unclear whether Dixon's examples are cases of noun incorporation or instrumental prefixes.

8.2.1 Reflexives and reciprocals

The reflexive suffix *-yeʔw* indicates that the same participant(s) function as semantic agent and patient. The core argument marking remains unaltered in the presence of *-yeʔw*. This is shown below.

66. Examples with reflexive suffix *-yeʔw* (Harrington 020-1128 and 020-1130)

66a. *noʔot pʰaʔmot č'imarot yekʰoxanat*
noʔot pʰaʔmot č'imar-ot y̠-ekʰo-xana-t
1SG DET person-DEF 1SG.A-kill-FUT-ASP
'I am going to kill him' [lit. 'I am going to kill this person']

66b. *pʰaʔmot noʔot čʰakʰoxanan*
pʰaʔmot noʔot č̠ʰ-akʰo-xana-n
3 1SG 1SG.P-kill-FUT-ASP
'He is going to kill me'

66c. *yekʰoyeʔwxanat noʔot*
*y̠-ekʰo-**yeʔw**-xana-t noʔot*
1SG.A-kill-REFL-FUT-ASP 1SG
'I am going to kill myself'

In examples 66a and 66c the first person agent prefix *y-* occurs, while in 66b there is a first person patient prefix *čʰ-*, given that a third person acts on a first. With the reflexive suffix the argument marking remains the same as without the reflexive suffix.

Reflexives can co-occur with transitivizing constructions, such as applicatives, or with detransitivizing constructions (see 8.2.2. and 8.2.4). While the applicatives precede the reflexive, the detransitivizing *-tta* or *-teʔw* (see 8.2.4) follow it.

67. Reflexive *-yeʔw* with applicative *-ʔna* (Harrington 020-1125)

    noʔot ʔik'oʔnayeʔwdinda
    *noʔot   ʔ-ik'o-**ʔna-yeʔw**-dinda*
    1SG   1SG.A-talk-APPL-REFL-PROG
    'I was talking to myself'

68. Reflexive *-yeʔw* with detransitivizing *-teʔw* (Harrington 020-1107)

    kumičin hakʰoyeʔwdeʔw
    *kumičin   h-akʰo-**yeʔw-deʔw***
    all   3-kill-REFL-DER
    'All killed themselves'

Like the reflexive, the reciprocal *-nwa* does not alter argument marking. It co-occurs with the agent rather than the patient affix.

69. Reciprocal *-nwa* (Harrington 020-1134)

69a. *načʰidot yanunwaxanat*
     *načʰidot   ya-nu-**nwa**-xana-t*
     1PL   1PL.A-growl-RECP-FUT-ASP
     '<u>We</u> are going to growl at <u>each other</u>'

69b. *kumičin čʰanut*
     kumičin   čʰa-nu-t
     all   1PL.P-growl-ASP
     'They all growl at <u>us</u>'

A reciprocal meaning may also result when a dual pronoun *mamotowa* occurs with a verb that contains the reflexive suffix *-yeʔw*. The reciprocal *-nwa* and the dual suffix on pronouns *-owa* have very similar shapes. They may derive from the same source.

70. Reflexive *-yeʔw* and independent dual pronoun (Harrington 020-1128)

    yakʰoʔyew mamotowa
    y-akʰo-ʔyew   mamot-owa
    1SG.A-kill-REFL   2SG-dual
    'Let's you and me kill each other'

8.2.2 Applicatives

Applicatives are directly attached to the verb stem to form new stems that require an additional participant. This participant is cast as core argument and can be marked pronominally on the verb depending on the hierarchical structure. Intransitives can change their transitivity by adding an applicative, such as from *ik'o* 'to talk' to *ik'oʔna* 'to talk to' with the applicative *–(ʔ)na*. Since applicatives function as word-formation devices, verb stems with applicatives can easily become lexicalized. To what extent the newly created verbs are lexicalized in Chimariko remains unclear.

There are three applicative suffixes: *-ʔna*, *-čan*, and *-ku*. Only examples with *-ʔna* occur in the narratives.

71. Applicative *-ʔna* in *ikoʔna* 'to talk to' (from 'Woman wanders')

č'imar heyʔewinda, kumičin čʰuk'oʔnan
*č'imar h-eyʔew-inda kumičin čʰ-**uk'o-ʔna**-n*
person 3-?-PROG all 1SG.P-talk-APPL-ASP
'The people are good,they all talk to me good'

72. Applicative *-ʔna* in *ikoʔna* 'to talk to' (from 'Mrs Bussell')

hamew xewunan, xok'oʔnanan
*hamew x-ewu-na-n x-**ok'o-ʔna**-na-n*
food NEG-give-NEG-ASP NEG-talk-APPL-NEG-ASP
'I did not give her dinner, I did not speak to her'

In example 71, the additional argument 'I' is treated as core and marked on the verb with the pronominal prefix *čʰ-*. No pronominal marking occurs in 72 due to the presence of the negative circumfix. In the following example a direction is cast as a core argument of a motion verb. Additional examples with applicatives are in Table 11.

73. Applicative *-ʔna* with direction as core argument (Harrington 020-1096)

73a. *hakimni*
h-aki-m-ni
3-wash.away-DIR-ASP
'She washed away'

73b. *waida hakiʔnamda*
*waida h-aki-**ʔna**-m-da*
east 3-wash.away-APPL-DIR-ASP
'She washed east' (She washed away toward the east)

Table 11: Word formation with applicatives (from Grekoff 012.010)

Applicative	Basic verb stem	New verb stem
-ʔna	*loč'* 'to drip'	*loč'iʔna* 'to drip onto'
-ʔna	*iwo* 'to sit'	*iwoʔna* 'to sit on'
-ʔna	*iwota* 'to be seated'	*iwoʔnata* 'to be seated on'
-ʔna	*awata* 'to hang'	*awaʔnata* 'to hang on'
-č'an	*č'oh* 'to drip'	*č'ohč'an* 'to drip onto'
-č'an	*wi* 'to get burnt'	*wič'an* 'to get burnt onto'
-č'an	*uṭan* 'to touch'	*uṭanč'an* 'to touch someone'
-ku	*itay* 'to pay something'	*itayku* 'to pay someone something'
-ku	*ikiʔ* 'to ask money in payment for something'	*ikiʔku* 'to ask someone money in payment for something'

8.2.3 Causatives

There are two causative constructions in Chimariko: (1) a morphological causative and (2) a periphrastic causative. The causative-benefactive suffix *-miy* adds a beneficiary or recipient. No examples occur in the narratives.

74. Causative-benefactive suffix *-miy* (Grekoff 012.027)

ama 'to eat'	=>	*amamiy* 'to feed, to give to eat'
luˀ 'to drink'	=>	*luˀ . . miy* 'to water, to give to drink'
oši 'suck (milk)'	=>	*ošimiy* 'to give to suckle'
iši 'to dress'	=>	*išimiy* 'to cover'

The periphrastic causative construction is formed with *ixaˀy* 'to make'. Pronominal marking occurs on both predicates. Given the limited number of examples, it remains unclear whether there are any restrictions or reductions in the verb morphology.

75a. 'Crawfish'
ˀaqʰa ˀelohqʰut ˀixaˀyta
ˀaqʰa ˀeloh-qʰut ˀ-ixaˀy-ta
water hot-liquid 1SG.A-cause-ASP
'I made the water hot'

75b. 'Cutting Navel'
hičʰu nexaˀy
hičʰu n-exaˀy
long IMP.SG-cause
'Make it long'

75c. Grekoff 012.027
minoˀk ˀixaˀyxanat
m-inoˀk ˀ-ixaˀy-xana-t
2SG-recover 1SG.A-make-FUT-ASP
'I am going to cure you' (Literally: 'I am going to cause you to recover')

75d. Grekoff 012.027
natolmu nixaˀy
n-atol-mu n-ixaˀy
IMP.SG-roll-DIR IMP.SG-make
'You roll it!' (Literally: 'You cause it to roll!')

75e. Grekoff 012.027
hisuhnuwuk čʰuxaˀyni
h-isuhnu-wu-k čʰ-uxaˀy-ni
3-wake-RET-PST 1SG.P-make-ASP
'He (rooster) woke me up'

Grekoff (012.027) lists the following example to illustrate the difference between the two causative constructions:

76. *ošimiy* 'have someone suck, give to suck'
oši ixaˀy 'make (let) someone (i.e. baby) suck'

The difference between the two constructions lies in the directness of the causation. Furthermore, it is likely that the morphological causative describes semantically one event, while the periphrastic causative describes semantically two events. There are not enough data, however, to examine the difference in detail.

8.2.4 Indefinite third person plural agent

There are two derivational suffixes, *-teˀw* and *-tta*, that are passive-like constructions in their semantic function. They refer to an indefinite third person plural agent, apply only to dynamic events rather than to states, and they background the agent and/or foreground the patient. In some instances, such as with *sideˀw* 'they said it, it was said', they have developed into fixed expressions. The constructions differ from passives in that they do not have a syntactic impact, i.e. there is no shift in the argument structure.

8.2.4.1 -teˀw/-deˀw. The derivational suffix *-teˀw/-deˀw* signals that an event has an indefinite third person plural agent. Hence, it backgrounds the agent. The suffix precedes any tense, aspect, or modal suffixes.

77. 'Woman Wanders'
hišehekteˀw, hexačideˀw, hišehet, k'oṭihut,
*h-išehe-k-**teˀw*** *h-exači-**deˀw*** *h-išehe-t* *k'oṭi-hu-t*
3-take.along-DIR-DER 3-steal-DER 3-take.along-ASP run.away-CONT-ASP
'(Bad Indians) took her along, they stole her, they took her along, she ran away'
. .
noˀot čušehemdeˀw k'oṭihut, ˀawa hida imamda
*noˀot čʰ-ušehe-m-**deˀw*** *k'oṭi-hu-t* *ˀawa* *hida* *i-mam-da*
1SG 1SG.P-take.along-DIR-DER run.away-CONT-ASP house lots 1SG.A-see- ASP
'They took me off, I fled, I saw lots of houses'

78. 'Crawfish'
hoputeˀw ˀama, txol makumčaxat q'ehčaxat
*h-opu-**teˀw*** *ˀama* *txol* *makum-čaxa-t* *q'e-h-čaxa-t*
3-mine-DER land crawfish perish-COMP-ASP die-3-COMP-ASP
'They mined the land, all crawfish perished, they died all'

79. 'Hollering at New River'
ˀapu xošektanat, himisamdudaˀn sideˀw,
ˀapu *x-ošekta-na-t* *himisamdu-daˀn* *si-**deˀw***
fire NEG-make-NEG-ASP devil-INF say-DER
'He made no fire, it must have been the devil, they said'

pačʰigut ˀapu, himisamdudaˀn sideˀw

pačʰigut	*ˀapu*	*himisamdu-daˀn*	*si-**deˀw***
no.more	fire	devil-INF	say-DER

'There was no fire, it must have been the devil they said'

In example 77 the main focus lies on the patient, the woman who is the main character of the narrative, and not on the agent, the bad Indians who took her away. The derivational suffix signals that the agent is backgrounded and unimportant. Although in example 78 the main focus does not lie on the patient, the land, *-teˀw* signals that the agent, the white people who mined the land, is unimportant and indefinite. In example 79 the verb *si* 'to say' and the derivational suffix have become a fixed expression together. There is no person or other marking on the verb apart from *-teˀw*. Similarly, the agent of the action is unimportant and indefinite.

8.2.4.2 -tta/-ta. As with the derivational suffix *-teˀw/-deˀw*, *-tta/-ta* signals that an event has an unidentifiable third person plural agent. Hence, it backgrounds the agent and foregrounds the patient. The suffix precedes any tense, aspect, or modal suffixes.

80. 'Crawfish'

ˀaqʰa ˀelohqʰut ˀixaˀyta, memat txolop ˀiwinqʰutta

ˀaqʰa	*ˀeloh-qʰut*	*ˀ-ixaˀy-ta*	*memat*	*txol-op*	*ˀ-iwin-qʰut-**ta***
water	hot-liquid	1SG.A-make-ASP	alive	crawfish-DEF	1SG.A-dump-liquid-**DER**

'I made the water hot, I dumped them alive, the crawfish, immersingly'

81. 'Fugitives at Burnt Ranch'

hek'omatta, hakʰodeˀ, č'imarop, xawiyop hakʰodeˀn

*h-ek'o-ma-**tta***	*h-akʰo-deˀ*	*č'imar-op*	*xawiy-op*	*h-akʰo-deˀ-n*
3-say-?-**DER**	3-kill-DER	person-DEF	Redwood.Indian-DEF	3-kill-DER-ASP

'The boy told (it), they killed the boy, the people, the Indians killed him'

82. 'Dailey Chased by the Bull'

xowetnat, hek'omatta, pʰaˀyit čʰuwetni sit

x-owet-na-t	*h-ek'o-ma-**tta***	*pʰaˀyit*	*čʰ-uwet-ni*	*si-t*
NEG-hook-NEG-ASP	3-say-?-**DER**	thus.say	1SG.P-hook-ASP	say-ASP

'But he did not hook him, he told (it), thus he said, he hooked me he said'

In example 80, the patient, crawfish, is central to the narrative and foregrounded, while in examples 81 and 82, it is unclear what semantic impact *-tta* has on the narrative. In both examples the word is identical in form and could be a lexicalized expression.

8.2.5 Noun incorporation

Noun incorporation is a special form of compounding whereby a nominal stem and a verbal stem together form a verb (Mithun 1986). The incorporated noun shows no morphological marking and bears no grammatical relation to the verb.

83. ‘Fugitives at Burnt Ranch’

hiṭawiˀmut, hičʰemta hiṭamtu

h-iṭa-wiˀmu-t	*h-ičʰe-mta*	*h-iṭa-mtu*
3-hand-take-ASP	3-say-PROG	POSS-hand-INST

‘He took his hand telling him (to go home), he led him by the hand’

84. ‘Woman wanders’

k’oṭihut, awa hita imamta ˀamaq’eˀta

k’oṭi-hu-t	*awa*	*hita*	*i-mam-ta*	*ˀama-q’e-ˀ-ta*
run.away-CONT-ASP	house	lots	1SG.A-see-ASP	country-die-1SG.A-ASP

‘I fled, I saw lots of houses, I will die in this country’

Noun incorporation is used in Chimariko for body parts or for locations. In example 83 *-ṭa-* ‘hand’ serves the function of an undergoer in the clause. This function tends to be associated with core arguments in other languages. However, the core argument is marked by a pronominal prefix referring to the person ‘him’ and not to the hand. The newly-created verb stem *iṭa-wiˀm* ‘to hand-take’ or ‘to take by the hand’ expresses a single concept. In example 84 the location where the event takes place, the country, is incorporated in the verb stem. Only a few examples occur in the data. It remains unclear how productive noun incorporation is in Chimariko, and to what extent the forms have been lexicalized. Some stems appear separately elsewhere, such as *amaˀ* ‘land, country’ and *q’e* ‘to die’, and they show a predictable semantic pattern.

8.2.6 Reduplication

Reduplication is a morphological process in which a root is partially or fully repeated for grammatical or semantic purposes. Chimariko has partial reduplication, mostly to signal event-internal pluractionality in verbs, i.e. a single event that is made up of different reiterated subparts (Garret 2001). The productivity of this process remains unclear, given that for most verbs only the reduplicated forms are attested in the data. In the reduplication process the final syllable, CV or CVC, is repeated and suffixed to the root. This process can be summarized as follows:

$$-C_1V_1\,(C_2)\;/\;C_1V_1\,(C_2)\_\_\_\_\_\_\;\#$$

The examples below illustrate this process. It must be noted, however, that the bases for most of the verbs are not attested in the data.

85. Grekoff 010.010

Polysyllabic verb stems: Final CV repeated

welu	>	*welulu*	‘act quickly’
wini	>	*winini*	‘be cold, shivering’
q’iwu	>	*q’iwuwu*	‘tremble’
txulu	>	*txululu*	‘roar’

q^{h}uyu	>	*q^{h}uyuyu*	'drizzle'
ček'i	>	*ček'ik'i*	'break'
xumu	>	*xumumu*	'be smashed'
q'amu	>	*q'amumu*	'talk a lot'
ṭ'ala	>	*ṭ'alala*	'ticking'
ničli	>	*ničlili*	'grind powder (with stick)'
nimitčili	>	*nimitčilili*	'grind powder (with foot)'

Polysyllabic verb stems: Final CVC repeated

čučax	>	*čučaxčax*	'hit'
ičxekim	>	*ičxekimkim*	'shake hands'
imeluš	>	*imelušluš*	'shake one's head to say no'
ituk'um	>	*ituk'umk'um*	'bend the basket'
ac'uxum	>	*ac'uxumxum*	'mash, break up lumps (of sugar or salt)'
ič^{h}axum	>	*ič^{h}axumxum*	'pound with fists'

Monosyllabic verb roots: CV repeated

q'i	>	*q'iq'i*	'belch'
ko	>	*koko*	'holler'

Monosyllabic verb roots: CVC repeated

p^{h}ot	>	*p^{h}otp^{h}ot*	'boil'
q^{h}ol	>	*q^{h}olq^{h}ol*	'growl'
p^{h}oq'	>	*p^{h}oq'p^{h}oq'*	'burst'
tos	>	*tostos*	'grumble'
wo^{ʔ}	>	*wo^{ʔ}wo^{ʔ}*	'bark'
tew	>	*tewtew*	'shake a rope up and down'
lax	>	*laxlax*	'be howling'
lap	>	*laplap*	'blinking'
^{ʔ}ew	>	*^{ʔ}ew^{ʔ}ew*	'warcry'
čin	>	*činčin*	'pound'
mos	>	*mosmos*	'to be itchy'

Partial reduplication has been attested only in verbs. At least three pairs occur in the data in both reduplicated and non-reduplicated form.

86. Grekoff 010.010

ko	'shout, holler' (once)	*koko*	'holler'
isuq'iwmu	'nod one's head' (once)	*isuq'iwq'iwmuta*	'nod one's head'
ituk'umu	'break (basket)'	*ituk'umk'um*	'bend (basket)'

Many examples of fully and partially reduplicated stems occur in the data. Some are shown below.

87. Harrington 020-0420
ˀešoq'ehta, wininihta
ˀešo-q'e-h-ta, ***winini**-h-ta*
cold-?-3-ASP shiver-3-ASP
'It is cold, he is shivering'

88. Harrington 020-0494
hitululuida hiṭa, ˀešoq'ehta
*h-**itulului**-da h-iṭa, ˀešo-q'e-h-ta*
3-rub-ASP POSS-hand cold-?-3-ASP
'He is rubbing his hands together, he is cold'

89. Harrington 020-0472
naṭaˀṭan
*n-**aṭaˀṭa**-n*
IMP.SG-chop-ASP
'You chop it!'

90. Harrington 020-0124
ṭemumuxanan
***ṭemumu**-xana-n*
thunder-FUT-ASP
'It is going to thunder'

91. Harrington 020-0137
ṭˀalalahtat ˀalaˀuleda, ṭewu ṭˀalalahtat
***ṭˀalala**-h-ta-t ˀalaˀuleda, ṭewu* ***ṭˀalala**-h-ta-t*
tick-3-?-ASP clock big tick-3-?-ASP
'The clock is ticking, it is ticking loud'

92. Harrington 020-0445
načʰot ˀewˀewčʰin
načʰot ***ˀewˀew**-čʰ-in*
1PL warcry-1PL.P-ASP
'We warcry'

93. Harrington 020-0410
hisuq'iwq'iwmudat
*h-isu-**q'iwq'iw**-mu-da-t*
3-face-nod-DIR-?-ASP
'He nods'

94. Harrington 020-0125
mamot laxlaxni
mamot ***laxlax**-ni*
2SG cackle-IMP.SG
'You cackle!'

95. Harrington 020-0415
himinapušpušmudat
*h-imina-**pušpuš**-mu-da-t*
3-back-bend-DIR-?-ASP
'He bends his back up and down'

96. Harrington 020-0357
pačʰi kokomdaˀ
pačʰi ***koko**-m-da-ˀ*
what holler-2SG-ASP-Q
'What are you hollering for'

97. Harrington 020-0428
ˀaqʰa pʰotpʰotit ˀelohqʰutta
ˀaqʰa ***pʰotpʰot**-it* *ˀeloh-qʰut-ta*
water boil-ASP hot-liquid-ASP
'It is boiling hot water'

98. Harrington 020-0119
qʰolqʰolit, wowoˀin
***qʰolqʰol**-it,* *wowoˀ-in*
growl-ASP bark-ASP
'(The dog) growls, he barks'

Reduplication functions primarily to indicate event-internal pluractionality (Garrett 2001), signalling that a single event on a single occasion is made up of several internal repeated sub-events or phases that together make one complex event.

99. Event-internal pluractionality (Grekoff 010.010)

q'iwuwu	'tremble'
qʰuyuyu	'drizzle'
ničlili	'grind powder (with stick)'
nimitčilili	'grind powder (with foot)'
ičxekimkim	'shake hands'
imelušluš	'shake one's head to say no'
ituk'umk'um	'bend the basket'
ac'uxumxum	'mash, break up lumps (of sugar or salt)'
tewtew	'shake a rope up and down'
ituluIuy	'pet (a cat)'
iničʰe hushus	'sniffle'

Reduplication can also indicate the pluralization of internal arguments, as in 100.

100. Pluralization of internal arguments (Grekoff 010.010)

uṭankimkim muta	'wiggle fingers'
ac'uxumxum	'mash, break up lumps (of sugar, salt)'
akʰakʰo	'kill many (of the enemy)'

Reduplication can also signal reciprocity as in the following example:

101. Reciprocity (Grekoff 010.010)

ičxekimkim	'shake hands'

While most reduplicated forms are events, states expressed with reduplication indicate a spatial distribution, as in 102a, or a distributive, as in 102b.

102a. Spatial distribution (Grekoff 010.010)

wilili	'be freckled'
čʰelili	'be freckled'

102b. Distributive (Grekoff 010.010)

amosmos	'to be itchy'
winini	'be cold, shivering'

While reduplication signals event-internal repetition for the most part, in some instances it could also be interpreted as event-external repetition (Garrett 2001).

103. Possible event-external repetition (Grekoff 019.004)

hatoltolta	'he beats repeatedly'
ˀaqʰuye hatoltolta	'he beats his tail repeatedly'

Other reduplicated forms are onomatopoeic, in addition to indicating repetition:

104. Onomatopoeia (Grekoff 010.010)

xoṭuṭu	'snore'
woˀwoˀ	'bark'

8.2.7 Nominalization

Verb stems are nominalized by adding the derivational suffix *-ew*. In some cases the nominalized verb stem has become lexicalized, and the verb base is no longer apparent. The third person pronominal prefix *h-* occurs in the nominalized forms.

105. Nominalizer *-ew*

ama 'to eat'	=>	*hamew* 'food'	('Woman wanders')
ik'o 'to talk'	=>	*hik'ew* 'talker'	(Harrington 020-1133)
?	=>	*hiṭiytew* 'fence'	('Dailey chased by the bull')
opu 'to work'	=>	*hopew* 'acorn soup'	('Woman wanders')

Grekoff also lists an instrumental nominalizer *-kuččʰa* (Grekoff 008.012). The same as with the nominalizer *–ew* a third person pronominal prefix *h-* occurs in the nominalized forms.

106. Instrumental nominalizer *-kučʰa*

106a. Harrington 020-0397
hičxemkučʰa
*h-ičxem-**kučʰa***
3-pull-NOM
'Wagon'

106b. Harrington 020-0423
hičxemrahaˀkučʰa
*h-ičxem-rahaˀ-**kučʰa***
3-pull-?-NOM
'Scales'

106c. Harrington 020-0431
hičhektatkučʰa
*h-iče-kta-t-**kučʰa***
3-pull-DIR-ASP-NOM
'Plow'

106d. Harrington 020-0491
ˀapu hišekoˀtkučʰa
*ˀapu h-išek-oˀt-**kučʰa***
fire 3-make-?-NOM
'Stove'

Verbs in relative clauses have a special suffix *-rop/-rot/-lop/-lot* that has been interpreted as a nominalizer by Grekoff. However, it only occurs in relative clause constructions, generally together with nominals. Therefore, it is viewed here as a suffix marking a dependent relationship in relative clauses (see also 12.3).

107. Nominalization with *-rop, -rot/-lop,-lot*

107a. Harrington 020-0476
noˀot ˀimiˀnanlop
*noˀot ˀ-imiˀna-n-**lop***
1SG 1SG.A-want-ASP-NOM
'My sweetheart' [Lit. 'The thing I want']

107b. Harrington 020-0483
ˀiṭi hisamhunirop
*ˀiṭi h-isamhuni-**rop***
man 3-dance-NOM
'He is a dancing man' [Lit. 'The man who is dancing']

107c. Grekoff 020.09
kimot č'imal huwaktulot
*kimot č'imal h-uwa-ktu-**lot***

DET person 3-go-DIR-DEP
'The person who arrived'

107d. Grekoff 020.09
*pʰaˀmot ˀahatew h-ahaˀta-**lot***
*pʰaˀmot ˀahatew h-ahaˀta-**lot***
DET money 3-?-DEP
'That one, the one who has money'

107e. Grekoff 020.09
pačʰimop ˀuleytop šičela hičʰemrop
*pačʰim-op ˀuleyt-op šičela h-ičʰem-**rop***
that-DEF little-DEF horse 3-pull-DEP
'The little thing of yours which the horse pulls' (=carriage)

107f. Grekoff 020.09
poˀqʰol sumusu hipinṭaylop čʰiselop
*poˀqʰol sumu-su h-ipinṭay-**lop** čʰisel-op*
apple like-be 3-?-DEP knife-DEF
'The knife to peel apples with'

8.2.8 Instrumental affixes

Dixon (1910:329) lists several instrumental prefixes deriving new verb stems. However, it is unclear whether Dixon's examples are cases of noun incorporation or some other form of compounding or instrumental prefixes. The affixes are summarized in Table 12.

Table 12: Instrumental affixes (Dixon 1910:329)

mitei-	'with the foot'
wa-	'by sitting on'
e-	'with end of long object'
a-	'with a long object'
me-	with the head'
tsu-	'with a round object'
tu-	'with the hand'

108. Dixon (1910:329)
*n-**a**-klucmu* 'knock over with bat'
*ni-**e**-klucmu* 'knock over with end of pole by thrust'
*ni-**mitci**-klucmu* 'knock over with foot'
*ni-**mitci**-kmu* 'roll log with foot'
*ni-**tu**-kmu* 'roll log with hand'
*ni-**wa**-tcexu* 'break by sitting on'

The prefix *ni-* in Dixon's examples is most likely an imperative.

8.2.9 Directional affixes

Many directional suffixes occur in Chimariko. They are directly attached to the verb stem and are followed by tense, aspect, or mood markers. The suffixes are summarized in Table 13.

Table 13: Directional affixes

-ktam /-tam	'down'	Berman (2001b:1050) Dixon (1910:319)
-ema/-enak	'into'	Dixon (1910:319)
-ha	'up'	Dixon (1910:319)
-hot	'down'	Dixon (1910:319)
-lo	'apart'	Berman (2001b:1050) Dixon (1910:319)
-ro	'up'	Dixon (1910:319)
-sku	'towards'	Dixon (1910:319)
-smu	'across'	Dixon (1910:319)
-tap	'out'	Dixon (1910:319)
-tku/-ku	Cislocative ('towards here')	Harrington 020-0004 Grekoff 008.012
-tmu/-mu	Transmotional ('towards there')	Harrington 020-0004 Grekoff 008.012
-kh	'motion towards here'	Berman (2001b:1050)
-m	'motion towards there'	Berman (2001b:1050)
-tpi	'out of '	Berman (2001b:1050) Dixon (1910:319)
-xun/-xunok	'in, into'	Dixon (1910:319) Grekoff 008.012
-qʰa	'along'	Grekoff 008.012
-pa	'off, away'	Grekoff 008.012
-qʰutu	'into water'	Grekoff 008.012
-č'ana	'to, toward'	Grekoff 008.012
-čama	'in, into'	Grekoff 008.012

109. Directional suffixes *-tku* and *-m* (from 'Fugitives at Burnt Ranch')

č'imar xotai heṭaheskut uwatkut, heṭaheskut č'utamdače
*č'imar xotai h-eṭahe-**sku**-t uwa-**tku**-t h-eṭahe-**sku**-t č'utamdače*
man three 3-run.away-DIR-ASP go-DIR-ASP 3-run.away-DIR-ASP Burnt Ranch
'Three men came as fugitives, they ran away to Burnt Ranch'
. .
nuwawum kella, č'imar epatteˀw, qʰomal uwamaˀ
*n-uwa-wu-**m** kella č'imar epat-teˀw qʰomal uwa-**m**-aˀ*
IMP.SG-go-RET-DIR that.way person sit-DER where go-DIR-Q
'You go home that way (gesturing with lips), where did that man go to?'

110. Directional suffix *-mu* (from 'Woman wanders')

naˀahunmu ˀawakunoi, haˀatpimda ˀiṭirop
*n-aˀahun-**mu** ˀawa-kunoi h-aˀa-tpi-m-da ˀiṭir-op*
IMP.SG-?-DIR house-inside 3-?-DIR-DIR-ASP man-DEF
'Take her in the house, the man came out (and found her)'

111. Directional suffix *-kta* (from 'Mrs Bussell')

masunu huwaktanhut šunuhullot
*masunu h-uwa-**kta**-nhu-t šunuhull-ot*
always 3-go-DIR-CONT-ASP old.woman-DEF
'Mrs. Bussell goes around all the time'

112. Directional suffix *-tapmu/-tamu* (from 'Dailey chased by the bull')

yečučutapmun, hiṭiytew yuc'uˀtamun
*ye-čuču-**tapmu**-n hiṭiytew y-uc'uˀ-**tamu**-n*
1SG.A-?-DIR-ASP fence 1SG.A-?-DIR-ASP
'I dodged, I jumped over the fence'

The suffix *-tapmu* in 112 combines most likely of *-tap* 'out' and *-mu* 'towards there'.

8.2.10 Suffix *-ma* of unclear meaning

The suffix *-ma* occurs in a few examples attached to the verb root and preceding other derivational suffixes. Therefore, it is treated as a derivational suffix. Its meaning, however, is unclear. It could be interpreted as an applicative.

113. Grekoff 003.005
noˀot čʰtxoˀmattataˀ xaralla wenčʰumtu
*noˀot čʰ-utxoˀ-**ma**-tta-taˀ xaralla wenčʰu-mtu*
1SG 1SG.P-?-?-DER-PST baby cradle-INST
'They brought me up in a baby basket.'

114. 'Crawfish'
ˀičiˀta, puqʰela ˀitxaˀmat
*ˀ-ičiˀ-ta puqʰela ˀ-itxaˀ-**ma**-t*
1SG.A-catch-ASP basket 1SG.A-put-?-ASP
'I caught them, I put them in a basket'

115. 'Dailey chased by the bull'
xowetnat, hek'omatta, pʰaˀyit čʰuwetni sit
*xo-wet-na-t h-ek'o-**ma**-tta pʰaˀyit čʰu-wet-ni si-t*
NEG-hook-NEG-ASP 3-say-?-DER thus.say 1SG.P-hook-ASP say-ASP
'But he did not hook him, he told, thus he said, he hooked me he said'

8.3 Verb morphology in areal-typological perspective

The languages of Northern California all have very elaborate inflectional and derivational verb morphologies distinguishing similar sets of categories. Inflectional categories include: pronominal reference, tense, aspect, and modal affixes. Derivational categories include: reduplication, noun incorporation, reflexives, reciprocals, causatives, and directional affixes, among others. While the set of categories distinguished is similar, there are many differences in the sub-categories and actual functions and uses of the affixes, as well as in the position with regard to the verb stem, i.e. prefixing or suffixing.

Pronominal affixes are either prefixed, suffixed, or both, with no areal preference for one or the other. Furthermore, they follow different grammatical systems of argument marking. Some distinguish agents and patients, some encode subjects and objects, some are governed by person hierarchies having either one or two arguments marked on the verb, and some follow a combination of these distinctions. Typologically uncommon features found in Chimariko, such as agent-patient distinctions and person hierarchies occur in many languages of the area: Hupa, Shasta, Karuk, Yurok, Wiyot, and Yana. However, the details of each systems vary. Mithun (in press) shows how core argument marking in Karuk, Yurok, and Yana could have developed into hierarchical systems through crystallization of frequent patterns. Following Mithun, in this process low-ranking agents are eliminated through passivization or simply omitted in certain contexts leaving only one argument overtly marked on the verb. The patterns of the pronominal systems in Chimariko and its neighbors are summarized in Table 14.

Table 14: Pronominal reference in Northern California

	Pronominal prefixes or suffixes	Number of arguments marked on the verb	Hierarchy	Agents and patients
Chimariko	Prefixes or suffixes	1 (sometimes 2)	1,2 >3 agent >patient	yes (first, some second person)
Wintu[1]	Suffixes	(1)	no	no
Hupa[2]	Prefixes	2	2>3	no
Shasta[3]	Prefixes and suffixes	1 or 2	2>3	no
Karuk[4]	Prefixes	1	2PL>1>2SG>3	yes (first person)
Yurok[5]	Suffixes (and some prefixes)	2	1PL>2>3SG>3PL	no
Wiyot[6]	Suffixes (and some prefixes)	2	no	yes (with passives)
Yana[7]	Suffixes	1	1, 2 >3 patient> agent	no
Achumawi[8]	Prefixes	?	no	no
Maidu[9]	Suffixes	?	no	no

[1] Pitkin 1984

[2] Golla 1970
[3] Silver 1966
[4] Bright 1957:59-62; Mithun 2008
[5] Robins 1958:47; Mithun in press
[6] Teeter 1964; Mithun 2008
[7] Sapir and Swadesh 1960; Mithun in press
[8] Olmsted 1966
[9] Shipley 1964 :45-47

Table 14 illustrates some of the differences between the pronominal systems in Northern California. Person hierarchies or agentive systems, both typologically rare features, occur in Chimariko and its immediate neighbors, as well as in the neighbors to the west. It is likely that they have developed through language contact, as suggested by Mithun (in press).

The languages in Northern California differ in the categories they distinguish in their tense, aspect, and mood systems. While some have an elaborate tense system, such as Shasta, others, such as Yurok, have no grammaticized tense system (Robins 1958:32). In general, aspect is marked in greater detail than tense. All languages also have a set of modal affixes. Modal categories are reflected either in the verb stem or through affixation. They include: negatives, interrogatives, potentials, speculatives, dubitatives, imperatives, and evidentials, among others. The general affixing pattern of tense, aspect, and mood is summarized in Table 15.

Table 15: Affixing pattern in tense/aspect/mood

	Tense	Aspect	Mood
Chimariko and immediate neighbors			
Chimariko	Suffixes	Suffixes	Suffixes
Wintu[1]	Suffixes	Suffixes	Suffixes
Hupa[2]	-	Prefixes	Prefixes
Shasta[3]	Prefixes	Prefixes/Suffixes	Prefixes
Distant neighbors to the west			
Karuk[4]	Suffixes	Suffixes	Suffixes
Yurok[5]	Preverbs	Prefixes (preverbs)	Preverbs Suffixes
Wiyot[6]	Preverbs	Preverbs	Preverbs
Distant neighbors to the east			
Yana[7]	Suffixes	Suffixes	Suffixes
Achumawi[8]	Suffixes	Suffixes	Suffixes
Maidu[9]	Suffixes	Suffixes	Suffixes

[1] Pitkin 1984:99-103
[2] Golla 1970:56-119
[3] Silver 1966:115-135, 162-164
[4] Bright 1957:86-115
[5] Robins 1958; Conathan 2004
[6] Teeter 1964:42-49
[7] Sapir and Swadesh 1960:11-13

[8] Olmsted 1966
[9] Shipley 1964 :37-53

Table 15 shows that while most languages encode tense, aspect, and mood in verbal suffixes, these categories are expressed in verbal prefixes or preverbal elements in four languages: Hupa, Shasta, Yurok, and Wiyot. These four languages occur in a geographically contiguous area. In many languages inflectional markers are either all prefixed or all suffixed. In Shasta all inflectional markers are prefixed, except for some aspectual suffixes. These suffixes may have developed through language contact with Wintu and Chimariko. Similarly, Yurok has modal suffixes that may have developed through contact with Karuk. Overall, the inflectional systems in the languages of Northern California have similar categories. However, they vary in their affixing pattern and fine details.

Similar to inflection, derivational processes creating new verb stems are much alike in Northern California. Such processes include: reduplication, noun incorporation, reflexives, reciprocals, causatives, and directional affixes, among others.

Reduplication is very common in western North America and Canada (Dryer et al. 2004). In northern California, reduplication is found in close neighbors (Wintu, Shasta) and in distant neighbors (Yurok, Karuk) of Chimariko, forming a contiguous area. No evidence for reduplication has been found in Hupa or Wiyot. It is not surprising that Hupa lacks reduplication, as this process does not occur in Athabaskan languages. Yana and Maidu, two distant neighbours of Chimariko to the east, also show reduplication.

Table 16: Reduplication in Northern California[1]

Chimariko and its immediate neighbors	
Chimariko	yes
Wintu	yes
Hupa	no
Shasta	yes
Distant neighbors to the west	
Karuk	yes
Yurok	yes
Wiyot	no
Distant neighbors to the east	
Yana	yes
Achumawi	no
Maidu	yes

[1] For sources see Table 15

Conathan (2004) shows that Yurok, Karuk, and Chimariko all have verbal reduplication with the semantics of event-internal pluractionality, and that in Yurok and Karuk this contrasts with another category expressing event-external reduplication (Garrett 2001). Wiyot, which is related to Yurok, does not have reduplication. As a result, Conathan (2004) concludes that in Yurok reduplication contrasting event-internal and event-external categories has developed due to contact with Karuk, Chimariko, and possibly other languages of the area. According to Conathan and Wood (2002), in both

Yurok and Karuk, pluractional reduplication indicates a continuous, bounded repetition of a semelfactive, but the Karuk pluractional additionally can be used with activities to indicate ongoing repetition of subphases. In Chimariko, reduplication seems to have been a productive process at some point given the different semantic functions and the occurrence with events and states. However, due to the limited number of lexical pairs showing base and reduplicated stem with different meanings, it appears that reduplication in Chimariko was highly lexicalized and not used productively at the time of data collection.

A less common word formation process is noun incorporation. It also occurs in Yana and Maidu, though not productively in the latter. In general, noun incorporation has a random distribution in California and does not seem to have been a productive process at the time of data collection for several languages (Sherzer 1976b). Only very few examples are attested in Chimariko.

A common phenomenon in Northern California is the presence of directional and instrumental verbal affixes. They occur in all of Chimariko's neighbors, but Yurok and Wiyot. While directionals are mostly suffixed, instrumentals are all prefixes. This is shown in Table 17. The two languages with directional prefixes, Wintu and Hupa, lack instrumental prefixes.

Table 17: Directional and instrumental affixes[1]

	Directional	Instrumental
Chimariko and its immediate neighbors		
Chimariko	Suffixes	Prefixes
Wintu	Prefixes	-
Hupa	Prefixes	-
Shasta	Suffixes	Prefixes
Distant neighbors to the west		
Karuk	Suffixes	Prefixes
Yurok	-	-
Wiyot	-	-
Distant neighbors to the east		
Yana	Suffixes	-
Achumawi	Suffixes	Prefixes
Maidu	Suffixes	Prefixes

[1] For sources see Table 15 and Sherzer 1976b

Voice alternations, transitivizing, and detransitivizing mechanisms are generally all expressed through verbal affixes in the languages of the area. Transitivizing mechanisms include causatives and applicatives, while detransitivizing processes include reflexives, reciprocals, and passive-like constructions.

To conclude, the languages of Northern California all have elaborate inflectional and derivational systems that are similar in the general categories they distinguish, but that differ in the distribution, functions, and uses of their sub-categories and in the position with regard to the verb stem.

9. SIMPLE SENTENCES

This chapter describes the structure of simple sentences, i.e. sentences with one predicate. Word order, argument structure, argument structure alternations, transitivity, and predicate nominals, among other topics, are treated.

9.1 Constituent order

Word order in the oral narratives is predominantly verb-final, as in examples 1 and 2. Verbs are underlined and clauses are in brackets in the examples.

1. 'Mrs Bussell'
ˀawaidače xowonat, šičel hiwontat
[ˀawa-ida-če x-owo-na-t] [šičel h-iwonta-t]
home-POSS-LOC NEG-stay-NEG-ASP horse 3-ride-ASP
'She does not stay at home, she goes around on horseback'

huwaktat, ˀiṭi sumusut, hopew ˀičʰuˀnan
[h-uwa-kta-t] [ˀiṭi sumu-su-t] [hopew ˀ-ičʰuˀna-n]
3-go-DIR-ASP man like-be-ASP acorn.soup 1SG.A-eat-ASP
'She goes around, like a man, "I would like to eat acorn soup"'

2. 'Fugitives at Burnt Ranch'
čʰaxakʰona, wečʰup čʰaxakʰona, ˀama xoliˀyu
[čʰa-xa-kʰo-na] [wečʰup čʰa-xa-kʰo-na] [ˀama xoliˀ-yu]
IMP.PL-NEG-kill-NEG some IMP.PL-NEG-kill-NEG country bad-ADM
'Don't kill them, some said don't kill them, lest it spoil the country'

yaxakʰonaxanˀi, makʰotaxantinda, k'otnihu
[ya-x-akʰo-na-xan-ˀi] [m-akʰo-ta-xan-tinda] [k'ot-ni-hu]
1PL.A-NEG-kill-NEG-FUT-ASP 2SG-kill-DER-FUT-PROG run.away-IMP.SG-CONT
'We won't kill them, he is going to kill you, run away'

In examples 1 and 2 all clauses are verb-final. However, five out of eleven clauses in these two examples consist of only the verb. Given the particular discourse structure attributed to the narratives (see chapter 13), it is unclear whether verb-final word order also occurs most often in conversation or other discourse genres.

In some clauses in the narratives obliques or noun phrases occur after the verb clause-finally.

3. 'Fugitives at Burnt Ranch'
č'imar xotai heṭaheskut uwatkut, heṭaheskut č'utamdače
[č'imar xotai h-eṭahe-sku-t] [uwa-tku-t] [h-eṭahe-sku-t ***č'utamdače****]*
man three 3-run.away-DIR-ASP go-DIR-ASP run.away-DIR-ASP Burnt Ranch
'Three men came as fugitives, they ran away to Burnt Ranch'

4. 'Mrs Bussell'
sinda, yuṭiˀi paačʰikun, kimass uwatkun, huwomni welmu
[si-nda] [yuṭi-ˀi paačʰikun] [kimass uwa-tku-n] [h-uwo-m-ni ***welmu****]*
say-PROG acorn-POSS no.more today go-DIR-ASP 3-go-DIR-ASP quickly
'She says, but my acorns are none, today she came, she went back home at once'

welmu uwomni, hamew xewunan, xok'oˀnanan
[welmu uwo-m-ni] [hamew x-ewu-na-n] [x-ok'o-ˀna-na-n]
quickly go-DIR-ASP food NEG-give-NEG-ASP NEG-talk-APPL-NEG-ASP
'At once she returned, I did not give her dinner, I did not speak to her'

In example 3, the locative oblique *č'utamdače* 'Burnt Ranch' occurs after the verb, and in 4 the manner adverbial *welmu* 'quickly'. Example 4 shows that the order of words can be attributed to the particular discourse style of the narratives whereby entire clauses are repeated switching the word order, and often adding a new piece of information (see chapter 13). The same clause *huwomni welmu* 'she returned at once' is repeated with verb-final word order. A similar repetition of an entire clause occurs in example 5.

5. 'On grandmother getting the hiccups'
mamot maš mipuhunmat hita, mamuš hita mipuhunmuˀ,
[mamot maš m-ipu-hunma-t ***hita****] [mamuš hita m-ipu-hunmu-ˀ]*
2SG but 2SG-work-DIR-ASP lots but.you lots 2SG-work-DIR-Q
'But you took lots, but did you take lots'

While the post-verbal order of adverbial elements can be attributed to the particular discourse style of the narratives, the post-verbal occurrence of nominal elements often correlates with known or previously mentioned information. These post-verbal nominals often occur with the suffixes *-op/-ot* marking definiteness.

6. 'Fugitives at Burnt Ranch'
hek'omatta, hakʰodeˀ, č'imarop, xawiyop hakʰodeˀn
[h-ek'o-ma-tta] [h-akʰo-deˀ ***č'imar-op xawiy-op****] [h-akʰo-deˀ-n]*
3-say-?-DER 3-kill-ASP person-DEF Redwood.Indian-DEF 3-kill-DER-ASP
'The boy told (it), they killed the boy, the people, the Indians killed him'

7. 'On grandmother getting the hiccups'
puneš ṭamma hiput, haˀumkiloˀta sankeˀnop
[puneš ṭamma h-ipu-t] [h-aˀumkiloˀ-ta ***sankeˀn-op****]*
once salmon.meal 3-work-ASP 3-?-ASP basket-DEF
'Once she took a mouthful of salmon-meal, she uncovered it, the pack basket'

8. 'Crawfish'
hiničxeˀkut, pʰiˀalop, hiničxeˀkut
[h-iničxeˀku-t ***pʰiˀal-op****] [h-iničxeˀku-t]*
3-smell-ASP bacon-DEF 3-smell-ASP
'They smelled it, that bacon, they smelled it'

In examples 5-8 the argument which occurs after the verb is known and has already occurred as a third person pronominal affix attached to the verb that precedes it. However, not all nominals that occur post-verbally have a suffix *-op/-ot*. Furthermore, the third person pronominal affix is sometimes omitted, since it is phonetically weak.

9. 'Fugitives at Burnt Ranch'
q^{h}omal uwama^ʔ č'imarop
[q^{h}omal uwa-m-a^ʔ ***č'imar-op****]*
where go-DIR-Q person-DEF
'Where did that man go to?'

10. 'Woman wanders'
hikeexananda č'imar
*[****h****-ikee-xana-nda č'imar]*
3-understand-FUT-PROG person
'She was understanding the people'

11. 'Postnatal seclusion'
hači^{ʔ}natat ^{ʔ}eloh, ^{ʔ}eloh hexa^{ʔ}yta, p'un hixopektat p^{h}uncar
[h-ači^{ʔ}nata-t ^{ʔ}eloh] [^{ʔ}eloh h-exa^{ʔ}y-ta] [p'un h-ixopekta-t ***p^{h}uncar****]*
3-lie-ASP hot hot 3-make-ASP one 3-watch-ASP woman
'She lies on a hot (rock, place), she makes it hot, she watches the woman'

In example 9 the third person pronominal prefix *h-* on *uwama^ʔ* 'he went there' is omitted, hence the post-verbal *č'imarop* 'that man' is not explicitly mentioned on the immediately preceding verb. Nevertheless, 'the man' is mentioned earlier in the narrative. In example 10 *č'imar* 'people' does not occur with the suffix marking definiteness. Hence, not all post-verbal nominal elements occur with *-op/-ot*. Given that third person pronominal affixes do not distinguish agent and patient forms, it is unclear which person is marked on the verb *hikeexananda* 'she was understanding them'. In example 11 the post-verbal *p^{h}uncar* 'woman' does not have a suffix marking definiteness. As with example 10, it is unclear which person is marked on the verb *hixopektat* 'she watches her'. Overall, although word order in the narratives is predominantly verb-final, it is not a rigid word order.

The order of elements within the noun phrase equally shows variation. Adjectives, numerals, and demonstratives precede or follow the noun.

12. 'Woman wanders'
kimot č'imarot niwo
kimot *č'imar-ot n-iwo*
this person-DEF IMP.SG-stay
'This man told her to stay there'

13. 'Mrs Bussell'
huwaktat masunu šunuhullot p^{h}a^{ʔ}mot

h-uwa-kta-t *masunu* *šunuhull-ot* ***pʰaˀmot***
3-go-DIR-ASP always old.woman-DEF that
'She always goes around, that old woman'

14. 'Fugitives At Burnt Ranch'
č'imar xotai heṭaheskut uwatkut
č'imar ***xotai*** *h-eṭahe-sku-t* *uwa-tku-t*
man three 3-run.away-DIR-ASP go-DIR-ASP
'Three men came as fugitives'
. .
yaxamamnan, ***p'un*** *ˀiṭilla ˀuleeda himamda*
ya-x-amam-na-n *p'un* *ˀiṭilla* *ˀuleeda* *h-imam-da*
1PL.A-NEG-see-NEG-ASP one boy sibling 3-see-ASP
We didn't see it, a boy saw it'

15. 'Woman wanders'
ˀičinšoll isiˀ yoxaˀidaˀn
ˀičinšoll ***isiˀ*** *y-oxaˀi-daˀn*
dress good 1SG.A-make-INF
'I am going to make a good dress'

16. Grekoff 020.006
ṭewu yekʰon ˀaˀa
ṭewu *y-ekʰo-n* *ˀaˀa*
big 1SG.A-kill-ASP deer
'I killed a large deer'

Nouns precede numerals and adjectives more often than the reverse. Hence, switching the order may correlate with a discourse or other expressive function.

The order of elements in the possessive construction does not vary. The possessor always precedes the possessed.

17. 'Cutting finger when cleaning salmon'
čʰuṭa ṭeyta yekʰutni čʰiselimtu, ˀumul yekʰutaˀče,
čʰu-ṭa ***ṭe-yta*** *y-ekʰut-ni* *čʰiseli-mtu* *ˀumul* *y-ekʰut-aˀče*
POSS-hand ?-POSS 1SG.A-cut-ASP knife-INST salmon 1SG.A-cut-ASP
'I cut my thumb with a knife, when I was cleaning a salmon'

18. Grekoff 020.006
Ladd ˀuwelayta qʰoqʰu
Ladd ***ˀuwela-yta*** *qʰoqʰu*
son-POSS two
'Ladd's two sons'

In 17 *čʰuṭa* 'my hand' is the possessor, and in 18 *Ladd* is the possessor. In the available data, except for the possessive, the noun most often precedes any accompanying elements in the noun phrase. However, occasionally the reverse order occurs.

9.2 Argument structure

Chimariko argument structure is based on agents and patients, as well as on a person hierarchy. Argument structure alternations are expressed entirely within the verb. They shape clause structure semantically rather than syntactically, and they serve lexical, semantic, and discourse purposes.

9.2.1 Agents, patients, and person hierarchy

In Chimariko core arguments are obligatorily marked on the predicate as pronominal affixes, whether coreferential nominals are also present in the clause or not.

19. 'Fugitives at Burnt Ranch'
č'imar xotai heṭaheskut uwatkut, heṭaheskut č'utamdače
[č'imar xotai   h-eṭahe-sku-t]   [uwa-tku-t]   [h-eṭahe-sku-t   č'utamdače]
man   three   3-run.away-DIR-ASP   go-DIR-ASP   run.away-DIR-ASP   Burnt Ranch
'Three men came as fugitives, they ran away to Burnt Ranch'

In example 19 there is a coreferential nominal *č'imar xotai* 'three men' in the first clause, while in the second and third clause there is no coreferential nominal. The phonetically weak third person pronoun *h-* has been dropped in the second clause, *uwatkut* 'they came'.

Argument marking shows an agent-patient distinction, but this occurs only for first persons in all instances (see also 8.1.1). In general, second and third persons do not show such a distinction except for second person plural forms in transitive clauses with third person actors (see example 22).

20. 'Woman wanders'
noˀot čušehemdeˀw k'oṭihut, ˀawa   hida imamda
*noˀot   **č**-ušehe-m-deˀw   k'oṭi-hu-t   ˀawa   hida   **i**-mam-da*
1SG   1SG.P-take.along-DIR-DER   run.away-CONT-ASP   house   lots   1SG.A-see-ASP
'They took me off, I fled, I saw lots of houses'

21. 'Fugitives at Burnt Ranch'
makʰotaxantinda, k'otnihu
***m**-akʰo-ta-xan-tinda   k'otnihu*
2SG-kill-DER-FUT-PROG   run.away
'He is going to kill you, run away'

ˀirˀir musunda mamot, k'otnihu
*ˀirˀir   **m**-usu-nda   mamot   k'ot-ni-hu*
stranger   2SG-be-ASP   2SG   run.away-IMP.SG-CONT
'You are a stranger, run away'

In example 20 the first person agent and patient prefixes, *č^h-* and *i-* respectively, differ, while in 21 the second person does not distinguish agent and patient forms. In both instances the pronominal prefix is *m-*. Second person plural affixes, however, show a distinction between agent and patient forms, *q^{h}o-/q^h-* and *q^{h}a-* respectively, as in 22.

22a. Harrington 020-1133
mamq^{h}edot nač^{h}idot q^{h}owanut
*mamq^{h}edot nač^{h}idot **q^{h}o**-wa-nu-t*
2PL 1PL 2PL-COLL-growl.at-ASP
'You (plural) growled at us'

22b. Harrington 020-1134
mamq^{h}edot q^{h}anudeˀw
*mamq^{h}edot **q^{h}a**-nu-deˀw*
2PL 2PL.P-growl.at-DER
'Did he growl at you (plural)?'

22c. Harrington 020-1126
q^{h}uk'oˀnan
***q^h**-uk'o-ˀna-n*
2PL-talk-APPL-ASP
'You talked to him'

22d. Harrington 020-1126
q^{h}ak'oˀnan
***q^{h}a**-k'o-ˀna-n*
2PL.P-talk-APPL-ASP
'He talked to you (plural)'

While a system where second person plural but not second person singular affixes show a distinction between agent and patient forms appears irregular and confusing, second person plural forms are also special in other Northern California languages, such as Karuk, and are used to show respect to elders (Mithun 2008). Due to the nature of the data, it remains unclear whether these are respect forms resulting from language contact or whether they stem from an elicitation process with no specific context.

The agent-patient distinction for first persons occurs with ditransitive, transitive, and intransitive clauses (see also 9.3, 9.4, and 9.5). It is reflected only in the pronominal affixes. Free pronouns show no distinction between agents and patients.

23a. Harrington 020-1118
noˀot ˀik'onip
noˀot ˀ-ik'o-nip
1SG 1SG.A-talk-PST
'I was talking'

23b. Harrington 020-1113
noˀot ṭewčʰuxanat
noˀot *ṭew-***čʰu***-xana-t*
1SG big-1SG.P-FUT-ASP
'I am going to be big'

23c. 'Woman wanders'
ˀiwo hita č'awund amew,
ˀ-iwo *hita* **čʰ***-awu-nd* *amew*
1SG-A-stay lots 1SG.P-give-PROG food
'I'll stay here, they gave me lots of food'

The agent-patient distinction seen in the pronominal affixes does not affect the clause syntactically, only semantically. In general, only one core argument is marked on the predicate following a hierarchy whereby speech act participants, i.e. first and second persons, are favored over third persons (see also 8.1.1). In clauses where only speech act participants occur both participants are marked (see example 28).

24. Harrington 020-1099
mokoxanaˀ
m*-oko-xana-ˀ*
2SG-tattoo-FUT-Q
'Are you going to tattoo her?

2>3 => 2

25. Harrington 020-1125
qʰak'oˀnaˀ
qʰa*-k'o-ˀna-ˀ*
2PL-talk-APPL-Q
'Was he talking to you?'

3>2 => 2

26. 'Fugitives at Burnt Ranch'
pʰaˀasitaˀče yekʰotinda, čʰaxaduˀxakon, wisseeda čʰumčaxa
pʰaˀasitaˀče **y***-ekʰo-tinda* **čʰa***-xaduˀx-akon* *wisseeda* *čʰu-m-čaxa*
that.why 1SG.A-kill-PROG 1PL.P-?-FUT downstream IMP.PL-DIR-COMP
'That's why I killed him, they will kill us, you all move down to B. Noble's place.'

1>3 => 1 3>1 => 1

27. 'Crawfish'
pʰiˀa yehatat, hiničxeˀkut, ˀičiˀta, puqʰela ˀitxaˀmat
pʰiˀa **y***-ehata-t* **h***-iničxeˀku-t* *ˀ-ičiˀta* *puqʰela* *ˀ-itxaˀma-t*
grease 1SG.A-have-ASP 3-smell-ASP 1SG.A-catch basket 1SG.A-put-ASP

'I had grease, they smelled it, I caught them, I put them in a basket'

1 => 1 3>3 => 3 1>3 => 1 1>3 => 1

The person hierarchy is summarized below:

1 > 3	=> 1 agent marked
2 > 3	=> 2 marked
3 > 1	=> 1 patient marked
3 > 2SG	=> 2 marked
3> 2PL	=> 2PL patient marked
1 > 2	=> 1 agent marked
2 > 1	=> 2 marked + 1 patient marked[1]
3 > 3	=> 3 marked

[1] The shapes of the first person patient markers here are different from the regular first person patient forms.

Generally only one argument is overtly marked on the verb. However, in clauses where only speech act participants occur, i.e first and second persons, a first person patient marker may occur in addition to the second person agent affix. Hence, first persons are always marked on the verb.

28. 2>1 2>3

28a. Harrington 020-1126
mamqʰedot qʰok'oˀnakunaxanaˀ
mamqʰedot ***qʰ-o-****k'o-ˀna-kuna-xana-ˀ*
2PL 2PL-1P-talk-APPL-NEG-FUT-Q
'Are you not going to talk to me?'

28b. Harrington 020-1126
mamqʰedot quk'oˀnaxanaˀ
mamqʰedot ***qʰ-u****k'o-ˀna-xana-ˀ*
2PL 2PL-talk-APPL-FUT-Q
'Are you going to talk to him?'

28c. Harrington 020-1128
mekʰoxanaˀ
m-e*-kʰo-xana-ˀ*
2SG-1P-kill-FUT-Q
'Are you going to kill me?'

28d. Harrington 020-1128
makʰoxanaˀ
m-a*kʰo-xana-ˀ*
2SG-kill-FUT-Q
'Are you going to kill him?'

28e. Harrington 020-1126
mek'oˀnaˀ
m-e*-k'o-ˀna-ˀ*
2SG-1P-talk-APPL-Q
'Are you talking to me?'

28f. Harrington 020-1125
pačʰi mik'oˀnaˀtitaˀ
pačʰi ***m-i****k'o-ˀna-titaˀ*
who 2SG-talk-APPL-Q
'Who were you talking to?'

Similarly, in imperative constructions a first person patient affix occurs in addition to the imperative affix. There are two sets of imperative affixes: *n-*, *ne-* for commands given to a single person and *čʰ-*, *čʰa-* for commands given to more than one person. The vowels, *e* and *a* respectively, indicate a first person patient, i.e. the fact that the undergoer of the action of the command is a first person.

29. 2SG>1 2SG>3

29a. Harrington 020-1125
nek'o^{ʔ}na
***n-e**-k'o-^{ʔ}na*
IMP.SG-1SG.P-talk-APPL
'Talk to me!'

29b. Harrington 020-1125
nik'o^{ʔ}na
n-ik'o-^{ʔ}na
IMP.SG-talk-APPL
'Talk to them!'

30. 2PL>1 2PL>3

30a. Harrington 020-1126
č^{h}ak'o^{ʔ}na
***č^h-a**-k'o-^{ʔ}na*
IMP.PL-1PL.P-talk-APPL
'Talk to us!'

30b. Harrington 020-1126
č^{h}uk'o^{ʔ}na
č^h-uk'o-^{ʔ}na
IMP.PL-talk-APPL
'Talk to him!'

The only patients marked in addition to an agent are first persons. The difference between the stem-initial vowel /i/ in 29b and /u/ in 30b is due to a morphophonemic process (see chapter 3). First persons are always marked on the verb, either as pronominal affixes following the person hierarchy, or as an additional affix in relationships involving speech act participants only.

9.2.2 Transitivity

Transitivity is marked minimally in Chimariko. Most often, only one participant is marked on the predicate, following the person hierarchy (see 9.2.1) and regardless of the transitivity of the clause. If that participant is a third person, its semantic role remains unclear, given that there is neither a formal distinction for semantic role nor for number in third person pronominal affixes. As a result, when a third person acts on another third person the relationship is not expressed. Overall, third person markers are phonologically least prominent and sometimes cluster with other morphemes.

31. 'Woman wanders'
hišehekte^{ʔ}w, hexačide^{ʔ}w, hišehet
h-išehek-te^{ʔ}w *h-exači-de^{ʔ}w* *h-išehe-t*
3-take.along-DER **3**-steal-DER **3**-take.along-ASP
'They took the woman along, they stole her, they took her along'
. .
xukeenan himelušušun, xukeenan,
Ø-x-ukee-na-n *Ø-hime-lušušu-n* *Ø-x-ukee-na-n*
3-NEG-know-NEG-ASP **3**-head-shake-ASP **3**-NEG-know-NEG-ASP
'She did not know, she shook her head, she did not know'

In example 31, the first three verbs have a third person prefix *h-*. However, it is unclear whether this affix refers to the actor 'they' or to the undergoer 'the woman'. In the last three verbs in example 31 the third person affix has been dropped.

Transitivity is marked morphosyntactically on the verb only in situations where a second person acts on a first person. In these situations, two participants are marked on the verb: the second person actor and the first person patient.

32. 2>1 2>3

32a. Harrington 020-1133
mamot mewanut
mamot ***m-e****-wa-nu-t*
2SG 2SG-1PL.P-COLL-growl.at-ASP
'You growled at us'

32b. Harrington 020-1133
mamot xačile monut
mamot xačile ***m****-onu-t*
2SG children 2SG-gowl.at-ASP
'You growled at the kids'

33. 2>1 2>2

33a. Harrington 020-1128
nexok^{h}ona
n-e*-x-ok^{h}o-na*
IMP.SG-1SG.P-NEG-kill-NEG
'Don't you kill us!'

33b. Harrington 020-1128
naxak^{h}o^{ʔ}yewna
na-x-ak^{h}o-^{ʔ}yew-na
IMP.SG-NEG-kill-REFL-NEG
'Don't kill yourself!'

Two participants are marked on the verb in examples 32a and 33a, where a second person acts on a first. The first person patient is marked as the vowel *-e-*. This patient marker is different from the agent-patient distinction in the pronominal affixes that occurs with first persons. The latter is not affected by the transitivity of the predicate. Patient marking in pronominal affixes occurs in both transitives and intransitives, and it does not presuppose the presence of two participants: an actor and an undergoer.

34a. Harrington 020-1118
no^{ʔ}ot ^{ʔ}ik'onip
no^{ʔ}ot ^{ʔ}-ik'o-nip
1SG 1SG.A-talk-PST
'I am talking'

34b. Harrington 020-1132
no^{ʔ}ot ^{ʔ}imičitxanan
no^{ʔ}ot ^{ʔ}-imičit-xana-n
1SG 1SG.A-kick-FUT-ASP
'I am going to kick you'

35a. Harrington 020-1113
no^{ʔ}ot ṭewč^{h}uxanat
*no^{ʔ}ot ṭew-****č^{h}u****-xana-t*
1SG big-1SG.P-FUT-ASP
'I am going to be big'

35b. 'Woman wanders'
no^{ʔ}ot č^{h}ušehemde^{ʔ}w
no^{ʔ}ot ***č^{h}****-ušehe-m-de^{ʔ}w*
1SG 1SG.P-take.along-DIR-DER
'They took me off (my folks)'

In example 34a the first person agent prefix ^{ʔ}- occurs in an intransitive clause 'I am talking' and in 34b. in a transitive clause 'I am going to kick you'. In 35a and 35b the first person patient affix occurs in an intransitive clause 'I am going to be big' and in a transitive clause 'They took me off'. The patient marking in intransitive clauses depends on the verb stem. Due to lexicalisation and semantic change, a clear patient category involving affectedness, involuntary actions or the lack of control is no longer observable for the verbs with patient markers, although many describe actions or states where the participant has no or limited control and is affected (see Mithun 1991). Predicates with patient markers include actions, such as *give a warcry, cry out, growl, yell (animal), blink, lose a child, choke, grow up, give out, hiccough, fall, and sneeze* and states, such as *be called, be mad, be old, be pregnant, have rheumatic pain, be rotting, be stiff, be exhausted, be angry, be soft, be decayed, be black, be red, be white, be stout, be robust, be big, have a rash, be afraid, and be hurt.* A number of verb stems can take either agent or patient affixes. These include actions, such as *shout, lie, heed, wardance, (woman) to ge married,* and states, such as *be alive, be hungry, be thirsty, be tired, be cold, be strong, be sick, be swift, grow, die, and sleep.* As can be seen, no clear semantic pattern can be determined. Both agents and patients can occur with inherent and uncontrolled states, as well as with controlled and uncontrolled actions. Nevertheless, with many of the verbs that take patient marking there is a lack of control and/or an impact on the patient (see 9.3.1).

To conclude, it seems that in Chimariko the hierarchical structure makes up for markers related to transitivity in other languages, such as having both core arguments being marked on the predicate. Nevertheless, if there is a first person, it always surfaces on the predicate as (1) a pronominal agent or patient affix or (2) as a patient marker in addition to the second person pronominal affix or the imperative affix. The formal agent-patient system is only residual and restricted to bound pronominal marking for first persons and second person plural forms. Similar systems are found in other Californian languages, such as Yana, Yurok, and Karuk.

Transitivity often involves the grammatical distinction between core and oblique arguments. However, only the first may influence the transitivity of a clause. Core arguments form a clear category. In general, they are marked on the predicate as pronominal affixes. Oblique arguments are marked with instrumental or comitative case suffixes or with locative suffixes. Not all obliques show case marking. Chimariko uses different strategies to describe the concepts found in some oblique arguments in other languages. These strategies often involve verbal affixes and may affect the pronominal core argument marking and the transitivity of the clause (see 9.2.3, 9.2.4).

9.2.3 Core versus oblique

In Chimariko, core arguments are a clear category since they are obligatorily marked on the predicate as pronominal affixes. The pronominal affixes occur regardless of whether referential nominals are present or not in the clause. Nominals that function as core arguments are unmarked for case.

Participants marked as obliques in other languages, such as beneficiaries, goals, locations, and instruments, among others, are expressed either within the verb as core arguments, by means of noun incorporation, applicatives, instrumental or directional affixes, and/or as independent nominals with or without case marking. Case marking occurs only with instruments and companions.

36. Beneficiary as core argument (Harrington 020-1124)

xačile kumičin noˀot čʰawut
xačile *kumičin* ***noˀot*** ***čʰ****-awu-t*
children all **1SG** **1SG.P**-give-ASP
'All the children gave it to me'

37. Directional affixes with and without accompanying nominal

37a. Without nominal (from 'Mrs Bussell)
kimass uwatkun, huwomni welmu
*kimass uwa-**tku**-n* *h-uwo-**m**-ni* *welmu*
today go-**DIR**-ASP 3-go-**DIR**-ASP quickly
'Today she came over here, she went back home at once'

37b. With nominal (from 'Dailey chased by the bull')
mušmuš čʰuwetni, yečučutapmun, hiṭiyteˀw yutc̓uˀtamun
mušmuš čʰ-uwet-ni *y-ečuču-tapmun* ***hiṭiyteˀw*** *y-uc̓uˀ-**tamun***
bull 1SG.P-hook-ASP 1SG.A-dodge-DIR fence 1SG.A-jump-**DIR**
'The bull hooked me, I dodged, I jumped over the fence'

haˀačʰamta, hipikmut Dailey, hixomet, hiṭiyteˀw hiwetta
haˀa-čʰa-m-ta *h-ipik-mu-t* *Dailey* *h-ixome-t* ***hiṭiyteˀw*** *h-iwet-ta*
come-1SG.P-DIR-ASP 3-?-DIR-ASP Dailey 3-miss-ASP fence 3-hook-ASP
'He took after me, he took after Dailey, he missed, he hooked the fence'

38. Direction cast as core of motion verb with applicative (Harrington 020-1096)

38.a *hakimni*
h-aki-m-ni
3-wash.away-DIR-ASP
'She washed away'

38b. *waida hakiˀnamda*
waida *h-aki-**ˀna**-m-da*
east 3-wash.away-APPL-DIR-ASP
'She washed east' (Lit. 'toward the east')

Examples 36-38 show how participants grammatically defined as obliques in some languages are expressed as a core arguments in 36 and 38, or as a directional affix with and without an independent nominal in 37. The independent nominal *hiṭiyteˀw* 'fence' in 37b shows no formal marking.

While most independent nominals are unmarked for a syntactic relationship, instruments and companions have case marking. In addition, some locations show a special marking.

39. Location without marking (from 'Crawfish')
pʰiˀa yehatat, hiničxeˀkut, ˀičiˀta, puqʰela ˀitxaˀmat
pʰiˀa *y-ehata-t* *h-iničxeˀku-t* *ˀ-ičiˀ-ta* ***puqʰela*** *ˀ-itxaˀ-ma-t*
grease 1SG.A-have-ASP 3-smell-ASP 1SG.A-catch-ASP basket 1SG.A-put-?-ASP
'I had grease, they smelled it, I caught them, I put them in a basket'

40. Instrument with case marking (from 'Cutting finger when cleaning salmon')
čʰuṭa ṭeyta yekʰutni čʰiselimtu, ˀumul yekʰutaˀče,
čʰu-ṭa ṭe-yta y-ekʰut-ni ***čʰiseli-mtu*** *ˀumul y-ekʰut-aˀče*
POSS-hand ?-POSS 1SG.A-cut-ASP knife-INST salmon 1SG.A-cut-ASP
'I cut my thumb with a knife, when I was cleaning a salmon'

41. Location with marking (from 'Woman Wanders')
naˀahunmu ˀawakunoi, pʰuncar isik ˀimatni
*na-ˀahun-**mu** **ˀawa-kunoi** pʰuncar isik ˀ-imat-ni*
IMP-take-DIR house-inside woman pretty 1SG.A-find-ASP
'Take her in the house, I found a pretty woman'

The independent nominal *puqʰela* 'basket' in 39 is unmarked, while the instrument in 40 occurs with an instrumental case suffix *-mtu/-mdu*, and the location in 41 occurs with a locative suffix *-kunoi*. In the available data, locative suffixes occur only with *ˀawa* 'house' and lexicalized in certain placenames. The instrumental case suffix *-mtu/-mdu* occurs with all instruments, as in 42a and 42b.

42. Instrumental case suffix *-mtu/-mdu*

42a. Harrington 020-0439
nakʰum hiˀaṭ'apṭ'apakučʰamdu
n-akʰu-m ***hiˀaṭ'apṭ'apakučʰa-mdu***
IMP.SG-cut-ASP scissors-INST
'Cut it with the scissors'

42b. Harrington 020-0401
hopew hopit hiṭamdu
hopew h-opi-t ***h-iṭa-mdu***
acorn 3-work-ASP POSS-hand-INST
'He eats acorn mush with fingers' (lit. 'he eats acorn with his hand')

The case suffix *-owa* marks accompaniment.

43a. Harrington 020-0532
pʰunsalyowa
*pʰunsal-y-**owa***
woman-POSS-ACOMP
'With his wife'

43b. Harrington 021-019
ˀuwelaˀowa
*ˀuwela-ˀ-**owa***
boy-POSS-ACOMP
'Together with my boy'

9.2.4 Argument structure alternations and voice

Alternations in argument structure are expressed entirely within the verb. They are achieved through verbal derivational affixes. Applicatives add a participant to the set of core arguments. This participant can occur pronominally if it is higher ranked on the hierarchy than other participants in the clause, as in example 44. Causatives add an agent to the set of core arguments, as in example 45.

44. Applicative *-ˀna: iko* 'to talk' => *ikoˀna* 'to talk to' (from 'Woman wanders')

č'imar heyˀewinta kumičin čʰuk'oˀnan
č'imar heyˀew-inta kumičin *čʰ-**uk'o**-**ˀna**-n*
person good-PROG all 1SG.P-talk-APPL-ASP
'The people are good,they all talk to me good'

. .
č'imariko ˀik'otinda
*č'imariko ˀ-**ik'o**-tinda*
Chimariko 1SG.A-talk-PROG
'I talk Chimariko'

45. Causative-benefactive *-miy* (Grekoff 012.027)

ama 'to eat'	=>	*amamiy* 'to feed, to give to eat'
luˀ 'to drink'	=>	*luˀ...miy* 'to water, to give to drink'
oši 'suck (milk)'	=>	*ošimiy* 'to give to suckle'

While applicatives and causatives are the only transitivizing mechanisms in Chimariko, there are several detransitivizing mechanisms: two passive-like constructions, reciprocals, and reflexives. All are expressed within the verb.

Two derivational suffixes, *-tta* and *-teˀw*, create passive-like constructions in their semantic function. *-teˀw* signals that the actor is an indefinite third person plural and therefore backgrounds the agent of an action. *-tta* signals that an action is carried out on a patient and foregrounds the patient. Examples 46-48 illustrate the use of *-teˀw.*

46. 'Woman Wanders'
hišehekteˀw, hexačideˀw, hišehet, k'oṭihut,
*h-išehek-**teˀw*** *h-exači-**deˀw*** *h-išehe-t* *k'oṭi-hu-t*
3-take.along-DER 3-steal-DER 3-take.along-ASP run.away-CONT-ASP
'(Bad Indians) took **her** along, they stole **her**, they took her along, she ran away'

. .
noˀot čušehemdeˀw k'oṭihut, ˀawa ħida imamda
*noˀot čʰ-ušehe-m-**deˀw*** *k'oṭi-hu-t* *ˀawa hida i-mam-da*
1SG 1SG.P-take.along-DIR-DER run.away-CONT-ASP house lots 1SG.A-see- ASP
'They took **me** off, I fled, I saw lots of houses'

47. 'Crawfish'
hopuṭeˀw ˀama, txol makumčaxat q'ehčaxat
*h-opu-**teˀw*** *ˀama txol* *makum-čaxa-t* *q'e-h-čaxa-t*
3-mine-DER land crawfish perish-COMP-ASP die-3-COMP-ASP
'They mined **the land**, all crawfish perished, they died all'

48. ‘Hollering at New River’

ˀapu xošektanat, himisamdudaˀn sideˀw

ˀapu	*xo-šekta-na-t*	*himisamdu-daˀn*	*si-**deˀw***
fire	NEG-make-NEG-ASP	devil-INF	say-DER

‘He made no fire, it must have been the devil, they said’

pačʰigut ˀapu, himisamdudaˀn sideˀw

pačʰigut	*ˀapu*	*himisamdu-daˀn*	*si-**deˀw***
no.more	fire	devil-INF	say-DER

‘There was no fire, it must have been the devil they said’

In example 46, the main character of the narrative is the woman. Hence the focus lies on the patient of the three verbs with the derivational suffix *-teˀw* which signals that the agent is indefinite and unimportant to the narrative. Similarly, in example 47, the actor of the mining is not important, but the fact that the land was mined and that as a result all crawfish perished. The main characters of this narrative are the crawfish. Hence, ‘they’, the agent of the mining, is backgrounded. In example 48, the derivational suffix *-teˀw* has created what seems to be a fixed expression indicating that something was said. In this example the verb *si* ‘to say’ occurs only with the suffix *-teˀw* lacking any pronominal or tense-aspect marking. The expression *sideˀw* ‘they said’ occurs twice clause-finally and could be interpreted as a lexicalized epistemic marker.

Examples 49-51 illustrate the use of *-tta*.

49. ‘Crawfish’

memat txolop ˀiwinqʰutta

memat	*txol-op*	*ˀ-iwin-qʰu-**tta***
alive	crawfish-DEF	1SG.A-dump-into.water-DER

‘I made the water hot, I dumped **them** alive, the crawfish, immersingly’

50. ‘Fugitives at Burnt Ranch’

hek’omatta, hakʰodeˀ, č’imarop, xawiyop hakʰodeˀn

*h-ek’o-ma-**tta***	*h-akʰo-deˀ*	*č’imar-op*	*xawiy-op*	*h-akʰo-deˀ-n*
3-say-?-DER	3-kill-DER	person-DEF	Redwood.Indian-DEF	3-kill-DER-ASP

‘The boy told (it), they killed the boy, the people, the Indians killed him’

51. ‘Dailey Chased by the Bull’

xowetnat, hek’omatta, pʰaˀyit čʰuwetni sit

x-owet-na-t	*h-ek’o-ma-**tta***	*pʰaˀyit*	*čʰ-uwet-ni*	*si-t*
NEG-hook-NEG-ASP	3-say-?-DER	thus.say	1SG.P-hook-ASP	say-ASP

‘But he did not hook him, he told (it), thus he said, he hooked me he said’

In example 49, the crawfish are again central to the narrative. Although the first person is marked on *ˀiwinqʰutta* ‘I dumped them’, given the person hierarchy, the crawfish, the patients of the action, are foregrounded by the *-tta* suffix in the verb. In examples 50 and 51 *hek’omatta* ‘he said it’ seems to be a lexicalized expression. In both cases it is unimportant who said it; the focus lies on what was said.

-tta and *-teˀw* occur only with dynamic events and do not affect argument marking, since their presence does not alter the person hierarchy. They function much like passives semantically in that they either background the agent or foreground the patient. They differ from passives in that there is no syntactic impact. Syntactically, the argument structure, as well as the argument marking, remains the same.

Reflexives and reciprocals also affect argument structure by detransitivizing, given that a single participant functions as semantic agent and patient. Like the two passive-like constructions, they do not alter argument marking.

52a. Harrington 020-1128
noˀot pʰaˀmot č'imarot yekʰoxanat
noˀot pʰaˀmot č'imar-ot y-ekʰo-xana-t
1SG DET person-DEF 1SG.A-kill-FUT-ASP
'I am going to kill him'

52b. Harrington 020-1128
pʰaˀmot noˀot čʰakʰoxanan
pʰaˀmot noˀot čʰ-akʰo-xana-n
3 1SG 1SG.P-kill-FUT-ASP
'He is going to kill me'

52c. Harrington 020-1128
yekʰoyeˀwxanat noˀot
*y-ekʰo-**yeˀw**-xana-t noˀot*
1SG.A-kill-REFL-FUT-ASP 1SG
'I am going to kill myself'

In the presence of a reflexive suffix, the agent marker *y-* occurs on the verb, as in 52c. The reflexive *-yeˀw* can co-occur with applicatives, as in 53, or with the passive-like construction, as in 54.

53. Harrington 020-1125
noˀot ˀik'oˀnayeˀwdinda
*noˀot ˀ-ik'o-**ˀna-yeˀw**-dinda*
1SG 1SG.A-talk-APPL-REFL-PROG
'I was talking to myself'

54. Harrington 020-1107
kumičin hakʰoyeˀwdeˀw
*kumičin h-akʰo-**yeˀw-deˀw***
all 3-kill-REFL-DER
'All killed themselves'

As with the reflexive, the first person agent marker occurs with reciprocals. This is shown in 55.

55. Harrington 020-1134
načʰidot yanunwaxanat
načʰidot ya-nu-nwa-xana-t
1PL 1PL.A-growl-RECP-FUT-ASP
'We are going to growl at each other'

No evidence for a category of middles has been identified in the data. Overall, argument structure alternations and alternations in voice are encoded entirely within the verb through derivational affixes. Such alternations are only semantic in nature and have no syntactic impact. They seem to serve semantic, lexical, and discourse functions rather than syntactic purposes.

9.3 Intransitive sentences

Intransitive sentences show no formal distinction from transitive or ditransitive clauses. As with the latter two, in most occasions only one participant is marked on the verb, and first persons show an agent-patient distinction. Sentences with predicate adjectives or predicate nominals are intransitive.

9.3.1 Agents and patients

First person patient markers can occur in transitive and intransitive clauses. In intransitives the patient marking depends on the verb stem. As a result of lexicalisation and semantic change, a clear patient category involving affectedness, involuntary actions, or the lack of control (see Mithun 1991) is no longer observable for the verbs with patient markers. However, many verb stems that take the patient affixes describe actions or states in which the participant has no or limited control and in which the patient is affected. Table 1 contains a list of verb stems that take only patient markers, and Table 2 summarizes the verb stems that can take both agent and patient affixes.

Table 1: Verb stems with first person patient markers (Grekoff 003.005)

Actions		States	
ˀewˀew	'give a warcry'	*šeeda*	'be called'
lax..mu	'cry out'	*čʰewu*	'have rheumatic pain'
qʰolqʰol	'growl (animal)'	*qʰayqʰay*	'be rotting'
laxlax	'yell'	*šičiˀ*	'be wet'
q'eˀ	'choke'	*turuˀ*	'be exhausted'
law..puk	'give out'	*ṭuk*	'be angry'
leči	'hiccough'	*wiˀ..mu*	'be soft, mushy'
woˀ..puk	'bark'	*lot'..hu*	'be decayed'
		lot'oˀ	'be black'
		čʰeleˀ	'be red'
		wiliˀ	'be white'
		meneˀ	'be stout, robust'
		ṭewu	'be big'
		wi	'be afraid'

Table 2: Verb stems with first person agent OR patient markers (Grekoff 003.005)

Actions		States	
koko	'holler, shout'	*^{ʔ}amemtu*	'be hungry'
q^{h}ap^{h}ama	'lie'	*^{ʔ}ešomtu*	'be cold'
maṭ'i	'heed, give heed'	*ma . . imat*	'be alive'
šiši	'wardance'	*^{ʔ}akhemtu*	'be thirsty'
yap^{h}a	'(woman) to get married'	*la . . puk*	'be tired'
		ṭ^{h}upu	'be strong'
		hic'a^{ʔ}	'be sick'
		lu^{ʔ}re	'be swift'
		^{ʔ}iṭi	'to grow, be big'
		q'e	'to die'
		po . . mu	'to sleep'

As can be seen in Tables 1 and 2, with many of the verbs that take patient marking there is a lack of control and/or an impact on the patient. Nevertheless, verb stems with similar meanings also occur with agent markers: *flee, snore, tremble, bleed,* and *get burnt*, among many others. As a result, no clear semantic pattern can be determined. Both agents and patients can occur with inherent and uncontrolled states, as well as with controlled and uncontrolled actions.

9.3.2 Predicate adjectives

Predicate adjectives function much like verbs, except that they occur only in intransitive clauses. They differ from intransitive verbs in that the same forms can also be used attributively (see 4.4).

56. *xoli^{ʔ}* 'bad'/*(h)isi^{ʔ}* 'good' as predicate adjectives (from 'Fugitives at Burnt Ranch')

č^{h}axak^{h}ona, weč^{h}up č^{h}axak^{h}ona, ^{ʔ}ama xoli^{ʔ}yu
č^{h}a-x-ak^{h}o-na weč^{h}up č^{h}a-x-ak^{h}o-na ^{ʔ}ama ***xoli^{ʔ}-yu***
IMP.PL-NEG-kill-NEG some IMP.PL-NEG-kill-NEG country bad-ADM
'Don't kill them, some said don't kill them, lest it spoil the country'

. .
xoli^{ʔ}ta^{ʔ}n hak^{h}ot, xawiy asunda, xukeenat
xoli^{ʔ}-ta^{ʔ}n *h-ak^{h}o-t xawiy asu-nda x-ukee-na-t*
bad-INF 3-kill-ASP Redwood.Indian be-PROG NEG-understand-NEG-ASP
'It is not right to kill him, he was a Redwood Indian, he didn't understand'

. .
hisi^{ʔ}meda^{ʔ}, maik isi^{ʔ}meda^{ʔ}, ^{ʔ}ama xoli^{ʔ}xanan
hisi^{ʔ}-me-da^{ʔ} *maik* ***isi^{ʔ}-me-da^{ʔ}*** *^{ʔ}ama* ***xoli^{ʔ}-xana-n***
good-ASP-INF ? good-ASP-INF country bad-FUT-ASP
'Everything is all right there now, it will be all right, the country will be all bad'

57. *(h)isiˀ* 'good' as attributive adjective (from 'Woman wanders')

hiwanda, čitx isiˀ isiˀdaˀn, ˀičinšoll isiˀ yoxaˀidaˀn
h-iwa-nda ***čitx*** ***isiˀ*** *isiˀ-daˀn* ***ˀičinšoll*** ***isiˀ*** *y-oxaˀi-daˀn*
3-go-PROG blanket good good-INF dress good 1SG.A-make-INF
'She was coming, good blanket, it must have been good, I will make a good dress'

In example 56 *xoliˀ* 'bad' and *(h)isiˀ* 'good' occur with verbal morphology and function as predicates, while in 57 *(h)isiˀ* 'good' occurs without any affixes but with an accompanying noun and functions as an attributive adjective.

Depending on the aspectual marking, the same roots can be used for states and for events, as shown below.

58. Harrington 020-1113
noˀot ṭewut
noˀot ***ṭewu****-t*
1SG big-ASP
'I am big'

59a. Harrington 020-1113
ˀiṭilla ṭewunta
ˀiṭilla ***ṭewu****-nta*
boy big-PROG
'The boy is growing up'

59b. Harrington 020-1113
noˀot ṭewčut
noˀot ***ṭew****-ču-t*
1SG big-1SG.P-ASP
'I am growing up'

60. 'Dailey chased by the bull'
haˀačʰakinta mušmuš ṭewu
haˀa-čʰa-kinta mušmuš ***ṭewu***
?-1SG.P-PROG bull big
'The (big) bull was taking after me'

In example 58 *ṭewu* 'be big' refers to a state, while in 59 *ṭewu* 'growing up, getting big' refers to an ongoing action. The same root but lacking any verbal inflection functions as an attributive adjective in example 60.

9.3.3 Predicate nominals

There are two strategies for forming predicate nominal clauses in Chimariko: (1) using the copula *su* 'to be' or (2) by attaching verbal affixes to nominal stems.

61. Predicate nominal with copula (from 'Fugitives at Burnt Ranch')

kimot ˀuˀir asunda, čʰakʰo, heṭaheshutaˀa sunda
kimot ***ˀuˀir*** ***asu-nda*** *čʰ-akʰo* *h-eṭahe-shu-taˀa* *su-nda*
these stranger be-ASP IMP.PL-kill 3-run.away-DIR-? be-PROG
'These are strangers, kill them, they are running away'

62. Predicate nominal with verbal morphology (from 'Hollering at New River')

himisamduda'n side'w,
***himisamdu-da'n** si-de'w*
devil-INF say-DER
'It must have been the devil, they said'

In example 61 the predicate nominal clause 'these are strangers' is formed with the copula *su* 'to be'. In 62, the verbal suffix *-ta'n* with an inferential meaning is attached to a noun to form a predicate.

In general, equational clauses are formed with the copula *su* 'to be', while existentials, possessives, and clauses with predicate obliques are formed by attaching verbal morphology to nominal stems.

63a. Equational clause with *su* 'to be' (from 'Fugitives at Burnt Ranch')

'ir'ir musunda mamot
'ir'ir ***m-usu-nda*** *mamot*
stranger 2SG-be-PROG 2SG
'You are a stranger'

63b. Equational clause with *su* 'to be' (from 'Fugitives at Burnt Ranch')

xawiy asunda
xawiy ***asu-nda***
Redwood.Indian be-PROG
'He was a Redwood Indian'

63c. Equational clause with *su* 'to be' (Grekoff 013-018)

no'ot 'awu-'i sunta
no'ot 'awu-'i ***su-nta***
1SG mountain-POSS be-PROG
'That's my mountain'

63d. Equational clause with *su* 'to be' (Grekoff 013-018)

'umula sunta
'umula ***su-nta***
salmon be-PROG
'That's salmon'

While in 63a and 63c there are two nominal elements, in 63b and 63d there is only one nominal element, *xawiy* 'Redwood Indian' and *'umula* 'salmon' respectively. However, the second nominal element could also be a pronominal affix on the copula. In this case the phonetically weak pronominal prefix *h-* has been dropped in both examples, i.e. in

63b and 63d. In examples 63a-d the copula *su* 'to be' occurs each time with the progressive aspect suffix *-nta.*

Existentials (64a-64c) and possessives (65a, 65b) occur without a copula, but with verbal morphology attached to nominal elements.

64. Existential clauses

64a. Grekoff 012-001
č^hisamlan
č^hisamla-n
bear-ASP
'That's a bear' (There is a bear)

64b. Grekoff 012-001
č'imaranta
č'imara-nta
person-PROG
'It's a person' (There is a person)

64c. Harrington 020-0657
ˀanoˀak'unat
ˀanoˀa-k'una-t
pitchwood-NEG-ASP
'It wasn't pitchwood'

65. Possessive clauses

65a. Harrington 020-0377
huwešahta č'anapa
huweša-h-ta *č'anapa*
horn-POSS-ASP snail
'The snail had horns'

65b. Grekoff 008.012
xama-m-ta
xama-m-ta
gray.hair-POSS-ASP
'You have gray hair'

66. Privative clauses

66a. Grekoff 008.012
ˀiṭiˀiškut
ˀiṭi-ˀi-šku-t
man-POSS-PRIV-ASP
'I have no husband'

66b. Grekoff 008.012
husotaškut
h-usot-ašku-t
POSS-eye-PRIV-ASP
'It has no eyes'

Examples 64-66 illustrate the fact that existential, possessive, and privative clauses are formed in the same way by adding verbal morphology to the nominal predicate.

9.4 Transitive sentences

Argument structure in Chimariko is based on agents and patients, as well as on a person hierarchy. In general, only one core argument is marked on the predicate, following a hierarchy whereby first and second persons are favored over third persons. Most transitive sentences show little or no evidence for their transitivity, given the person hierarchy and the fact that having two nominals in the same clause is rare. There is only one instance where transitivity is formally marked on the predicate:

when a second person acts on a first person both are marked on the verb.

67. Transitive clauses with two participants overtly marked on the verb

67a. Harrington 020-1126
mek'oˀnaˀ
m-e-*k'o-ˀna-ˀ*
2SG-1P-talk-APPL-Q
'Are you talking to me?"

67b. Harrington 020-1128
mekʰoxanaˀ
m-e-*kʰo-xana-ˀ*
2SG-1SG.P-kill-FUT-Q
'Are you going to kill me?'

9.5 Ditransitive sentences

Ditransitive sentences are rare in the available data. Some examples are given below.

68. 'Woman wanders'
pʰuncar ˀimatni, hamew nawu
pʰuncar ˀ-imat-ni hamew n-awu
woman 1SG.A-find-ASP food IMP.SG-give
'I have found a woman, give her food'

69a. Harrington 020-0556
čʰatqawukni
čʰ-atqawuk-ni
1SG.P-take.away-ASP
'He grabbed it away from me'

69b. Harrington 020-0557
natqaywuk xalallot
n-atqaywuk xalall-ot
IMP.SG-take.away baby-DEF
'Take it away from the baby'

70. Harrington 020-0432
metqaytanta ˀahatew
m-e-tqayta-nta ˀahatew
2SG-1SG.P-take.away-PROG money
'You cheated me' (Literally: You took away the money from me)

71. Harrington 020-0441
čʰaxawunatinta ˀahadew
čʰ-a-xa-wu-na-tinta ˀahadew
IMP.PL-1P-NEG-give-NEG-ASP money
'Don't give me money'

In example 68, the imperative form *nawu* 'give!' and the additional independent nominal *hamew* 'food' indicate that the clause has three core arguments. However, only two arguments are expressed overtly: the imperative pronominal and the independent nominal. In example 69b there is formal evidence for one or two participants: the imperative form and the independent nominal *xalallop* 'the baby'; the other arguments are inferred from context. The clauses in examples 70 and 71 have three core arguments, all expressed overtly. In both examples there is an imperative prefix, a first person patient marker, and an independent nominal which is not coreferential with the other two arguments.

72. Harrington 020-0393
pač^hi mewuxanaʔ xopunewʔi noʔot
pač^hi *m-e-wu-xana-ʔ* *xopunew-ʔi* *noʔot*
what 2SG-1SG.P-give-FUT-Q gun-POSS 1SG
'What will you give me for my gun?'

The clause in example 72 has four arguments: an interrogative pronominal, a second person pronominal, a first person pronominal, and an independent nominal. However, not all four seem to be core arguments, since *wu* 'to give' can occur with three arguments (see example 68). Nevertheless, there is no formal marking identifying *xopunewʔi* 'for my gun' as oblique, and similar arguments are often cast as core.

In the available data most ditransitives occur with a small set of verbs: *wu* 'to give something to someone', *atqaywuk* 'to grab something away from someone', or *tey* 'to pay someone'.

9.6 Noun phrases

There is no formal evidence for a cohesive noun phrase in Chimariko. There is no concord marking, there are no observable co-occurrence restrictions, and the ordering of elements within the noun phrase is only rigid for possessives, where the possessor precedes the possessed, as in example 73.

73. Grekoff 020.006
Ladd ʔuwelayta q^hoq^hu
Ladd *ʔuwela-yta* *q^hoq^hu*
son-POSS two
'Ladd's two sons'

Noun phrases containing three elements are rare in the available data. They often involve a possessive construction as in examples 73, 74, and 75.

74. Harrington 020-0050
tiʔla himaʔ wiliʔi
tiʔla *h-imaʔ* *wiliʔi*
woodpecker POSS-head red
'Red woodpecker heads'

75. Harrington 020-0412
maṭupin hoxu hič^hu šičela
maṭupin *h-oxu* *hič^hu* *šičela*
nasty POSS-nose long dog
'A nasty long-nosed dog'

Some noun phrases with three elements include numerals, adjectives, and determiners, as in 76-79.

76. Grekoff 020.006
tiˀla p'un ṭewu
tiˀla p'un ṭewu
bird one large
'One large bird'

77. Harrington 020-0493
ˀawa hičʰekčʰa meneˀe
ˀawa hičʰekčʰa meneˀe
house paint white
'White house paint'

78. Grekoff 020.006
koˀot pʰunsal p'un
koˀot pʰunsal p'un
DET woman one
'This particular one woman'

79. Harrington 020-0070
pʰaˀmot Zach Bussell pʰunsalye
pʰaˀmot Zach Bussell pʰunsal-ye
DET woman-POSS
'That (there) wife of Zach Bussell'

Noun phrases cannot form clauses by themselves. Often, noun phrases that are core arguments are cross-referenced on the predicate as pronominal affixes, as in 80-81.

80. 'Fugitives at Burnt Ranch'
č'imar xotai heṭaheskut uwatkut
***č'imar xotai h**-eṭahe-sku-t uwa-tku-t*
man three 3-run.away-DIR-ASP go-DIR-ASP
'Three men came as fugitives, they ran away to Burnt Ranch'

81. 'Fugitives at Burnt Ranch'
hek'omatta, hakʰodeˀ, č'imarop, xawiyop hakʰodeˀn
*h-ek'o-ma-tta **h**-akʰo-deˀ **č'imar-op xawiy-op h**-akʰo-deˀ-n*
3-say-?-DER 3-kill-ASP person-DEF Redwood.Indian-DEF 3-kill-DER-ASP
'The boy told (it), they killed the boy, the people, the Indians killed him'

In some cases a noun forms a noun phrase by itself, with or without possessive, locative or other morphemes attached.

82a. Harrington 021-0197
ˀuwelaiowa
ˀuwela-i-owa
boy-POSS-NUM
'Together with my boy'

82b. Harrington 020-0532
pʰunsalyowa
pʰunsal-y-owa
woman-POSS-NUM
'With his wife'

83. Grekoff 020.006
č'imal huwatkun ˀawamiče
č'imal *h-uwa-tku-n* ***ˀawa-mi-če***
person 3-go-DIR-ASP house-POSS-LOC
'Someone has come to our house'

9.6.1 Definiteness

Definite and indefinite articles do not occur in Chimariko. However, Chimariko has a suffix *-ot/-ut/-op* that occurs with nouns, pronouns, and determiners and indicates definiteness. It occurs with animate and inanimate arguments. Most often, these arguments have been previously mentioned in the discourse, are identifiable, and are important to the narrative, as in the following examples.

84. 'Fugitives at Burnt Ranch'
hek'omatta, hakʰoteˀ č'imarop, xawiyop hakʰoteˀn
h-ek'o-ma-tta h-akʰo-teˀ ***č'imar-op*** ***xawiy-op*** *h-akʰo-teˀ-n*
3-say-?-DER 3-kill-DER person-DEF Indian-DEF 3-kill-DER-ASP
'He (the boy) told (it), they killed the boy, the people, the Indians killed him'.

85. 'Fugitives at Burnt Ranch'
memat txolop ˀiwinqʰutta
memat ***txol-op*** *ˀ-iwin-qʰut-ta*
alive crawfish-DEF 1SG.A-dump.liquid-DER
'I dumped them alive, the crawfish, immersingly'

86. 'Crawfish'
hiničxeˀkut, pʰiˀalop, hiničxeˀkut
h-iničxeˀku-t ***pʰiˀal-op*** *h-iničxeˀku-t*
3-smell-ASP bacon-DEF 3-smell-ASP
'They smelled it, that bacon, they smelled it'

The same suffix also indicates definiteness in elicited sentences without prior mention in discourse, as in 87-88.

87. Harrington 020-1093
šičelot čʰawin, čʰutpai, čʰawin
šičel-ot *čʰ-awi-n* *čʰ-utpa-i* *čʰ-awi-n*

dog-DEF 1SG.P-be.afraid-ASP 1SG.P-bite-MOD 1SG.P-be.afraid-ASP
'I am afraid of the dog, he might bite, I am afraid'.

88. Harrington 020-1120
ˀiṭinot hičiyat
ˀiṭin-ot *h-ičiya-t*
man-DEF 3-have.sores-ASP
'The man had sores on him'.

Indefinite arguments are unmarked as in the following example.

89. 'Woman wanders'
ˀuluidaˀe nahak ˀičinšolla, pʰuncar ˀimatni, hamew nawu
ˀuluida-ˀe *n-ahak* ***ˀičinšolla*** ***pʰuncar*** *ˀ-imat-ni* ***hamew*** *n-awu*
sister-POSS IMP.SG-bring dress woman 1SG.A-find-ASP food IMP.SG-give
'My sister, bring me a dress, I have found a woman, give her food'

9.7 Verb phrases

There is no evidence of a verb phrase constituent larger than the verb itself in Chimariko. There are no auxiliaries. Arguments are marked on each verb, and verbs can form sentences by themselves.

9.7.1 Co-occurrence of pronominal, aspectual, and modal marking

Each verb has a pronominal affix or an imperative marker. However, the third person pronominal affix is sometimes dropped, since it is phonetically weak. Except for verbs with imperative markers, most verbs are marked for aspect.

90. 'On grandmother getting the hiccups'
ˀaqʰa nawum, luˀni, ˀaqʰa luˀit haṭu
ˀaqʰa ***n-awum*** ***luˀ-ni*** *ˀaqʰa* ***luˀ-it*** *haṭu*
water IMP.SG-give drink-IMP.SG water drink-ASP then
'Give her water, drink, she drank then [water]'

91. 'Cutting navel'
hinoˀyta, hisuma nitix, xalallop, nakʰohoshu k'una
h-inoˀy-ta *hi-suma* ***n-itix*** *xalall-op* ***n-akʰohoshu*** *k'una*
3-bear-ASP POSS-face IMP.SG-wipe baby-DEF IMP.SG-cut NEG
'She bears it, wipe his face, (of) that baby, don't cut it'

In example 90 the two forms with the imperative marker, *n-* and *-ni* respectively, are unmarked for aspect, while the third verb has an aspect marker *-t*. Similarly, in example 91 the two forms with the imperative marker *n-* are unmarked for aspect, while the third verb, *hinoˀyta* 'she bears it', has an aspect marker *-ta*.

In general, verbs are marked either for mood or aspect (see chapter 8). However, some verbs occur with both modal and aspectual affixes.

92. 'Fugitives at Burnt Ranch'
čʰaxakʰona, wečʰup čʰaxakʰona, ˀama xoliˀyu

čʰa-xa-kʰo-na	*wečʰup*	*čʰa-xa-kʰo-na*	*ˀama*	***xoliˀ-yu***
IMP-NEG-kill-NEG	some	IMP-NEG-kill-NEG	country	bad-ADM

'Don't kill them, some said don't kill them, lest it spoil the country'

93. 'Dailey chased by the bull'
muwetteˀta makʰomet

m-uwet-teˀta	***m-akʰo-me-t***
2SG-hook-COND	2SG-kill-MOD-ASP

'If he had hooked you, he would have killed you right'

The last verb in 92 *xoliˀyu* 'lest it spoil it' occurs with a modal suffix, the same as the first verb in 93 *muwetteˀta* 'if he had hooked you', while the second verb in 93 *makʰomet* 'he would have killed you' has both a modal and an aspectual suffix. Imperative, admonitive, interrogative, conditional, evidential, speculative, and inferential affixes do not co-occur with aspectual affixes.

94. 'Fugitives at Burnt Ranch'
nuwawum kella, č'imar epatteˀw, qʰomal uwamaˀ č'imarop

n-uwa-wu-m	*kella*	*č'imar*	*epat-teˀw*	*qʰomal*	***uwa-m-aˀ***	*č'imar-op*
IMP.SG-go-RET-DIR	that.way	person	sit-DER	where	go-DIR-Q	person-DEF

'You go home that way (gesturing with lips), where did that man go to?'

95. 'Fugitives at Burnt Ranch'
načʰidot yakʰorot xukeenat, qʰakʰodaˀn xoliˀtaˀn

načʰidot	*y-akʰo-rot*	*x-ukee-na-t*	***qʰ-akʰo-daˀn***	***xoliˀ-taˀn***
1PL	1PL.A-kill-DEP	NEG-understand-NEG-ASP	2PL-kill-INF	bad-INF

'We killed him, he didn't understand, you killed him, it is not right'

The interrogative *-aˀ* in 94 does not co-occur with aspect marking. In example 95, the inferential *-taˀn* does not co-occur with aspect marking.

9.7.2 Dependency

In general, all verbs are independent and can form sentences by themselves. The only syntactically dependent clauses are relative clauses and some adverbial clauses. Verbs in relative clauses occur with a suffix *-lop/-rop* indicating dependency. Relative clauses cannot form sentences by themselves (see 12.3). In the following two examples the relative clauses are internally headed and in brackets (see 12.3). The heads of the relative clauses are boldfaced. In 97, the relative pronoun *map'un* is the head (see 12.3).

96. Harrington, 20-1103
[mo?a ***pʰuncar*** ***h****-uwa-tku-****rop****]* *pʰa?yi-nip*
yesterday woman 3-go-DIR-DEP say-PST
'That woman who came yesterday told me'

97. 'Hopping game'
hucume?kʰamta, himantamorop map'un, hi?amta
h-ucu-me?kʰam-ta *[****h****-iman-tamo-****rop*** ***map'un****]* ***h****-i?am-ta*
3-hop-?-ASP 3-fall-DIR-DEP that.one 3-?-DER
'He beats, those fellows that went down got beaten.

Adverbial clauses referring to a time are formed with a special verbal suffix *-lla* or *-ta?če*. They lack any tense, aspect, or modal marking, but occur with pronominal marking on the verb. It is unclear whether these adverbial clauses can occur by themselves, due to the limited amount of data.

98. Adverbial clause with *-lla* (Harrington 020-1106)

98a. *yemall uwatkun*
*[y-ema-****ll****]* *uwa-tku-n*
1SG.A-eat-DEP go-DIR-ASP
'He came, when I was eating.'

98b. *xemanalla uwatkun*
*[x-ema-na-****lla****]* *uwa-tku-n*
NEG-eat-NEG-DEP go-DIR-ASP
'He came, when I was not eating.'

9.8 Sentence structure in areal-typological perspective

Syntactic structures of simple sentences are similar in many Northern California languages. Word order with respect to the major clause constituents, i.e. arguments and predicates, is for the most part free and determined by pragmatics in Wintu, Shasta, Karuk, Yurok, Wiyot, and Maidu, as in Chimariko. However, certain preferences have been noted in several grammars indicating that SVO, SOV, and SV orders occur most often. The order of nominal elements within a noun phrase has rarely been described, possibly due to the limited occurrence of complex noun phrases with many elements in those languages. In Wintu modifiers precede the noun (Pitkin 1984:14), and in Shasta possessors precede the possessed (Silver 1966), as in Chimariko. In other languages of California, as in Wappo, the order of nominal elements is relatively fixed.

Transitivizing and detransitivizing mechanims, such as applicatives, causatives, reflexives, reciprocals, and passive-like constructions, are encoded through verbal derivational affixes in Wintu, Shasta, Hupa, and other languages of the area. Shasta has a passive construction similar to that of Chimariko. In Shasta there are prefixes on the verb indicating a third person indefinite actor (Silver 1966). Hupa also has a similar construction with an indefinite third person actor (Golla 1970).

In the languages of Northern California noun phrases generally do not occur with any linking morphology. A rigid order of the elements in a noun phrase has only been noted for Wintu where the modifier precedes the noun (Pitkin 1984). Verbs are generally independent and can form clauses by themselves. Overall, the syntactic structures and the syntactic behaviour are very similar in the languages of Northern California.

10. QUESTIONS

This chapter describes the strategies used to form yes/no and question-word questions, as well as the structure of answers to questions.

10.1 Yes/no questions

Yes/no questions are formed by adding an interrogative suffix predicate-finally. There are three different interrogative suffixes: *-(a)ˀ*, *-titaˀ/-itaˀ*, and *-pʰuˀ*. It is unclear how their meanings and functions differ from one another. All three also occur in question-word questions.

1. 'On grandmother getting the hiccups'
mamot maš mipuhunmat hita, mamuš hita mipuhunmuˀ
*mamot maš m-ipu-hunma-t hita mamuš hita m-ipu-hunmu-**ˀ***
2SG but 2SG-work-DIR-ASP lots but.you lots 2SG-work-DIR-Q
'But you took lots, but did you take lots'

2. Harrington 020-0470
mamot č'imartidaˀ
*mamot č'imar-**tidaˀ***
2SG perso-Q
'Are you a person?'

3. Grekoff 019-001
map'unamsudaˀ
*map'una-m-su-da-**ˀ***
that.one-2SG-be-ASP-Q
'Is that you?'

4. Harrington 020-1101
moxokonaˀ
*mo-x-oko-na-**ˀ***
2SG-NEG-tattoo-NEG-Q
'Did you not tattoo?'

5. Harrington 020-1103
mamot q'emkunatitaˀ
*mamot q'e-m-kuna-**titaˀ***
2SG die-2SG-NEG-Q
'Did you not die?'

6. Harrington 020-0468
mamatidaˀ
*m-ama-**tidaˀ***

2SG-eat-Q
'Are you eating?'

7. Harrington 020-1199
pʰaˀmot hamapʰuˀ
*pʰaˀmot h-ama-**pʰuˀ***
3 3-eat-Q
'Did that fellow eat?'

In the available data, *-(a)ˀ* occurs most frequently. *-(a)ˀ* and *-titaˀ/-itaˀ* occur in positive and negative clauses with verbal and with nominal predicates. *-pʰuˀ* occurs rarely in the examined data. All three interrogative suffixes have a glottal stop as final element.

In addition, Berman lists two other interrogative suffixes *-a* and *-ye*, based on examples with a final glottal stop which corresponds to an interrogative suffix. Hence, Berman's *-a* could correspond to *-(a)ˀ*, and *-ye* most likely has a different function.

8. Berman 2001b:1051
maweyaˀ
*m-awey-**aˀ***
2SG-angy-Q
'Are you angry?'

9. Berman 2001b:1051
makʰoyeˀ
*m-akʰo-**ye**-ˀ*
2SG-kill-?-Q
'Are you going to kill me?'

10.2 Question-word questions

Question-word questions are formed with an interrogative pronoun clause-initially, in addition to a predicate-final interrogative suffix (see 10.1). There are only minor similarities in the shapes of the different interrogative pronouns found in Harrington. The suffix *-lla* of unclear meaning occurs in *qʰomalla* 'where' and *ˀawilla* 'who'. Several interrogative pronouns have an initial back velar stop /q/ or /qʰ/. Dixon (1910:322) lists eight different interrogative pronouns. According to Dixon, they are all derived from a single stem *qo-* or *qa-*. Dixon's forms are very similar to the ones recorded by Harrington, as can be seen in Table 1.

Table 1: Interrogative pronouns (Dixon, 1910:322; Harrington)

Dixon	Harrington	Gloss
qomas or *awilla*	*ˀawilla*	who
qâtci or *pātci*	*pačʰaˀ, pačʰi*	what
qomalla	*qʰomal(la)*	where
qosidadji	*qʰositaˀče*	why
	pačʰaˀaqʰositaˀče	what for (what-why)
qâsuk	*qʰosuk*	when
qâtala		how many
qâtcu		how far
qâtramdu		how often

Some interrogative pronouns show similarities with other kinds of pronouns or words:

Interrogative pronoun		Other pronoun or word	
qosidadji	'why'	*pʰaˀasitaˀče*	'that's why'
pačʰaˀaqʰositaˀče	'what for'	*pʰaˀasitaˀče*	'that's why'
qʰomalla	'where'	*malla*	'there'

Examples with question-word questions are given below.

10. 'Woman wanders'
pačʰaˀa qʰuduqʰmuˀ
pačʰaˀa *qʰ-uduqʰmu-ˀ*
what 2PL-?-Q
'What have you been doing?'

11. 'On grandmother getting the hiccups'
pačʰaˀ qʰosumsiˀ, pačʰi misekmuˀ
pačʰaˀ *qʰ-osumsi-ˀ* ***pačʰi*** *m-isekmu-ˀ*
what 2PL-do-Q what 2SG-swallow-Q
'What did you all do, what did you swallow?'

12. Harrington 020-0656
pačʰi čʰak'oṭeteˀw načʰitot
pačʰi *čʰa-k'o-ṭe-teˀw* *načʰitot*
what 1PL.P-say-?-DER 1PL
'What are they saying about us?'

13. Harrington 020-1133
pačʰaˀaqʰositaˀče mamqʰedot qʰonutidaˀ
pačʰaˀaqʰositaˀče *mamqʰedot qʰ-onu-**tidaˀ***
what.for 2PL 2PL-growl.at-Q
'What did you growl at him for?'

14. 'Fugitives at Burnt Ranch'
qʰoqʰ uwadokta, č'imara, qʰomall akʰodeˀ
qʰoqʰ uwa-do-kta č'imar-a ***qʰomall*** *akʰo-de-ˀ*
two go-?-DIR man-? where kill-DER-Q
'Two got back here home, where did they kill him?'
. .
qʰomalla qʰuktaˀ
qʰomalla *qʰ-ukta-ˀ*
where 2PL-DIR-Q
'Where have you been?'

15. 'Fugitives at Burnt Ranch'
nuwawum kella, č'imar epatteˀw, qʰomal uwamaˀ

n-uwa-wu-m *kella* *č'imar* *epat-teˀw* ***qʰomal*** *uwa-m-**aˀ***
IMP.SG-go-RET-DIR that.way person sit-DER where go-DIR-Q
'You go home that way (gesturing with lips), where did that man go to?'

16a. Harrington 020-0467
ˀawilla musudaˀ
ˀawilla *m-usu-da-**ˀ***
who 2SG-be-ASP-Q
'Who are you?'

16b. Harrington 0202-0467
qʰomas musudaˀ
qʰomas *m-usu-da-**ˀ***
who 2SG-be-ASP-Q
'Who are you?'

17. Harrington 020-1124
ˀawilla hawuˀ
ˀawilla *h-awu-**ˀ***
who 3-give-Q
'To whom did he give it?

18. Grekoff 019.018
awilla mič'utaˀ
awilla *m-ič'u-ta-**ˀ***
who 2SG-hit-ASP-Q
'Who hit you?'

19. Harrington 020-0469
awillida muxattititaˀ
awill-ida *m-uxatti-**titaˀ***
who-? 2SG-shoot-Q
'Who shot you?'

Examples 10-19 illustrate the use of different question words in combination with the interrogative suffixes *-(a)ˀ* or *-titaˀ*. In example 12 the interrogative suffix is missing. It is unclear whether this is due to language attrition or data collection issues or to the potential omissability of the interrogative suffix. The derivational suffix *-teˀ(w)* does co-occur with interrogative suffixes, as in *hokoteˀpʰuˀ* 'is s/he tattooed?' (Harrington 020-1094).

10.3 Answers

Answers to question-word questions are entire clauses containing the requested information, as in the following two examples.

20. 'Fugitives at Burnt Ranch'
qʰomalla qʰuktaˀ, q'owan, ˀawaktahinta,
qʰomalla qʰu-kta-ˀ q'owan ˀ-awa-kta-hinta
where 2PL-DIR-Q ? 1SG.A-go-DIR-PROG
'Where have you been? (I was) just taking a walk'

21. Harrington 020-1124
ˀawilla hawuˀ. pʰaˀmot hawun
ˀawilla h-awu-ˀ pʰaˀmot h-awu-n
who 3-give-Q that 3-give-ASP
'To whom did he give it? He gave it to that fellow.'

Answers to yes/no questions are either positive or negative. Positive answers contain the positive particle *himow* 'yes', while negative answers contain a negative particle *paačikun/pačikut* 'no'. In general, the particles are followed by an entire clause. However, answers with just the particle *himow* 'yes' also occur.

22. Positive answers to yes/no questions

22a. 'On grandmother getting the hiccups'
mamuš hita mipuhunmuˀ, himow, hita ˀipuhunmut.
mamuš hita m-ipu-hunmu-ˀ ***himow*** *hita ˀ-ipu-hunmu-t*
but.you lots 2SG-work-DIR-Q yes lots 1SG.A-work-DIR-ASP
'But did you take lots? Yes, I took lots.'

22b. Harrington 020-1199
hamadeˀwpʰuˀ, himow, hamadeˀw
h-ama-deˀw-pʰuˀ ***himow*** *h-ama-deˀw*
3-eat-DER-Q yes 3-eat-DER
'Did they all eat? Yes, they ate.'

22c. Harrington 020-1125
nač̌ʰot mexekʰoˀnanaxanaˀ, himow
nač̌ʰot m-e-x-ekʰo-ˀna-na-xana-ˀ ***himow***
1PL 2SG-1P-NEG-talk-APPL-NEG-FUT-Q yes
'Aren't you going to talk to us? Yes.'

23. Negative answers to yes/no questions

23a. Harrington 020-1128
makʰoˀyewxanaˀ, paačikun, xakʰoˀyewkuč̌ʰaˀnan
m-akʰo-ˀyew-xana-ˀ ***paačikun*** *x-akʰo-ˀyew-kuč̌ʰaˀ-na-n*
2SG-kill-REFL-FUT-Q no NEG-kill-REFL-NOM-NEG-ASP
'Are you going to kill yourself? No, I am not going to kill myself.'

23b. Harrington 020-1104
mamot pʰaˀyidaˀnčimiˀ, noˀot pač̌ʰikut, pʰaˀxuyinat
mamot pʰaˀyidaˀnčimi-ˀ noˀot ***pač̌ʰikut*** *pʰaˀxuyinat*
2SG you.believe.it-Q 1SG no I.don't believe.it
'Do you believe it? No, I don't believe it.'

10.4 Question formation in areal-typological perspective

The question formation strategies in the languages of Northern California show similarities and differences. The languages compared include Chimariko, Wintu, Shasta, Hupa, Karok, Yurok, Wiyot, and Maidu. All languages have two kinds of questions: (1) question-word questions and (2) yes/no questions. These are formed with different strategies. In many of the languages compared all question words are based on the same root or morpheme, and they show formal similarities to other kinds of pronouns. There are two main differences among the eight languages compared: (a) the type of the interrogative marker, i.e. prefix, suffix, or particle, and (b) the presence or absence of the interrogative marker in question-word questions. Chimariko, Wintu, and Maidu form yes/no questions with an interrogative suffix, while Hupa, Karok, Yurok, and Wiyot form yes/no questions with a particle or postposition occurring either clause-finally or after the questioned constituent. Wintu has an interrogative prefix, which is typologically uncommon. Chimariko, Wintu, Shasta, and Maidu include an interrogative marker in their question-word questions, while Hupa, Karok, Yurok, and Wiyot do not. In general, question words occur clause-initially. Overall, the question formation processes in the eight languages compared are very similar. The different question formation strategies are summarized in Table 2.

Table 2: Question formation strategies in Northern California

	Question-word questions	Yes/no questions
Chimariko	clause-initial question word AND interrogative verb-final suffix	interrogative verb-final suffix
Wintu[1]	clause-initial question word AND interrogative verb-final suffix	interrogative verb-final suffix
Shasta[2]	question word AND interrogative prefix	interrogative prefix
Hupa[3]	question word	clause-final particle
Karok[4]	question word	sentence particle (?)
Yurok[5]	clause-initial question word	particle
Wiyot[6]	clause-initial question word AND verb in subjunctive form	postposition
Maidu[7]	clause-initial question word AND interrogative modal suffix	interrogative modal suffix

[1] Pitkin 1984:61,101

[2] Silver 1966:133-135

[3] Golla 1970:237

[4] Bright 1957

[5] Robins 1958:1549-152

[6] Teeter 1964:32, 45, 68, 103-104

[7] Shipley 1964:50-51, 60-61

11. NEGATION

This chapter describes clausal negation. In addition, strategies used to form negative imperatives and admonitives, negative existentials, and negative questions and answers are presented. No examples of constituent negation occur in the available data.

11.1 Clausal negation

Chimariko has three different strategies for negating clauses: (1) the verbal circumfix *x-. . -na*, (2) the suffix *-kuna/-k'una/-ˀna*, and (3) the particle *kuna/k'una*. The circumfix *x-. . -na* occurs only with the verb stem classes that take pronominal prefixes; *-kuna/-k'una/-ˀna* occurs with all verb stem classes and with predicate nominals. Both may be followed by other modal or by tense-aspect suffixes. It is unclear whether the negation circumfix and suffix differ semantically. The negative particle *kuna/k'una* occurs in negative imperatives and in negative predicate nominal clauses (see 8.1.3.2, 8.1.3.4, and 11.2).

1. Clausal negation with verbal circumfix *x-. . -na* (from 'Fugitives at Burnt Ranch')

   yaxak^{h}onaxanˀi, mak^{h}otaxantinda
   *ya-**x**-ak^{h}o-**na**-xan-ˀi*   *m-ak^{h}o-ta-xan-tinda*
   1PL.A-NEG-kill-NEG-FUT-ASP   2SG-kill-DER-FUT-PROG
   'We won't kill them, he is going to kill you'

2. Clausal negation with verbal circumfix *x-. . -na* (from 'Mrs Bussell')

   ˀawaidače xowonat
   ˀawa-ida-če   ***x**-owo-**na**-t*
   home-POSS-LOC   NEG-stay-NEG-ASP
   'She does not stay at home'

3. Clausal negation with verbal circumfix *x-. . -na* (from 'Mrs Bussell')

   welmu uwomni, hamew xewunan, xok'oˀnanan
   *welmu   uwo-m-ni   hamew **x**-ewu-**na**-n   **x**-ok'o-ˀna-**na**-n*
   quickly go-DIR-ASP   food   NEG-give-NEG-ASP   NEG-talk-APPL-NEG-ASP
   'At once she returned, I did not give her dinner, I did not speak to her'

4. Clausal negation with suffix *-kuna* (Harrington 020-1103)

   q'ehkunacoˀol
   *q'e-h-**kuna**-coˀol*
   die-3-NEG-MOD
   'Maybe he doesn't die'

5. *-kuna* and *x- . . -na* with the same verb stem (Harrington 020-1105)

5a. *yemakunaxanat*
*y-ema-**kuna**-xana-t*
1SG.A-eat-NEG-FUT-ASP
'I am not going to eat'

5b. *xemanaxanat*
***x**-ema-**na**-xana-t*
NEG-eat-NEG-FUT-ASP
'I am not going to eat'

The person prefix is sometimes omitted with the negative circumfix *x-..-na*, as in examples 2 and 3. This occurs with third person and first person singular agent pronouns, most likely due to their weak phonological structure, *h-* and *ˀ-* respectively. The negative circumfix *x-..-na* attaches to the verb root directly, allowing only derivational suffixes between the root and the negative marker, such as the applicative *-ˀna* in *xok'oˀnanan* 'I did not speak to her' (example 3). The suffix *-kuna* follows the person marking on the verb. This is shown in Table 1. Example 5 illustrates that *x- . . -na* and *-kuna* can occur with the same verb stem with no change in the translation.

Table 1: Morpheme templates with negative affixes

(Person)	Negative **x-**	Root	Derivation	Negative **-na**	Tense/Aspect/Mood

Root	Person	Negative **-kuna**	Tense/Aspect/Mood

In negative predicate nominal or predicate adjective clauses, the negative suffix *-kuna/-k'una/-ˀna* or the negative particle *kuna/k'una* occur.

6. Negative predicate nominal clause with *-k'una* (Harrington 020-0470)

mamot čimarmik'unatinda
*mamot čimar-mi-**k'una**-tinda*
2SG person-2SG-NEG-PROG
'You are not an Indian'

7. Negative predicate adjective clause with *-k'una* (Grekoff 1996:54)

hisiˀk'unaxananta
*hisiˀ-**k'una**-xana-nta*
good-NEG-FUT-ASP
'They will not be good (ones).'

11.2 Negative imperatives and admonitives

Negative imperatives (prohibitives) are formed in two ways: (1) with the negative circumfix *x- . . -na* or (2) with the negative particle *kuna/k'una*. Given that the negative suffix and the negative particle have the same form (-)*kuna/k'una*, and given that imperatives have no tense/aspect suffixes, it is sometimes unclear whether *kuna/k'una* is a suffix or a particle, as it always occurs in final position, i.e. as the final morpheme of the predicate or immediately following the predicate. In the available data, *kuna/k'una* occurs as a suffix or as a particle.

8. Negative imperative with circumfix *x-*. . *-na* (from 'Fugitives at Burnt Ranch')

čʰaxakʰona, wečʰup čʰaxakʰona, ˀama xoliˀyu

*čʰa-***x***-akʰo-***na**	*wečʰup*	*čʰa-***x***-akʰo-***na**	*ˀama*	*xoliˀ-yu*
IMP.PL-NEG-kill-NEG	some	IMP.PL-NEG-kill-NEG	country	bad-ADM

'Don't kill them, some said don't kill them, lest it spoil the country'

9. Negative imperative with circumfix *x-*. . *-na* (Harrington 020-1128)

nexokʰona
*n-e-***x***-okʰo-***na**
IMP.SG-1P-NEG-kill-NEG
'Don't kill us!'

10. Negative imperative with circumfix *x-*. . *-na* (Harrington 020-1128)

naxakʰoˀyewna
*na-***x***-akʰo-ˀyew-***na**
IMP.SG-NEG-kill-REFL-NEG
'Don't kill yourself!'

11. Negative imperative with particle *k'una* (from 'Cutting navel')

hinoˀyta, hisuma nitix, xalallop, nakʰohoshu k'una

h-inoˀy-ta	*hi-suma*	*n-itix*	*xalall-op*	*n-akʰohoshu*	***k'una***
3-bear-ASP	POSS-face	IMP.SG-wipe	baby-DEF	IMP.SG-cut	NEG

'She bears it, wipe his face, (of) that baby, don't cut it (the navel)'

12. Negative imperative with suffix *-kuna* (Harrington 020-1132)

nunuˀ nemičitkuna

nunuˀ	*n-e-mičit-***kuna**
?	IMP.SG-1P-kick-NEG

Don't you kick me!

In examples 11 and 12 the negative imperatives are formed with *kuna/k'una*. These two examples illustrate the fact that *kuna/k'una* occurs in word-final or clause-final position. As a result, it could be interpreted either as a suffix or as a final particle here.

The negative admonitive is formed with the admonitive suffix *-teˀq* and a negative marker. The negative marker is either the first element of the negative circumfix, i.e. *x-*, or the suffix *-k'una* in a reduced form *-k'u*, depending on the verb stem class.

13. Negative admonitive with *x-... -teˀq* (Grekoff 012.018)

xačile hik'omuda exaˀixanat, xoxačiteˀq, pačʰaˀa xahaˀdeˀq
xačile h-ik'o-muda exaˀi-xana-t ***x**-oxači-**teˀq*** *pačʰaˀa* ***x**-ahaˀ-**deˀq***
children 3-talk-? make-FUT-ASP NEG-steal-ADM anything NEG-pick.up-ADM
'He praises the children, never steal, don't pick up anything'

14. Negative admonitive with *-k'u-teˀq* (Grekoff 012.018)

xahaˀdeq pačʰaˀa, hitxattakon, qʰapʰamahk'uteˀq
x**-ahaˀ-**deq *pačʰaˀa* *h-itxa-tta-kon* *qʰapʰamah-**k'u-teˀq***
NEG-pick.up-ADM anything 3-put-DER-FUT lie-NEG-ADM
'Let it lie there and don't pick it up, never lie'

11.3 Negative existential and possessive clauses

Negative existential clauses can be formed in the same way as negative predicate nominal clauses with the negative suffix *-kuna/-k'una/-ˀna* or the negative particle *kuna/k'una*.

15. Negative existential with suffix *-k'una* (Harrington 020-0657)

ˀanoˀak'unat
*ˀanoˀa-**k'una**-t*
pitchwood-NEG-ASP
'It's not pitchwood' (There is no pitchwood)

16. Negative existential with suffix *-ˀna* (Grekoff 012-001)

č'imaraˀnanta
*č'imara-**ˀna**-nta*
person-NEG-PROG
'It's not a person' (There is no person)

There is also a second negative existential construction formed with *paačʰikun/pačʰigut* 'none'.

17. Negative existential with *paačʰikun* (from 'Mrs Bussell')

sinda, yuṭiˀi paačʰikun, kimass uwatkun, huwomni welmu
si-nda *yuṭi-ˀi* ***paačʰikun*** *kimass* *uwa-tku-n* *h-uwo-m-ni* *welmu*
say-PROG acorn-POSS none today go-DIR-ASP 3-go-DIR-ASP quickly
'She says, but my acorns are none, today she came, she went back home at once'

18. Negative existential with *pačʰigut* (from 'Hollering at New River')

himedašur ˀapu pačʰigut, ˀawa qʰoqʰ huhooidat
himedašur ˀapu ***pačʰigut*** *ˀawa qʰoqʰ h-uhooida-t*
next.morning fire none house two 3-?-ASP
'The next morning there was no fire, there were two houses here too'

In examples 17 and 18 the negative morpheme *paačʰikun/pačʰigut* occurs in verbless existential clauses and functions as a predicate. However, it shows no verbal morphology in these examples. The negative morpheme is identical to *paačikun* 'no' that occurs in negative answers (see 11.5). *paačʰikun/pačʰigut* also occurs in negative equational clauses where it may be interpreted as a negative copula.

19. Negative equational clause with *pačʰikut* (Grekoff 020-006)

map'un noˀot paačʰikut
map'un noˀot ***paačʰikut***
that.one 1SG NEG
'That wasn't me.'

The negative *paačʰikun/pačʰigut* can also occur with verbal suffixes as in the following example:

20. Negative *pačʰikut* with verbal morphology (Harrington 020-0500)

pačʰikudinda
pačʰiku*-dinda*
NEG-ASP
'I have none at all' (Answer to 'Have you lots of deer meat?')

Negative possessive clauses are formed with the privative suffix *-(a)šku*.

21. Negative possessive with the privative *-(a)šku* (Grekoff 008.012)

21a. *ˀiṭiˀiškut*
*ˀiṭi-ˀi-****šku****-t*
man-POSS-PRIV-ASP
'I have no husband'

21b. *husotaškut*
*h-usot-****ašku****-t*
POSS-eye-PRIV-ASP
'It has no eyes'

11.4 Negative conditionals

Conditional clauses are negated using the same negation strategies as other clauses, i.e. conditional clauses with predicate nominals are negated with *(-)kuna/k'una/-ˀna*, while conditional clauses with verbal predicates are negated with *x-...-na* or *-kuna/-k'una/-ˀna*. The scarcity of examples in the available data leads only to a tentative description of negative conditionals. Real conditions and hypothetical conditions are negated in the same way with the negative marker preceding the conditional suffix or clitic.

22. -*k'una* as separate word with modal marker (from 'Hollering at New River')

*himisamdu k'uno*ˀ*op* ˀ*ap hišektakon*

himisamdu	***k'un*=*o*ˀ*op***	ˀ*ap*	*h-išekta-kon*
devil	NEG=COND	fire	3-make-FUT

'If it is not a devil, he will make a fire'

23a. Harrington 020-1107

*mallak'uwamnate*ˀ*ta xak*ʰ*ottameta*ˀ

*mallak'-uwa-m-**na**-te*ˀ*ta*	*x-ak*ʰ*o-tta-me-ta*ˀ
there-go-DIR-NEG-COND	NEG-kill-DER-MOD-PST

'If he hadn't gone there, they wouldn't have killed him.'

23b. Harrington 020-1107

*mallak'uwamnate*ˀ*ta xak*ʰ*ottameta*ˀ

*malla-**k'u**-wa-m-**na**-te*ˀ*ta*	*x-ak*ʰ*o-tta-me-ta*ˀ
there-NEG-go-DIR-NEG-COND	NEG-kill-DER-MOD-PST

'If he hadn't gone there, they wouldn't have killed him.'

23c. Grekoff 012.020

malla	*huwamte*ˀ*ta*	*xak*ʰ*ottatqi*
malla	*h-uwa-m-te*ˀ*ta*	*h-ak*ʰ*o-tta-tqi*
there	3-go-DIR-COND	3-kill-DER-INT

'If he had gone there, he would not have got killed'

Example 22 shows a real condition with a predicate nominal. The conditional clitic =*so*ˀ*op* is attached to the negative particle *k'una*. Examples 23a and 23b are identical with slightly different parsing: in 23b *k'u* is interpreted as part of a negative circumfix. Example 23c illustrates that the interpretation in 23b is more likely. In general, the negative marker *k'u* does not function as a part of the negative circumfix and it does not occur before the root. Given that this is the only example of that sort, it may be interpreted as being the result of language attrition.

11.5 Negative questions and answers

Negative questions are formed using the same strategies as found in clausal negation (see 11.1). The negative marker always precedes the question marker.

24. Harrington 020-1101

*moxokona*ˀ

*mo-**x**-oko-**na**-*ˀ

2SG-NEG-tattoo-NEG-Q

'Did you not tattoo?'

25. Harrington 020-1103
mamot q'emkunatitaˀ
*mamot q'e-m-**kuna**-titaˀ*
2SG die-2SG-NEG-Q
'Did you not die?'

Negative answers contain the negative particle *paačikun/pačikut* 'no'. The particle is followed by an entire clause that is negated.

26. Negative answers with *paačikun* 'no' (Harrington 020-1128)

makʰoˀyewxanaˀ, paačikun, xakʰoˀyewkučʰaˀnan
m-akʰo-ˀyew-xana-ˀ ***paačikun*** ***x**-akʰo-ˀyew-kučʰaˀ-**na**-n*
2SG-kill-REFL-FUT-Q no NEG-kill-REFL-NOM-NEG-ASP
'Are you going to kill yourself? No, I am not going to kill myself.'

27. Negative answers with *pačʰikut* 'no' (Harrington 020-1104)

mamot pʰaˀyidaˀnčimiˀ, noˀot pačʰikut, pʰaˀxuyinat
mamot pʰaˀyidaˀnčimi-ˀ noˀot ***pačʰikut pʰaˀxuyinat***
2SG you.believe.it-Q 1SG no no believe.it
'Do you believe it? No, I don't believe it.'

11.7 Negation in areal-typological perspective

The negation strategies in the languages of Northern California are very similar and include negative suffixes and negative adverbs or particles that precede the predicate. The strategies are summarized in table 2.

Table 2: Negation strategies in Northern California

	Negation strategies
Chimariko	Circumfix *x-...na;* suffix/particle (-)*kuna/k'una*
Wintu[1]	Suffix *-mina*; negative preverb (possibility, prohibitive) + *-mina*
Shasta[2]	Adverb *ma* (precedes whatever is being negated)
Hupa[3]	Particle *do* (precedes whatever is being negated)
Neighbors to the northwest	
Karok[4]	Adverb *pu* (precedes whatever is being negated)
Yurok[5]	Preverbal particles (*nimi, mos, pa's*)
Wiyot[6]	Preverb (*ki, ko*); suffix (*-ah, -ih*)
Neighbors to the east	
Maidu[7]	Suffix *-men*

[1] Pitkin 1984:121-122
[2] Silver 1966:133-135
[3] Golla 1970

[4] Bright 1957
[5] Robins 1958:110-111
[6] Teeter 1964:37-38
[7] Shipley 1964:44

While the negation strategies are very similar, the actual forms of the negative morphemes differ from language to language. Noticeable is the position of the negative morpheme either before of after the negated constituent in geographically contiguous areas. In Chimariko and two of its neighbors to the east, Wintu and Maidu, the negative morpheme is suffixed, while in the languages to the north and west of Chimariko, i.e. Shasta, Hupa, Yurok, Wiyot, and Karok, the negative morpheme occurs preverbally. In Wiyot it occurs pre- or postverbally.

Table 3: Position of negative morpheme

	Negative morpheme before or after the negated constituent
Chimariko	after
Wintu	after
Shasta	before
Hupa	before
Neighbors to the northwest	
Yurok	before
Wiyot	before and after
Karok	before
Neighbors to the east	
Maidu	after

In general, the negation strategies described in the grammars of Northern California refer to clausal negation. Constituent negation is rarely mentioned. Special negative forms for imperatives and conditionals are uncommon.

12. COMPLEX SENTENCES

This chapter describes the structure of complex sentences, i.e. clause coordination, complement clauses, relative clauses, and adverbial clauses. There is morphosyntactic evidence for clause combining in relative clauses and adverbial clauses, as well as in the complementation construction with *imiˀna* 'to want'.

12.1 Coordination

There is no morphosyntactic clause coordination. Chimariko does not have a conjunction with the meaning 'and'. Other words, however, may be analyzed as clause connectives (see 5.8.5). The word *haṭu* 'then' could be either an adverb or a conjunction. No morphological or syntactic criteria point to one or the other. Nevertheless, adverbs occur most often clause-initially, while *haṭu* 'then' occurs clause-finally.

1. 'On grandmother getting the hiccups'

luˀni, ˀaqʰa luˀit haṭu
luˀ-ni ˀaqʰa luˀ-it ***haṭu***
drink-IMP.SG water drink-ASP then
'Drink, she drank then.'

hisekmut, hisiˀta haṭu. hita hisekmutaˀ
h-isekmu-t hisiˀ-ta ***haṭu*** *hita h-isekmu-taˀ*
3-swallow-ASP good-ASP then lots 3-swallow-INF
'She swallowed, and then she was all right. I guess she took a little too much.'

2. 'Cutting navel'

hinoˀyta, hisuma nitix, xalallop, nakʰohoshu k'una
h-inoˀy-ta hi-suma n-itix xalall-op n-akʰohoshu k'una
3-bear-ASP POSS-face IMP.SG-wipe baby-DEF IMP.SG-cut NEG
'She bears it, wipe his face, (of) that baby, don't cut it (the navel)'

nunuˀ, ˀaweye hinoˀylala haṭu, nihuy, nataqmu honapu,
nunuˀ ˀaweye h-inoˀy-lala ***haṭu*** *n-ihuy n-ataqmu honapu*
? sac 3-bear-? thereupon IMP.SG-wash IMP.SG-tie.up navel
'Let it be, she bears the sac thereupon, wash him, tie the navel'

12.2 Complementation

In general, there is no morphosyntactic complementaion in Chimariko (Jany 2004). However, constructions with *imiˀna* 'to want' show a morphological reduction in the predicate that occurs in the complement clause. According to Dixon (1995), languages with no grammatical complementation employ complementation strategies to express the range of semantic concepts which are coded by complements in other languages. Four strategies are used in Chimariko to encode the semantic concepts expressed by complements in some languages: (1) separate sentences with no linking morphology, (2) verbal morphology, (3) attitude words, and (4) *imiˀna* 'to want' with a complement clause.

12.2.1 Complementation strategies

There are no complementizers or other particles related to complements with the four complementation strategies: (1) morphosyntactically independent clauses, (2) verbal affixes, (3) attitude words, and (4) *imiˀna* 'to want' with a complement clause. Furthermore, putative complements are never marked as arguments in a main clause.

12.2.1.1 Separate clauses. One strategy used in Chimariko to deal with the semantic concepts found in complementation in other languages is juxtaposing separate clauses. The clauses show no reduction of the predicate in the putative complement or any other restrictions. Morphosyntactically, they function as independent clauses. The following three semantic classes of predicates occur with this strategy (see Noonan 1985): (1) utterance predicates, (2) commentative predicates (Noonan, 1985), and (3) immediate perception predicates. Examples are given below. Clauses are enclosed in square brackets, and complement-taking predicates are boldfaced.

3. Complements with utterance predicates (from 'Dailey chased by the bull')

Dailey hik'ot mušmuš č^{h}uwetni
[Dailey ***h-ik'o-t]*** *[mušmuš č^h-uwet-ni]*
Dailey 3-say-ASP bull 1SG.P-hook-ASP
'Dailey said: the bull hooked me'

4. Complements with utterance predicates (from 'Hollering at New River')

himisamdudaˀn sideˀw
[himisamdu-daˀn] ***[si-deˀw]***
devil-INF say-DER
'It must have been the devil, they said'

Example 3 shows that both clauses are fully inflected including a person and an aspect marker. The same aspect suffixes, *-t* and *-ni*, also occur in other independent clauses not involving any semantic concepts associated with complementation. In example 4 the utterance predicate *sideˀw* 'they said' lacks pronominal marking. The verb *si* 'to say' does not occur with pronominal marking in the available data.

Only direct quotation occurs in Chimariko. There are no indirect quotations. Sometimes, direct quotation is not introduced by an utterance predicate, as in example 5, where the story simply switches between a narration in the third person and a direct speech segment.

5. Direct quotation without an introducing utterance predicate (from 'Fugitives at Burnt Ranch')

č'imar xotai heṭaheskut uwatkut, heṭaheskut č'utamdače
č'imar xotai h-eṭahe-sku-t wa-tku-t h-eṭahe-sku-t č'utamdače
man three 3-run.away-DIR-ASP go-DIR-ASP run.away-DIR-ASP Burnt Ranch
'Three men came as fugitives, they ran away to Burnt Ranch'

kimot ˀuˀir asunda, čʰakʰo, heṭaheshutaˀa sunda
kimot ˀuˀir asu-nda čʰ-akʰo h-eṭahe-shu-taˀa su-nda
these stranger be-PROG IMP.PL-kill 3-run.away-DIR-? be-PROG
'These are strangers, kill them, they are running away'

The second line in example 5 is a direct quote. It employs the imperative form in *čʰakʰo* 'kill them', which is used only in direct speech. No utterance predicate introduces the direct discourse segment.

Commentative predicates express an attitude towards the truth value of the complement and provide a comment in the form of an emotional reaction, an evaluation, or a judgement (Noonan 1985). In Chimariko they occur with fully inflected clauses.

6. Complements with commentative predicates (from 'Fugitives at Burnt Ranch')

xoliˀtaˀn hakʰot, xawiy asunda, xukeenat
*[**xoliˀ-taˀn**] [h-akʰo-t] xawiy asu-nda x-ukee-na-t*
bad-INF 3-kill-ASP Redwood.Indian be-ASP NEG-understand-NEG-ASP
'It is not right to kill him, he was a Redwood Indian, he didn't understand'

načʰidot yakʰorot xukeenat, qʰakʰodaˀn xoliˀtaˀn
*načʰidot ya-kʰo-rot x-ukee-na-t [qʰ-akʰo-daˀn][**xoliˀ-taˀn**]*
1PL 1PL.A-kill-DEP NEG-understand-NEG-ASP 2PL-kill-INF bad-INF
'We killed him, he didn't understand, you killed him, it is not right'

xoliˀtaˀn, qʰakʰot, hetaxawi uwatkukon
*[**xoliˀ-taˀn**] [qʰ-akʰo-t] heta-xawi uwa-tku-kon*
bad-INF 2PL-kill-ASP many-Redwood.Indians go-DIR-FUT
'It is not right, you killed him, lots of Redwood Indians will come'

The clauses containing the information commented on, *hakʰot* 'he killed him' and *qʰakʰodaˀn* 'you killed him', have fully inflected predicates, including pronominal and tense/aspect/modal marking. The commentative predicate *xoliˀ* 'to be bad' has a modal affix, but no pronominal marking. However, the phonologically weak third person affix is sometimes omitted.

Immediate perception predicates also occur in multi-clausal constructions with fully inflected clauses, as in the examples below.

7. Complements with immediate perception predicates (from 'Woman wanders')

ˀikeedinda, ˀiwoxandinda
*[ˀ-**ikee-dinda**]* *[ˀ-iwo-xan-dinda]*
1SG.A-understand-ASP 1SG.A-sit.down-FUT-PROG
'I understand that I will stay here'

8. Complements with immediate perception predicates (Harrington 020-1103)

8a. *q'ehta ˀikeeneq*
[q'e-h-ta] *[ˀ-**ikee-neq**]*
die-3-ASP 1SG.A-hear-PST
'I heard that he was dead.'

8b. *q'ehtinta ˀimamnip*
[q'e-h-tinta] *[ˀ-**imam-nip**]*
die-3-PROG 1SG.A-see-PST
'I saw him die.'

Example 7 illustrates that shared arguments, such as the first person agent, appear in each clause. In examples 7, 8a, and 8b all predicates are fully inflected with pronominal and tense and/or aspect marking.

12.2.1.2 Verbal morphology. The second strategy used in Chimariko to deal with the semantic concepts found in complementation in other languages is to encode this information in the verbal morphology. Complement-taking predicates in some languages correspond to modal suffixes in Chimariko. The following two semantic classes occur with this strategy: (1) propositional attitude predicates and (2) modal predicates.

Propositional attitudes refer to the truth value of a clause (Noonan 1985). They are encoded in modal suffixes, as in the following examples. Such suffixes include *-taˀ(n)*, *-tiˀarhiniˀ*, and *-(a)l*, among others.

9. Propositional attitude (from 'On grandmother getting the hiccups')

hisekmut, hisiˀta haṭu hita hisekmutaˀ
h-isekmu-t *hisiˀ-ta* *haṭu* *[hita h-isekmu-**taˀ**]*
3-swallow-ASP good-ASP then lots 3-swallow-INF
'She swallowed, and then she was all right. I guess she took a little too much.'

10. Propositional attitude (Harrington 020-1103)

q'ehxantiˀarhiniˀ
*[q'e-h-xan-**tiˀarhiniˀ**]*
die-3-FUT-MOD
'I guess that he is going to die'

11. Propositional attitude (Harrington 020-1103)

q'ehkunal
[q'e-h-kuna-l]
die-3-NEG-MOD
'I guess he doesn't die'

A deontic modal meaning, corresponding to complement-taking predicates in some languages, occurs in example 12.

12. Deontic modal (from 'On grandmother getting the hiccups')

ˀisekmu čisit, xakimnan, xotalla hipuhunmateˀqʰ, sit
*ˀ-isekmu čі-si-t x-akim-na-n [xotalla h-ipu-hunma-**teˀqʰ**] si-t*
1SG.A-swallow ?-say-ASP NEG-?-NEG-ASP a.little 3-work-DIR-ADM say-ASP
'I tried to swallow it, but it wouldn't go down, a little (salmon-meal) one <u>should</u> put (in his mouth), she said.'

12.2.1.3 Attitude words. The third strategy used in Chimariko to deal with the semantic concepts found in complementation in other languages is attitude words. Attitude words show no morphology and are invariant. Only one such word, corresponding to a predicate of knowledge, occurs in the available data: *čʰeq* 'to know'.

13. Attitude word corresponding to a predicate of knowledge (Harrington 020-1102)

13a. *mamot q'emxan čʰeqhiniˀ*
*mamot q'e-m-xan **čʰeq**=hiniˀ*
2SG die-2SG-FUT know=?
'You know that you are going to die'

13b. *pʰaˀmot q'ehxan čʰeqhiniˀ*
*pʰaˀmot q'e-h-xan **čʰeq**=hiniˀ*
3 die-3-FUT know=?
'He knows that he is going to die'

13c. *kumičin četpaˀxanan čʰeqhiniˀ*
*kumičin četpaˀ-xana-n **čʰeq**=hiniˀ*
all ?-Fut-ASP know=?
'All know that they are going to die'

or: *četpaˀxanan čʰeq kumičin=hiniˀ*
*četpaˀ-xana-n **čʰeq** kumičin=hiniˀ*
?-FUT-ASP know all=?

In examples 13a-c the actor of *čʰeq* 'to know' is the same as the actor in the respective complement clause. The predicates in the complement clauses are marked for person and tense/aspect. The phonologically weak third person marker is omitted in 13c. The attitude word is invariant and does not occur with any apparent person or tense/aspect marking. The clitic *=hiniˀ* is of unclear meaning.

12.2.1.4 imiˀna 'to want'. The fourth strategy used in Chimariko to deal with the semantic concepts found in complementation involves *imiˀna* 'to want'. *imiˀna* 'to want' can occur in simple sentences with nominal arguments (as in example 17) or in complex sentences with clausal arguments (as in examples 14 and 15).

14. Desiderative *imiˀna* 'to want' with clausal arguments (Grekoff 004.008)

yuwom imiˀnan

y-uwo-m	***imiˀna**-n*
1SG.A-go-DIR	want-ASP

'I want to go home'

15. Desiderative *imiˀna* 'to want' with clausal arguments (Grekoff 012.014)

yečiˀpʰa ˀimiˀnan pʰimečʰu

y-ečiˀ-pʰa	*ˀ-**imiˀna**-n*	*pʰimečʰu*
1SG.A-buy-?	1SG.A-want-ASP	hide

'I want to buy the hide'

In examples 14 and 15 *imiˀna* 'to want' takes clausal arguments. The complements of *imiˀna* 'to want', *yuwom* 'I go home' and *yečiˀpʰa pʰimečʰu* 'I buy hide' respectively, show pronominal marking, but no tense, aspect, or modal suffixes. Hence, there is a reduction in the verb morphology in the complement clause. *yuwom* 'I go home' in 14 and *yečiˀpʰa pʰimečʰu* 'I buy hide' in 15 cannot function as independent clauses, since they lack tense, aspect and modal marking.

The desiderative verb *imiˀna* 'to want' can appear as a suffix, as in example 16. In 16, the suffix *imiˀna* 'to want' is negated, while the verb root *q'e* 'to die' is not negated. If *imiˀna* 'to want' is separated from the root *q'e* 'to die', it is fully inflected with a negative circumfix and an aspect suffix, while *q'e* 'to die' occurs only with pronominal marking.

16. Desiderative *imiˀna* 'to want' in complex predicate (Harrington 020-1102)

q'eˀxo-miˀnanan
*q'e-ˀ-x-**omiˀna**-na-n*
die-1SG.A-NEG-want-NEG-ASP
'I don't want to die'

It is unclear whether the desiderative *imiˀna* 'to want' can function as both: (a) an independent predicate, as in examples 14-15 and (b) a verbal suffix forming a complex predicate, as in example 16. It is possible that *q'eˀ* 'I die' and *xomiˀnanan* 'I don't want to' in 16 are in fact two separate words that have been written together by mistake.

Example 17 illustrates that *imiˀna* 'to want' also occurs in simple clauses with nominal arguments.

17. Desiderative *imiˀna* 'to want' with nominal arguments (from 'Woman wanders')

ˀimiˀnan, ˀama ˀimiˀnan
***ˀ-imiˀna**-n* *ˀama* ***ˀ-imiˀna**-n*
1SG.A-want-ASP country 1SG.A-want-ASP
'I want it, I want this country'

It is likely that the periphrastic causative construction with *ixaˀy* 'to make, to cause' also shows reduction in the predicate of the complement. Due to the limited amount of examples in the available data, however, a detailed analysis is not possible (see 8.2.3).

12.3 Relative clauses

There are two relativization strategies in Chimariko: (1) internally headed relative clauses and (2) headless relative clauses. Relative clauses that are internally headed are formed with a special verbal suffix *-rop/-rot/-lop/-lot*. Sometimes, the relative pronoun *map'un* is the head. This is shown below. Relative clauses are in brackets, heads are boldfaced, and the special verb form is underlined.

18. 'Hopping Game'
pusuw iṭaˀṭarop malla p'un huwatmut, map'un
[pusuw iṭaˀṭa-rop malla ***p'un]*** *h-uwa-tmu-t map'un*
stick chop-DEP there one 3-go-DIR-ASP that.one
'One gets to the stick, he gets to (the) stick'

hucumeˀkʰamta, himantamorop map'un, hiˀamta
h-ucu-meˀkʰam-ta [h-iman-tamo-rop ***map'un]*** *h-iˀam-ta*
3-hop-?-ASP 3-fall-DIR-DEP that.one 3-?-DER
'He beats, those fellows that went down got beaten.

19. Harrington 20-1097
map'un hokoteˀrot yečiˀ ˀimiˀnan
[map'un *h-oko-teˀ-rot] y-ečiˀ ˀi-miˀn-an*
that.one 3-tattoo-DER-DEP 1SG.A-buy 1SG-want-ASP
I want to buy that engraved one.

20. Harrington 20-1103
moˀa pʰuncar huwatkurop pʰaˀyinip
[moˀa ***pʰuncar*** *h-uwa-tku-rop] pʰaˀyi-nip*
yesterday woman 3-go-DIR-DEP thus.say-PST
'That woman who came yesterday told me.'

21. Grekoff 020-009
načʰot yak'orop pʰaˀasu hik'ot
[načʰot ya-k'o-rop ***pʰaˀasu]*** *h-ik'o-t*
1PL 1PL-talk-DEP that.kind 3-talk-ASP
'What we talk, she talked.'

22. Grekoff 012.014
č^{h}eˀnew yewurop hačmukč^{h}a č^{h}awun
*[**č^{h}eˀnew** y-ewu-rop] hačmukč^{h}a č^h-awu-n*
bread 1SG-give-DEP axe 1SG.P-give-ASP
'For the bread I gave him, he gave me an axe.'

In examples 18-22 the relative clause always precedes the main clause. The heads of the relative clauses, *p'un* 'one' and *map'un* 'that one' in 18, *map'un* 'that one' in 19, *p^{h}uncar* 'woman' in 20, *p^{h}aˀasu* 'that kind' in 21, and *č^{h}eˀnew* 'bread' all occur within the relative clause and either precede or follow the dependent predicate. The dependent predicate occurs with a suffix *-rop/-rot* to mark dependency and, in general, with a pronominal affix. There are no tense, aspect, or modal suffixes on the dependent verb forms.

It is unclear whether there are any restrictions on what can be relativized in Chimariko. In the available data there are examples only of relativized third person arguments. The relativized arguments can serve a variety of roles in the relative clause. They are either actors, as in examples 18 and 20, or undergoers, as in examples 19, 21, and 22.

The second relativization strategy used in Chimariko is headless relative clauses, as in examples 23-25.

23. Harrington 020-0483
q'exanrop hiˀenda
[q'e-xan-rop] h-iˀen-da
die-FUT-DEP 3-groan-ASP
'The person about to die groans'

24. Grekoff 012.014
yewuxan ˀahatew hexačilop šičelaˀi
y-ewu-xan ˀahatew [h-exači-lop šičela-ˀi]
1SG.A-give-FUT money 3-steal-DEP dog-POSS
'I'll give you money for the stealing by my dog.'

25. Harrington 020-0386
šitoita hik'orop hek'oˀnačaxat
[šito-ita h-ik'o-rop] h-ek'o-ˀna-čaxa-t
mother-POSS 3-tell-DEP 3-say-APPL-COMP-ASP
'She told her mother everything' ('What she told her mother, she told her all')

As with internally headed clauses, the verb form in the headless relative clause occurs with a suffix *-rop/-lop* marking dependency.

The same suffix marking dependency in relative clauses *-rop/-lop* has been interpreted by Grekoff as a nominalizer. Nominalized expressions occur with other suffixes, such as for example the nominalizer *-ew*, and are different from the relative clause constructions with *-rop/-lop*.

26. Nominalizations with the nominalizer *-ew*

ama 'to eat'	=>	*hamew* 'food'	('Woman wanders')
ik'o 'to talk'	=>	*hik'ew* 'talker'	(Harrington 020-1133)
?	=>	*hiṭiytew* 'fence'	('Dailey chased by the bull')
opu 'to work'	=>	*hopew* 'acorn soup'	('Woman wanders')

27. Relative clause constructions with *-rop, -rot/-lop,-lot*

27a. Grekoff 012-009
*kimot č'imal h-uwa-ktu-**lot***
*kimot č'imal h-uwa-ktu-**lot***
DET person 3-go-DIR-DEP
'The person who arrived'

27b. Harrington 020-0136
hitaˀnat noˀot ˀik'erop
*h-itaˀna-t noˀot ˀ-ik'e-**rop***
3-write-ASP 1SG 1SG.A-talk-DEP
'He wrote my language'

27c. Harrington 020-0689
pačʰimop ˀuleytop šičela hičʰemrop
*pačʰim-op ˀuleyt-op šičela h-ičʰem-**rop***
that-DEF little-DEF horse 3-pull-DEP
'The little thing of yours which the horse pulls' (=carriage)

The expressions in example 27 differ from the expressions in example 26 in that the predicate with the dependent suffix *-rop/-lop* can take arguments, and thus still functions as a predicate. The expressions in example 26 can only function as arguments and cannot take any other arguments. Nevertheless, all expressions occur with the third person prefix *h-*. Although the expressions with *-rop/-lop* are noun-like in that they (1) lack any tense, aspect, or modal affixes and (2) do not form independent clauses by themselves, they are verb-like in that they (1) can take arguments and (2) take pronominal marking. Given that these clauses are restrictive, i.e. they identify the respective referents, rather than being nominalizations, they are better interpreted as headless relative clauses. However, some could have developed into lexicalised expressions, as in the following example.

28. Harrington 020-1106

28a. *hamadeˀrop malla*
h-ama-deˀ-rop malla
3-eat-DER-DEP there
'Eating place'

28b. *hamadeˀlop malla ˀawa*
h-ama-deˀ-lop malla ˀawa
3-eat-DER-DEP there house
'Restaurant'

12.4 Adverbial clauses

There are two types of adverbial clauses in Chimariko: (1) those referring to a time and (2) those referring to a condition.

12.4.1 Time, place, manner

Adverbial clauses referring to a time are formed with special verbal suffixes. There are two suffixes: *-lla* and *-taˀče*. It is unclear how they differ in use and meaning. Adverbial clauses are in brackets.

29. Adverbial clause with *-lla* (Harrington 020-1106)

29a. *yemall uwatkun*

*[y-ema-**ll**]*	*uwa-tku-n*
1SG.A-eat-DEP	go-DIR-ASP

'He came, when I was eating.'

29b. *xemanalla uwatkun*

*[x-ema-na-**lla**]*	*uwa-tku-n*
NEG-eat-NEG-DEP	go-DIR-ASP

'He came, when I was not eating.'

30. Adverbial clause with *-taˀče* (from 'Cutting finger when cleaning salmon')

čʰuṭa ṭeyta yekʰutni čʰiselimtu, ˀumul yekʰutaˀče,

čʰ-uṭa	*ṭe-yta*	*y-ekʰut-ni*	*čʰiseli-mtu*	*[ˀumul*	*y-ekʰu-**taˀče**]*
POSS-hand	?-POSS	1SG.A-cut-ASP	knife-INST	salmon	1SG.A-cut-ASP

'I cut my thumb with a knife, when I was cleaning a salmon'

The predicate in the adverbial clause lacks any tense, aspect, or modal suffixes, but it occurs with pronominal marking. It is unclear whether the aspectual suffix *-lla* is a clitic attached to the end of an adverbial clause. In example 31 a meaning 'while' or 'when' for *-lla* is likely, similar to the one in example 29. Only one such example occurs in the available data.

31. 'Crawfish'

ˀaqʰa yeˀaqʰtut čitxayamulla

ˀaqʰa	*y-eˀa-qʰtu-t*	*[čitxa-yamu-lla]*
water	1SG.A-?-liquid-ASP	blanket-without-while

'I went immersingly into the water being naked'

Sometimes, clauses with conditional suffixes are translated as adverbial clauses referring to time (see also 12.4.2). This could be due to vague translations, as only two such examples occur in the available data.

32a. Adverbial clause with *-seˀta* (Harrington 020-1096)

hitakseˀta hop'unhut
*[h-itak-**seˀta**] h-op'u-nhu-t*
3-rain-COND 3-work-CONT-ASP
'(Frank) is working while it is raining.'

32b. Adverbial clause with *=soˀop* (Harrington 020-1098)

ˀiṭinsoˀop ˀiwonhoxantinta noˀot
*ˀiṭin=**soˀop** ˀ-iwo-nho-xan-tinta noˀot*
man=COND 1SG.A-stay-CONT-FUT-PROG 1SG
'When she grows up I will marry her'

Clauses referring to a place are formed as relative clauses (see 12.3). No adverbial clauses indicating manner occur in the available data.

12.4.2 Conditionals

There are three different conditional clause constructions with three different markers: (1) *-teˀta*, (2) *-seˀta*, and (3) *=soˀop*. (1) describes conditions that cannot be fulfilled, as they refer to events in the past, i.e. hypothetical conditions. (2) and (3) refer to conditions that may be fulfilled, i.e. real conditions. It is unclear how (2) and (3) differ in use and meaning. Only one example occurs with (2). While (3) *=soˀop* is a clitic, there is not enough evidence to define all three markers as clitics.

33a. Example with *-teˀta* (from 'Hollering at New River')

muwetteˀta makʰomet
*[m-uwet-**teˀta**] m-akʰo-me-t*
2SG-hook-COND 2SG-kill-MOD-ASP
'If he had hooked you, he would have killed you right.'

33b. Example with *-teˀta* (Harrington 020-1107)

mallak'uwamnateˀta xakʰottametaˀ
*[mallak'-uwa-m-na-**teˀta**] x-akʰo-tta-me-taˀ*
there-go—DIR-NEG-COND NEG-kill-DER-MOD-PST
'If he hadn't gone there, they wouldn't have killed him.'

33c. Example with *-teˀta* (Harrington 020-1106)

malla huwamteˀta xakʰottatqi
*[malla h-uwa-m-**teˀta**] h-akʰo-tta-tqi*
there 3-go-DIR-COND 3-kill-DER-INT
'If he had gone there, he would not have got killed'

33d. Example with *-teʔta* (Harrington 020-1106)

malla huwamteʔta hakʰoteʔtiʔarhin
*[malla h-uwa-m-**teʔta**] h-akʰo-teʔ-tiʔarhin*
there 3-go-DIR-COND 3-kill-DER-MOD
'If he had gone there, they might have killed him'

34. Examples with *-seʔta* (Grekoff 020.009)

hamew č'imal huwatku seʔta hawut
*hamew [č'imal h-uwa-tku **seʔta**] h-awu-t*
food person 3-go-DIR COND 3-give-ASP
'If someone comes, one offers them food'

35a. Examples with *=soʔop* (Harrington 020-1106)

mamasoʔop yenuwešxanʔi
*[m-ama=**soʔop**] y-enuweš-xan-ʔi*
2SG-eat=COND 1SG.A-whip-FUT-ASP
'If you eat that thing, I'm going to whip you.'

35b. Examples with *=soʔop* (Harrington 020-1132)

nemičicoʔop pusuwamdu yetxanan
*[nemi-či=**coʔop**] pusuwa-mdu y-et-xana-n*
kick-1SG.P=COND stick-INST 1SG.A-hit-FUT-ASP
'If you kick me, I'll hit you with a stick'

With hypothetical conditions, as in example 33, the verb in the main clause occurs with a potential suffix *-me* or some other modal suffix. With real conditions, the verb in main clause occurs with a future suffix *-xana* or *-(a)kon* or an aspectual suffix *-t*, as in examples 34 and 35. The conditional constructions are summarized in Table 1.

Table 1: Conditional clauses

	Main clause	Conditional clause
Hypothetical condition	Potential *-me* Modal *-tiʔarhin* Intensive modal *-(i)tqi*	*-teʔta*
Real condition	Aspect *-t*	*-seʔta*
Real condition	Future *-xana/-kon*	*=soʔop*

The conditional marker *=soʔop* can also be attached to other types of words, such as nouns or the negative particle *k'una*. It is a clitic attached to the clause it marks as a condition.

36. *=soˀop* attached to other kinds of words (from 'Hollering at New River')

kowmilot himisamtu hapukʰeˀxanat, himisamdu k'unoˀop

kow-mi-lot	*himisamtu*	*h-apukʰeˀ-xana-t*	*[himisamdu*	*k'un=**oˀop**]*
holler-POSS-NOM	devil	3-steal-FUT-ASP	devil	NEG=COND

'The devil will steal your voice, if it is not a devil'

...

ˀap hišektakon, č'imarsoˀop, xošektanakon

ˀap	*h-išekta-kon*	*[č'imar=**soˀop**]*	*x-ošekta-na-kon*
fire	3-make-FUT	person=COND	NEG-make-NEG-FUT

'He will make a fire, if a person, he does not make a fire'

12.5 Complex sentences in areal-typological perspective

Clause combining is not described in great detail in the grammars of Northern California languages. However, most languages have a set of clause connectives occurring at the beginning or at the end of clauses. Clause connectives, like *hatu* 'then' in Chimariko, occur in Wintu, Shasta, Hupa, Karok, Yurok, and Maidu. In general, they do not take any affixes and are invariant.

Complementation or relativization strategies are not treated in any of the grammars describing neighboring languages. Hupa has a set of words which correspond semantically to complement-taking predicates with meanings such as 'I wonder', 'I wish', and 'I guess' (Golla 1970). However, they have no verbal morphology. Typologically, complement clauses of utterance predicates show no reduction of the predicate and can function as independent clauses in most languages (Dryer et al. 2004), as occurs in Chimariko. Relativization strategies have been described for some California languages, such as Wappo, which has headless relative clauses, just like Chimariko (Thompson et al 2006).

Adverbial clauses are described for some of the languages. Wintu, Hupa, and Maidu have temporal and/or conditional clauses formed with special verbal suffixes marking dependency; the same strategy occurs in Chimariko.

To conclude, more detailed descriptions of clause combining strategies in Northern California languages are needed in order to compare Chimariko coordination, complementation and relativization strategies, and adverbial clauses to neighboring languages.

13. DISCOURSE STRUCTURE

This chapter describes Chimariko discourse structure. Data are available for one discourse genre only: oral narratives. Eleven narratives are examined, two long stories and nine short texts.

13.1 Couplets and information flow

The narratives examined have similar structure and style with many repetitions of single words and even of entire clauses. The consistent repetitions are not random, but rather deliberate and regular. A repeated segment often elaborates on a particular point of the narrative adding a new piece of information or emphasizing a main point. The following examples illustrate this. Repetitions are underlined.

1. 'Fugitives at Burnt Ranch'
nač^{h}idot yak^{h}orot xukeenat, q^{h}ak^{h}oda^{ʔ}n xoli^{ʔ}ta^{ʔ}n
nač^{h}idot ya-k^{h}o-rot x-ukee-na-t q^{h}a-k^{h}o-da^{ʔ}n xoli^{ʔ}-ta^{ʔ}n
1PL 1PL.A-kill-DEP NEG-understand-NEG-ASP 2PL-kill-INF bad-INF
'We killed him, he didn't understand, you killed him, it is not right'

xoli^{ʔ}ta^{ʔ}n, q^{h}ak^{h}ot, hetaxawi uwatkukon
xoli^{ʔ}-ta^{ʔ}n q^{h}a-k^{h}o-t heta-xawi uwa-tku-kon
bad-INF 2PL-kill-ASP many-Redwood.Indians go-DIR-FUT
'It is not right, you killed him, lots of Redwood Indians will come'

The second line in example 1 elaborates on what had just been said. The story introduces the result of the action described in the first line: a man killed another man of a different tribe, which is not right because that man did not understand the language. As a result, many Indians from that other tribe will come for vengeance.

2. 'Mrs Bussell'
masunu huwaktanhut šunuhullot,
masunu h-uwa-kta-nhu-t šunuhull-ot
always 3-go-DIR-CONT-ASP old.woman-DEF
'Mrs. Bussell goes around all the time,'

huwaktat masunu šunuhullot p^{h}a^{ʔ}mot
h-uwa-kta-t masunu šunuhull-ot p^{h}a^{ʔ}mot
3-go-DIR-ASP always old.woman-DEF that
'She goes around all the time, that old woman.'

In example 2 the entire clause is repeated with a different word order and with the addition of 'that one', which emphasizes the main character of the narrative: Mrs. Bussell, the old woman.

3. 'Woman wanders'
q^{h}omall iṭanku muwaka$^?$,
q^{h}omal iṭan-ku m-uwa-k-a$^?$
where ?-DIR 2SG-go-DIR-Q
'Where do you come from?'

xukeenan himelušušun, xukeenan
x-ukee-na-n hime-lušušu-n x-ukee-na-n
NEG-know-NEG-ASP head-shake-ASP NEG-know-NEG-ASP
'She did not know, she shook her head, she did not know.'
. .
'hisikni p^{h}uncar', xukeenan hiko$^?$da$^?$
'h-isik-ni p^{h}uncar' x-ukee-na-n h-iko$^?$-da$^?$
3-pretty-ASP woman NEG-know-NEG-ASP 3-talk-PST
' "Pretty woman", she couldn't talk'

In example 3 one word is repeated twice, *xukeenan* 'she did not know'. The first repetition stresses the fact that the woman does not know where she came from. The second repetition adds a new piece of information: the woman cannot answer the question because she does not speak the language. The main point is that the woman can not communicate with the people.

Repetitions of single words are sometimes used to intensify an action, rather than to emphasize a main point, as in the following example.

4. 'On Grandmother getting the hiccups'
hipuhunmut, hisekmimi$^?$nat, lečit lečit
h-ipu-hunmu-t hi-sekm-imi$^?$na-t leči-t leči-t
3-work-DIR-ASP 3-swallow-want-ASP hiccup-ASP hiccup-ASP
'She put some in her mouth, she tried to swallow it, she hiccoughed'

The repetitive structure in example 4 is different from the stylistic repetitions. It does not add any new information, and it is not used to emphasize the main point of the storyline. Rather, this repetition mimics the event, the hiccup, which is generally composed of many repetitive sub-events. The repetition intensifies the event.

Furthermore, the repetition in example 4 is different from the ones in the previous examples in that it occurs within the same prosodic constituent. Prosodic units are marked in the data by punctuation, i.e. by commas and periods. Given the lack of sound recordings of connected speech, prosody can not be examined in detail. However, taking into consideration the punctuation, it is clear that the repetitions generally do not occur in the same prosodic unit. This is illustrated in example 5.

5. 'Dailey chased by the bull'
č^{h}uwetni sit, hawitomta, xowetnat, hek'omatta
č^h-uwet-ni si-t h-awi-tom-ta x-owet-na-t h-ek'o-ma-tta
1SG.P-hook-ASP say-ASP 3-afraid-?-ASP NEG-hook-NEG-ASP 3-say-?-DER
'He hooked me he said, he was scared, but he did not hook him, he told.'

p^{h}a^{ʔ}yit č^{h}uwetni sit, xowetnat, p^{h}uncarye p^{h}a^{ʔ}yit
p^{h}a^{ʔ}yit č^{h}-uwet-ni si-t x-owet-na-t p^{h}uncar-ye p^{h}a^{ʔ}yit
thus.say 1SG.P-hook-ASP say-ASP NEG-hook-NEG-ASP woman-POSS thus.say
'Thus he said, he hooked me he said, but it did not hook him, so his wife said.'

Example 5 shows that the repetitions occur in different prosodic units which are divided by commas. Again, the main points of the narrative are reiterated. They are two different opinions: Dailey claims that the bull hooked him, while his wife claims that this is not true.

Mithun (1992) shows for Central Pomo how narratives and stretches of conversation are structured in couplets, i.e. 'pairs of intonationally and semantically parallel lines' used to 'make special points of importance to the discourse as a whole' (Mithun 1992: 112). Although intonational patterns cannot be examined for Chimariko, a couplet structure similar to the one described by Mithun is sometimes apparent.

6. 'Woman wanders'
č'imarot hisikinda, hisikni č'imara nunu^{ʔ},
č'imar-ot hisik-inda hisik-ni č'imar-a nunu^{ʔ}
person-DEF good-PROG good-ASP person-? ?
'Good folks, the people are good.'

7. 'Mrs Bussell' (same as example 2)
masunu huwaktanhut šunuhullot
masunu h-uwa-kta-nhu-t šunuhull-ot
always 3-go-DIR-CONT-ASP old.woman-DEF
'Mrs. Bussell goes around all the time,'

huwaktat masunu šunuhullot p^{h}a^{ʔ}mot
h-uwa-kta-t masunu šunuhull-ot p^{h}a^{ʔ}mot
3-go-DIR-ASP always old.woman-DEF that
'She goes around all the time, that old woman.'

8. 'Cutting finger when cleaning salmon'
č^{h}uṭa ṭeyta yek^{h}utni č^{h}iselimtu, ^{ʔ}umul yek^{h}uta^{ʔ}če
č^{h}u-ṭa ṭe-yta y-ek^{h}ut-ni č^{h}iseli-mtu ^{ʔ}umul y-ek^{h}ut-a^{ʔ}če
POSS-hand ?-POSS 1SG.A-cut-ASP knife-INST salmon 1SG.A-cut-DEP
'I cut my thumb with a knife, when I was cleaning a salmon'

^{ʔ}umul yek^{h}uta^{ʔ}če č^{h}uṭa ṭeyta yek^{h}utni
^{ʔ}umul y-ek^{h}ut-a^{ʔ}če č^{h}u-ṭa ṭe-yta y-ek^{h}ut-ni
salmon 1SG.A-cut-DEP POSS-hand ?-POSS 1SG.A-cut-ASP
'Cleaning the salmon I cut my thumb.'

The repetitions or couplets in examples 6-8 represent semantically parallel lines. A parallel intonation seems likely. Overall, they are used to emphasize the main points in the narrative. The following example illustrates how the repetitions are used throughout an entire narrative to reiterate the main events of the narrative.

9. 'Crawfish'

šur txol hetat
šur *txol* *hetat*
formerly crawfish they.were.many
'Formerly there were many crawfish'

ˀaqʰaqʰut hiˀektaˀxat, hetat
ˀaqʰaqʰut *h-iˀekta-ˀxa-t* *hetat*
river 3-swim-COMP-ASP they.were.many
'They swam all in the river, they were many'

hiničxeˀkut, pʰiˀalop, hiničxeˀkut
h-iničxeˀku-t *pʰiˀal-op* *h-iničxeˀku-t*
3-smell-ASP bacon-DEF 3-smell-ASP
'They smelled it, that bacon, they smelled it,

ˀaqʰa yeˀaqʰtut čitxayamulla
ˀaqʰa *y-eˀa-qʰtu-t* *čitxa-yamu-lla*
water 1SG.A-?-liquid-ASP blanket-without-DEP
'I went into the water being naked'

pʰiˀa yehatat, hiničxeˀkut, ˀičiˀta, puqʰela ˀitxaˀmat
pʰiˀa *y-ehata-t* *h-iničxeˀku-t* *ˀ-ičiˀta* *puqʰela* *ˀ-itxaˀ-ma-t*
bacon 1SG.A-have-ASP 3-smell-ASP 1SG.A-catch basket 1SG.A-put-?-ASP
'I had grease, they smelled it, I caught them, I put them in a basket'

ˀaqʰa ˀelohqʰut ˀixaˀyta, memat txolop ˀiwinqʰutta
ˀaqʰa *ˀeloh-qʰut* *ˀ-ixaˀy-ta* *memat* *txol-op* *ˀ-iwin-qʰu-t-ta*
water hot-liquid 1SG.A-make-ASP alive crawfish-DEF 1SG.A-dump-liquid-DER
'I made the water hot, I dumped them alive, the crawfish, immersingly'

hikuytam hupʰo ˀaqʰuye hikuyta, hoputeˀw ˀama
h-ikuytam *hupʰo* *ˀaqʰuye* *h-ikuyta* *hopu-teˀw* *ˀama*
3-taste.good leg tail 3-taste.good mine-DER land
'The leg tails taste good, they taste good, they mined the land.'

txol makumčaxat q'ehčaxat
txol *makum-čaxa-t* *q'e-h-čaxa-t*
crawfish perish-COMP-ASP die-3-COMP-ASP
'All crawfish perished all, they died all'

In example 9 there are four important points in the narrative: (1) at some point in time there were many crawfish, (2) they were easy to catch with bacon, (3) they taste good, and (4) now they are all gone. All four points are repeated at least once.

13.2 Discourse structure in areal-typological perspective

The same rhetorical style that occurs in Chimariko is also found in many other American indigenous languages, such as Central Pomo, Haida, Kwakiutl, Chinook, and many others (Mithun 1992; Hymes 1981, 2003). Furthermore, it is also apparent in Wintu and Wiyot. In Central Pomo, this repetitive pattern has been described in terms of intonation and the discourse as a whole (Mithun 1992, 2000). Mithun shows how the couplet structure in Central Pomo is used for the main points in a narrative and important points in conversation. Following Mithun (2000:8) 'the information is often presented in a series of statements: a basic clause followed by successive elaborations'. Hymes (1981, 2003) examines the organization of entire narratives in various Native American languages in terms of sequences and units. He concludes that the equivalent units marked by repetition and parallelism form part of a larger structure involving verses, stanzas, and scenes. Overall, repetitive pattern in oral narratives are very common. They occur in many different languages and cultures with an oral tradition.

14. SUMMARY: CHIMARIKO IN AREAL-TYPOLOGICAL PERSPECTIVE

There are various factors that make languages the same or different: the physiological properties of humans, the need to communicate and to convey messages, genetic affiliation, and language contact, among others. Often, it is difficult to distinguish shared linguistic features attributed to genetic affiliation from those attributed to language contact, in particular if there is intense contact for centuries, and if there are no written records, as with Chimariko. The present work is intended to address this and other issues related to language contact by identifying similarities to neighboring languages attributed to language contact rather than to genetic affiliation. In addition, this work is meant to show how the linguistic structures and phenomena found in Chimariko relate to those in other languages of the world. The following paragraphs include a typological profile of Chimariko with a special emphasis on typological highlights and a summary and discussion of similarities to neighboring languages that may be due to the intense and extended language contact.

The typological profile of Chimariko comprises the following features: (1) head-marking, (2) mainly suffixes, (3) mostly agglutinating, (4) synthetic to polysynthetic, (5) verb-final word order, and (6) no preference in the order of nominal elements. In general, as with many other Native American languages, Chimariko packages a large amount of information in its verbs. In Chimariko core arguments are obligatorily marked on the verb (see 4.6, 8.1.1, and 9.2) and possession is marked on the possessed (see 4.1 and 5.1.1). Case-marking occurs with instruments and companions (see 5.1.4). Other nominal syntactic relations are unmarked (see 5.1.4). With regard to fusion, Chimariko appears to be mostly agglutinating. In general, word-internal morpheme boundaries are easily recognizable (see 3). Roots and affixes are clearly separable with one exception: most verb roots have an initial vowel which sometimes fuses with certain prefixes (see 3.1 and 3.2). However, fusion may be harder to detect given the nature of the data. It could occur in the tense-aspect marking which is not fully understood at this point (see 8.1.2). Chimariko is mainly suffixing, but personal pronouns and possessors are either prefixed or suffixed (see 3.1, 5.1.1, and 8.1.1). In terms of synthesis, Chimariko is synthetic to polysynthetic. There are many different verbal affixes, and verbs are often composed of three or more morphemes (see chapter 8). Yet sometimes, only two or three morphemes occur in one verb, and there are numerous mono-morphemic words. As for basic word order, Chimariko seems to be verb final, though the limited amount and kind of data does not yield a clear picture (see 9.1). With regard to the order of nominal elements within a noun phrase, the modifier either precedes or follows the modified with no apparent preference or restrictions (see 9.1).

Chimariko exhibits a number of interesting typological features. A typologically uncommon feature is the complex system of argument marking based on agents and patients, as well as a hierarchy favoring speech act participants, i.e. first and second persons, over third persons (see 9.2). Both, agentive and hierarchical argument systems, are rare in the world's languages and have strong areal distributions (Mithun, 2008, in press). Similar systems also occur in other Northern California languages, such as Hupa, Shasta, Karuk, Yurok, Wiyot, and Yana.

Larger structures and clause combining strategies also show some typologically striking properties. Alternations in argument structure, i.e. changes in the relationship between the predicate and its arguments, comparable to passives in other languages, shape argument structure only semantically without having a syntactic impact (see 9.2.4). They are achieved through verbal derivational affixes (see 8.2). Another striking feature is the near absence of clause combining syntax. The semantic concepts expressed as complements in some languages are coded using one of four different strategies: (1) separate sentences with no linking morphology, (2) verbal morphology, (3) attitude words, and (4) *imiʔna* 'to want' with a complement clause (see 12.2). Clause combining syntax occurs with relative clauses and some adverbial clauses (see 12.3 and 12.4). Relative clauses are internally headed or headless and show a special verb form with a nominalizing suffix (see 12.3).

The textual material studied exhibits a special style with many word and clausal repetitions, whereby a basic statement is followed by successive elaborations. It seems likely that such elaborations were linked intonationally to the basic clause. However, while intonation may have played a role in discourse structure, clause combining, and elsewhere in the language, it can not be examined here due to the lack of sound recordings of connected speech.

While Chimariko shows many typologically striking features, it also shares many grammatical traits with neighboring languages. Areally, Chimariko is situated within the Northern California linguistic area along with the Hupa, Shasta, Wintu, and others. Northern California is characterized by great genetic diversity: there are twenty language families and several linguistic isolates with no known related languages represented. Prior to European contact, many small groups speaking different languages lived here for centuries in close contact with each other through trade and intermarriage, suggesting a considerable amount of bilingualism and multilingualism. While the relationships between immediate neighbors were intimate, contact with distant groups was practically nonexistent. This fact explains why Chimariko shares more traits with its immediate neighbors Wintu and Shasta than with the more distant neighbors to the east and west.

Genetically, Chimariko is considered by some linguists to be a Hokan language, grouped with its northern neighbor Shasta. However, the long history of language contact, multilingualism, and intermarriage in California makes it difficult to distinguish distant genetic relationship from ancient language contact. Following a subdivision of Hokan into Northern Hokan (a) Karuk, Chimariko, and Shasta, (b) Yana, and (c) Pomoan, Chimariko is more closely related to Shasta and Karuk than to other languages within the Hokan stock. Shasta, however, is also an immediate neighbor of Chimariko, and effects of language contact are likely to occur. While there are many striking similarities between Chimariko and Shasta in terms of phonology and grammatical structure, less phonological convergence is apparent between Chimariko and Karuk. This is probably due to the close contact between immediate neighbors in the area, i.e. Chimariko and Shasta, and the lack of contact between more distant groups, i.e. Chimariko and Karuk.

Of Chimariko's close neighbors, Hupa shares the fewest features with Chimariko. The Chimariko are said to have been tributary to the larger and more powerful Hupa at the time of European contact in the early nineteenth century (Powers 1877). This relationship could have affected the outcome of the language contact process. It would be expected that Chimariko adopted more Hupa features than the reverse; but no evidence for such an outcome has been found. This may be due to major structural differences between the two languages. Of Chimariko's close neighbors, Hupa is structurally most different in that it is highly polysynthetic and predominantly prefixing. Wintu and Shasta are much like Chimariko in that they are synthetic to polysynthetic, and, contrary to Hupa, they are predominantly suffixing. Although Wintu and Shasta share these features with Chimariko, they differ in other grammatical traits. Wintu has a nominal case system, and both Wintu and Shasta encode possession with a morpheme on the possessor, unlike Chimariko. While the languages diverge in some grammatical traits they also converge in others.

Contrary to previous studies (Conathan 2005) this work shows that there is phonological convergence in Northern California, i.e. the sound inventories of close neighbors are much alike. Phonological features, such as large consonant inventories with three series of stops, plain, aspirated, and glottalized, show strong areal distributions as a result of language contact. Syllable structure and phonotactic restrictions, such as the lack of onsetless syllables, and stress systems are equally shared among the different languages. Other common areal features include: a) a distinction between alienable and inalienable possession, b) emphatic, locative, and instrumental affixes on nouns, c) pronominal dual forms, d) pronominal, directional, and instrumental affixes on verbs, and e) reduplication and noun incorporation as word formation processes. These shared traits all occur in genetically unrelated languages from four major language families and stocks: Penutian, Athabaskan, Algic, and Hokan. The following paragraphs summarize the main findings of the areal comparisons conducted for each chapter of this grammar including an overall assessment of the similarities.

Many of the phonological traits found in Chimariko also occur in other languages of the area, in particular in its close neighbors (see 2.5). They include: an aspirated stop series, the presence of the back velar *q*, and the lack of obstruent voicing. The phoneme inventories are largest in and around Chimariko and smaller to the west and east of its territory. In general, traits are concentrated in contiguous areas. While certain Chimariko traits are not shared with Shasta, such as a large phoneme inventory, the presence of the back velar *q*, and the lack of gemination, these are shared with its direct neighbors to the west, hence still forming a contiguous area. Overall, Chimariko patterns more like Wintu and Hupa in terms of its phonology and less like Shasta. An areally unique trait of Chimariko is the presence of retroflex apicals. This trait is common in Central California, but is generally absent in Northern California. Syllable structure and phonotactic restrictions are shared by most languages of the area. Again Shasta patterns differently from Chimariko, Wintu, and Hupa in that it allows complex onsets and codas. Only very few complex onsets and codas are possible in Chimariko.

Stress systems show many similarities in the languages of Northern California (see 2.5). Immediate neighbors of Chimariko: Hupa, Shasta, and Wintu, all show weight-sensitive stress systems. While their weight hierarchies are slightly different, all have CVV as their heaviest syllable. Given that stress is easily transferred through language contact, it is likely that the languages in Northern California have shifted their stress patterns as a result of multilingualism in the area. For Chimariko it can be speculated that vowel length on stressed syllables was developing as a contact phenomenon, given the weight-sensitive stress systems of neighboring languages with CVV as the heaviest syllable type.

Morphophonemic processes are generally very language-specific. Therefore, no areal features have been identified (see 3.4). However, processes which are similar in general though different in detail are found in many Northern California languages. For the most part, these are cross-linguistically very common processes, such as vowel elision due to VV sequences at morpheme boundaries or consonant loss to avoid impermissible consonant clusters. As with morphophonemics, there are no surprising similarities with word classes (see 4.9).

Nominal morphology exhibits several similarities between Chimariko and its close neighbors: Wintu, Shasta, and Hupa (see 5.5). In all four languages suffixing is far more frequent than prefixing. However, this is not surprising since it is a general pattern found in the world's languages (Mithun 2003). The main difference among the four languages is that Wintu has a nominal case system. As a result, possession in Wintu is marked on the possessor with a genitive suffix. Although Shasta does not have a case system as Wintu does, possession is marked in a very similar way in both languages: a suffix on the possessor and independent pronouns. Hence, both languages mark possession on the dependent, contrary to Chimariko and Hupa which also show many similarities. Both mark possession on the possessed and show an alienable/inalienable distinction, a common feature in California according to Sherzer (1976b:118-9). Such a distinction also occurs in Wintu. While in Chimariko core arguments are unmarked for case, two kinds of arguments exhibit case marking: instruments and companions. It is possible that these case markings have developed as a result of language contact with Wintu. However, the forms of the suffixes show no similarities to the Wintu forms. The case suffix marking accompaniment is very similar to the dual suffix on pronouns and reciprocal suffix on verbs. Hence, it may have developed from the dual. Instrumental suffixes on nouns are very common in Northern California. They also occur in Shasta. Locative suffixes on nouns are equally common and occur in all four languages. In Chimariko, they are not considered case markings as they are not obligatory.

Pronominal morphology exhibits several similarities, as well as differences, between Chimariko and its neighbors (see 6.5). In addition to a singular-plural distinction, Chimariko and Wintu have a pronominal dual, which is absent in Shasta and Hupa. Wintu and Shasta have independent possessive pronouns which do not occur in Chimariko and Hupa. A common trait among all four languages is having equal or similar shapes for demonstratives and third person pronouns. This is a very common trait in California and along the entire Pacific Coast (Dryer et al. 2004), though not uncommon elsewhere in the world.

The languages of Northern California all have very elaborate inflectional and derivational verb morphologies distinguishing similar sets of categories (see 8.3). Inflectional categories include: pronominal reference, tense, aspect, and modal affixes. Derivational categories include: reduplication, noun incorporation, reflexives, reciprocals, causatives, and directional affixes, among others. While the set of categories distinguished is similar, there are many differences in the sub-categories and actual functions and uses of the affixes, as well as in the position with regard to the verb stem, i.e. prefixing or suffixing. Typologically uncommon features, such as agent-patient distinctions and person hierarchies occur in many languages of the area. Chimariko, Hupa, and Shasta all show person hierarchies, but only Chimariko distinguishes agents and patients. The pronominal affixes are either prefixed or suffixed in Chimariko and Shasta, while only suffixes occur in Wintu and only prefixes in Hupa. Tense, aspect, and modal categories are all encoded in verbal affixes. In general, in Chimariko and Wintu these are suffixes, while in Hupa and Shasta they are prefixes. Most languages encode tense, aspect, and mood in verbal suffixes. However, these categories are expressed in verbal prefixes or preverbal elements only in four Northern California languages: Hupa, Shasta, Yurok, and Wiyot, together forming a geographically contiguous area. Overall, the inflectional systems in the languages of Northern California fall into similar categories. Nevertheless, they vary in their affixing pattern and fine details. Similarly, derivational processes creating new verb stems are much alike across Northern California. Reduplication occurs in Chimariko, Wintu, and Shasta, but not in Hupa. This is not surprising, as this process does not occur in Athabaskan languages. A less common word formation process is noun incorporation. It has a random distribution in California and does not seem to have been a productive process at the time of data collection for several languages (Sherzer 1976b). Only very few examples are attested in Chimariko. Directional and instrumental affixes on verbs are very common in California. With regard to these affixes, Chimariko and Shasta differ greatly from Hupa and Wintu. Hupa and Wintu lack instrumental affixes, and they have directional prefixes rather than suffixes, as occur in Chimariko and Shasta.

No striking cross-linguistic similarities or differences have been found among syntactic structures and patterns (see 9.8). Transitivizing and detransitivizing mechanims, such as applicatives, causatives, reflexives, reciprocals, and passive-like constructions, are encoded through verbal derivational affixes in Wintu, Shasta, Hupa, and in other languages of the area. Verbs are generally independent and can form clauses by themselves.

The question formation strategies in the languages of Northern California show similarities and differences (10.4). There are two main differences among the languages: (1) the type of the interrogative marker, i.e. prefix, suffix, or particle, and (2) the presence or absence of the interrogative marker in question-word questions. Chimariko and Wintu form yes/no questions with an interrogative suffix, while Hupa has a clause-final particle. Wintu has an interrogative prefix, which is typologically uncommon. Chimariko, Wintu, and Shasta, include an interrogative marker in their question-word questions, while Hupa does not. Overall, Chimariko and Wintu show most similarities in their question formation strategies.

The negation strategies in the languages of Northern California are very similar and include negative suffixes and negative adverbs or particles that precede the predicate (see 11.7). Noticeable is the position of the negative morpheme either before or after the negated constituent in geographically contiguous areas. In Chimariko and two of it neighbors to the east, Wintu and Maidu, the negative morpheme is suffixed, while in the languages to the north and west of Chimariko, i.e. Shasta, Hupa, Yurok, Wiyot, and Karok, the negative morpheme occurs preverbally.

Clause combining strategies are not described in great detail in the grammars of Northern California languages. However, most languages have a set of clause connectives occurring at the beginning or at the end of clauses. Another similarity is the formation of adverbial clauses through verbal suffixes marking dependency. They occur in Chimariko, Wintu, and Hupa.

The discourse style that occurs in Chimariko narratives is also found in many other American indigenous languages, such as Central Pomo, Haida, Kwakiutl, Chinook, and others (Mithun 1992; Hymes 1981, 2003). A repetitive pattern in oral narratives is very common and occurs in many different languages and cultures with an oral tradition.

To conclude, similarities and language contact phenomena between Chimariko and other Northern California languages include: phoneme inventories, stress systems, reduplication, the distinction between alienable and inalienable possession, noun incorporation, directional and instrumental suffixes on verbs, and agentive and/or hierarchical person marking, among others. The main similarities between Chimariko and its close neighbors, Shasta, Wintu, and Hupa are summarized in Table 1.

Table 1: Similarities between Chimariko and its close neighbors and Karuk

Feature	Chimariko	Shasta	Wintu	Hupa	Karuk
Large consonant inventory (30 or more)	x		x	x	
Aspirated stops	x		x	x	
Back velar *q*	x		x	x	
Complex onsets	x (limited)	x			x (limited)
Complex codas	x (limited)	x		x (limited)	
Vowel assimilation across affixes	x	x	x		x
Nominal case	x (limited)		x		
Possession on possessed	x			x	x
Possessive prefixes	x			x	x
Possessive suffixes	x	x	x		
Definiteness on nouns	x	x	x		
Pronominal dual	x		x		x
Pronominal prefixes	x	x		x	x
Pronominal suffixes	x	x	x		
Person hierarchy	x	x		x	x
Tense suffixes	x		x		x
Aspect suffixes	x	x	x		x
Mood suffixes	x		x		x
Reduplication	x	x	x		x
Directional suffixes	x	x			x
Instrumental prefixes	x	x			x
Negative morpheme after negated constituent	x		x		
Interrogative verb-final suffix	x		x		
Question word AND interrogative affix	x	x	x		
Quinary Numeral System	x	x			x

From Table 1 it is apparent that Chimariko shares more features, a total of sixteen out of twenty-five, with its unrelated neighbour Wintu than with Shasta which, according to some linguists, is related to Chimariko. Chimariko and Shasta share fourteen out of twenty-five features, the same number of features that Chimariko shares with its distant neighbour Karuk. All three, Chimariko, Shasta, and Karuk, are identified by some linguists as being Hokan. Hokan is a linguistic stock based on a series of often problematic hypotheses about distant genetic relationship (see 1.2). While this work is not intended to prove or disprove a genetic relationship, it may serve as a starting point for future Hokan studies.

Table 1 also shows that Chimariko shares the fewest features with Hupa. This is not surprising, given that Hupa is structurally most different. While there seem to be no restrictions as to what can be borrowed, it appears that great structural divergence between two languages, as with Chimariko and Hupa, may slow down the process of structural borrowing. Nevertheless, it may have only a minor impact on lexical borrowing.

In examining possible language contact features, this work has focused on structural borrowing rather than on lexical borrowing. It is likely that lexical borrowing was pervasive and that some words, such as *mušmuš* 'bull' (see 5.2.3), are originally from a more distant languages, but have entered the language through a close neighbor.

Furthermore, language attrition and contact with English need to be considered when examining the Chimariko data. Major structural borrowing from English is not expected due to the relatively recent contact and forced assimilation. Lexical borrowing, however, occurs occasionally, as in the following example.

1. English borrowing (Grekoff 012.014)

   hatqawukta šəvəlop
   h-atqa-wu-k-ta **šəvəl**-*op*
   3-take.away-RET-PST-DER shovel-DEF
   'They took the shovel away from him'

To conclude, comparing grammatical features of Chimariko to those of its neighbors has yielded results similar to those of Haas (1976), supporting her statement that 'most languages bear more resemblance to their adjacent unrelated neighbors than they do to their congeners' (1976:353). This work has shown that linguistic traits are often concentrated in geographically contiguous areas even if the languages are genetically unrelated.

APPENDICES

i. Narratives

i.i Introduction to the narratives

The following corpus includes eleven narratives: two longer stories and nine shorter texts. The narratives comprise personal stories heard or experienced by Sally Noble, Harrington's main consultant, as well as texts with general information, such as how to catch and prepare crawfish. While nine of the narratives stem directly from Harrington's field notes, the remaining two are drawn from Grekoff's notes.

The narratives are broken down into lines for easy reading and glossing. The division into lines does not reflect the spacing in the original source. The lines are randomly grouped together as they best fit the page. However, text separation by punctuation in the original source has been considered for the division into lines. Couplets are not explicitly grouped together nor marked in this corpus.

The translations were provided by one of the two sources: Harrington or Grekoff. Where a translation was missing or incomplete in the sources, it has been provided by the author. The added translations appear in square brackets. Glossing is the sole responsibility of the author. A few unclear glosses are indicated by question marks.

i.ii Fugitives at Burnt Ranch (Source: Harrington 021-0007)

1. *č'imar xotai heṭaheskut uwatkut,*
č'imar xotai h-eṭahe-sku-t uwa-tku-t
man three 3-run.away-DIR-ASP go-DIR-ASP
'Three men came as fugitives'

2. *heṭaheskut č'utamdače*
h-eṭahe-sku-t č'utamdače
run.away-DIR-ASP Burnt Ranch
'They ran away to Burnt Ranch'

3. *kimot ˀuˀir asunda, čʰakʰo, heṭaheshutaˀa sunda*
kimot ˀuˀir asu-nda čʰ-akʰo h-eṭahe-shu-taˀa su-nda
these stranger be-ASP IMP.PL-kill 3-run.away-DIR-? be-ASP
'These are strangers, kill them, they are running away'

4. *čʰaxakʰona, wečʰup čʰaxakʰona, ˀama xoliˀyu*
čʰa-x-akʰo-na wečʰup čʰa-x-akʰo-na ˀama xoliˀ-yu
IMP.PL-NEG-kill-NEG some IMP.PL-NEG-kill-NEG country bad-ADM
'Don't kill them, some said don't kill them, lest it spoil the country'

5. *yaxakʰonaxanˀi, makʰotaxantinda, k'otnihu*
ya-x-akʰo-na-xan-ˀi m-akʰo-ta-xan-tinda k'otnihu
1PL.A-NEG-kill-NEG-FUT-ASP 2SG-kill-DER-FUT-PROG run.away
'We won't kill them, he is going to kill you, run away'

6. *ˀirˀir musunda mamot, k'otnihu*

ˀirˀir	*m-usu-nda*	*mamot*	*k'ot-ni-hu*
stranger	2SG-be-ASP	2SG	run.away-IMP.SG-CONT

'You are a stranger, run away'

7. *nuwawum, xukeenatinda*

n-uwa-wu-m	*x-ukee-na-tinda*
IMP.SG-go-RET-DIR	NEG-understand-NEG-PROG

'Go home, you don't understand'

8. *hiṭawiˀmut, hičʰemda, hiṭamdu*

h-iṭa-wiˀmu-t	*h-ičʰe-mda*	*h-iṭa-mdu*
3-hand-take-ASP	3-say-PROG	POSS-hand-INST

'He took his hand telling him (to go home), he led him by the hand'

9. *nuwawum kella, č'imar epatteˀw,*

n-uwa-wu-m	*kella*	*č'imar*	*epat-teˀw*
IMP.SG-go-RET-DIR	that.way	person	sit-DER

'You go home that way (gesturing with lips)'

10. *qʰomal uwamaˀ č'imarop*

qʰomal	*uwa-m-aˀ*	*č'imar-op*
where	go-DIR-Q	person-DEF

'Where did that man go to?'

11. *ˀuˀir asunda, xukeenanda*

ˀuˀir	*asu-nda*	*x-ukee-na-nda*
stranger	be-ASP	NEG-understand-NEG-ASP

'He is a stranger, he doesn't understand'

12. *qʰoqʰ uwadokta, č'imara, qʰomall akʰodeˀ*

qʰoqʰ	*uwa-do-kta*	*č'imar-a*	*qʰomall*	*akʰo-de-ˀ*
two	go-?-DIR	man-?	where	kill-DER-Q

'Two got back here home, where did they kill him?'

13. *qʰomalla qʰuktaˀ, q'owan, ˀawaktahinta*

qʰomalla	*qʰu-kta-ˀ*	*q'owan*	*ˀ-awa-kta-hinta*
where	2PL-DIR-Q	?	1SG.A-go-DIR-PROG

'Where have you been?, just taking a walk'

14. *yaxamamnan, p'un ˀiṭilla ˀuleeda himamda*

ya-x-amam-na-n	*p'un*	*ˀiṭi-lla*	*ˀuleeda*	*h-imam-da*
1PL.A-NEG-see-NEG-ASP	one	man-DIM	sibling	3-see-ASP

'We didn't see it, a boy saw it'

15. *hek'omatta, hakʰodeˀ, č'imarop, xawiyop hakʰodeˀn*
h-ek'o-ma-tta h-akʰo-deˀ č'imar-op xawiy-op h-akʰo-deˀ-n
3-say-?-DER 3-kill-ASP person-DEF Redwood.Indian-DEF 3-kill-DER-ASP
'The boy told (it), they killed the boy, the people, the Indians killed him'

16. *xoliˀtaˀn hakʰot, xawiy asunda, xukeenat*
xoliˀ-taˀn h-akʰo-t xawiy asu-nda x-ukee-na-t
bad-INF 3-kill-ASP Redwood.Indian be-ASP NEG-understand-NEG-ASP
'It is not right to kill him, he was a Redwood Indian, he didn't understand'

17. *načʰidot yakʰorot xukeenat, qʰakʰodaˀn xoliˀtaˀn*
načʰidot y-akʰo-rot x-ukee-na-t qʰ-akʰo-daˀn xoliˀ-taˀn
1PL 1PL.A-kill-DEP NEG-understand-NEG-ASP 2PL-kill-INF bad-INF
'We killed him, he didn't understand, you killed him, it is not right'

18. *xoliˀtaˀn, qʰakʰot, hetaxawi uwatkukon*
xoliˀ-taˀn qʰa-kʰo-t heta-xawi uwa-tku-kon
bad-INF 2PL-kill-ASP many-Redwood.Indians go-DIR-FUT
'It is not right, you killed him, lots of Redwood Indians will come'

19. *pʰaˀasitaˀče yekʰotinda, čʰaxaduˀxakon, wisseeda čʰumčaxa*
pʰaˀa-sitaˀče y-ekʰo-tinda čʰa-xaduˀx-akon wisseeda čʰu-m-čaxa
that-why 1SG.A-kill-PROG 1PL.P-?-FUT downstream IMP.PL-DIR-COMP
'That's why I killed him, they will kill us, you all move down to Billy Noble's place'

20. *čʰumeečoda, xoliˀ, qʰudukmuda'n, pačʰaˀa qʰuduqʰmuˀ*
čʰ-umeečo-da xoliˀ qʰ-udukmu-da'n pačʰaˀa qʰ-uduqʰmu-ˀ
IMP-?-DER bad 2PL-?-INF what 2PL-?-Q
'You watch around, circle round, what have you been doing?'

21. *hisiˀmedaˀ, maik isiˀmedaˀ, ˀama xoliˀxanan*
hisiˀ-me-daˀ maik isiˀ-me-daˀ ˀama xoliˀ-xana-n
good-?-PST ? good-?-PST country bad-FUT-ASP
'Everything is all right down there now, it will be all right, the country will be all bad'

i.iii Woman Wanders (Source: Harrington 021-0031)

1. *hišehekteˀw, hexačideˀw, hišehet, k'oṭihut*
h-išehek-teˀw h-exači-deˀw h-išehe-t k'oṭi-hu-t
3-take.along-DER 3-steal-DER 3-take.along-ASP run.away-CONT-ASP
'Bad Indians took the woman along, they stole her, they took her along, she ran away'

2. *hamadeˀw imedašur, hiwot, haˀat pimda, hixodat,*
h-ama-deˀw imedašur h-iwo-t haˀat pim-da h-ixoda-t
3-eat-DER morning 3-sit.down-ASP ? ?-ASP 3-watch-ASP
'They were eating breakfast, she sat down, a man came out, he saw her'

3. *qʰomall iṭanku muwakaˀ, xukeenan*
qʰomal iṭan-ku m-uwa-k-aˀ x-ukee-na-n
where ?-DIR 2SG-go-DIR-Q NEG-know-NEG-ASP
'Where do you come from? She did not know'

4. *himelušušun, xukeenan*
hime-lušušu-n xu-kee-na-n
head-shake-ASP NEG-know-NEG-ASP
'She shook her head, she did not know'

5. *ˀuluidaˀe nahak ˀičinšolla, pʰuncar ˀimatni, hamew nawu*
ˀuluida-ˀe n-ahak ˀičinšolla pʰuncar ˀ-imat-ni hamew n-awu
sister-POSS IMP.SG-bring dress woman 1SG.A-find-ASP food IMP.SG-give
'My sister, bring me a dress, I have found a woman, give her food'

6. *naˀahunmu ˀawakunoi, haˀat pimda ˀiṭirop,*
n-aˀa-hun-mu ˀawa-kunoi h-aˀa-tpi-m-da ˀiṭir-op
IMP.SG-?-CONT-DIR house-inside 3-?-DIR-DIR-ASP man-DEF
'Take her in the house, the man came out (and found her)'

7. *pʰuncar isik ˀimatni*
pʰuncar isik ˀ-imat-ni
woman pretty 1SG.A-find-ASP
'I found a pretty woman'

8. *yaxodayex, č'imarot uwaktut, hixodateˀw pʰuncarot*
ya-xoda-yex č'imar-ot uwa-ktu-t h-ixoda-teˀw pʰuncar-ot
1PL.A-watch-? person-DEF go-DIR-ASP 3-watch-DER woman-DEF
'Let us go and see her, lots of people came and looked at her'

9. *'hisikni pʰuncar', xukeenan hikoˀdaˀ*
'h-isik-ni pʰuncar' x-ukee-na-n h-ikoˀ-daˀ
3-pretty-ASP woman NEG-know-NEG-ASP 3-talk-PST
'"Pretty woman", she couldn't talk'

10. *hisiˀta pʰuncarop, hamew it exaˀita, hisiˀta*
hisiˀta pʰuncar-op hamew it exaˀi-ta hisiˀta
good woman-DEF food lots cause-DER good
'The new woman, cooked lots of food'

11. *hiwot, hamew it hihailukla*
h-iwo-t hamew it hihailukla
3-sit.down-ASP food lots ?
'She stayed, she got lots of food outside'

12. *q'ehexawinanda, ˀamaida umusunda*
q'e-he-x-awi-na-nda ˀama-ida umu-su-nda
?-3-NEG-afraid-NEG-ASP country-POSS like-be-ASP
'She was not afraid, it was like her country'

13. *hikeyinda, ˀaqʰa sinda, hikeexananda č'imar*
h-ikey-inda ˀaqʰa si-nda h-ikee-xana-nda č'imar
3-understand-PROG water say-ASP 3-understand-FUT-PROG person
'She understood now, she knew what to call water, she was understanding the people'

14. *ˀamanilla ikeeda hik'ot, hošem ik'ot*
ˀama-ni-lla ikee-da h-ik'o-t hošem ik'o-t
country-LOC-DEP understand-ASP 3-talk-ASP good talk-ASP
'She understood it now, she talked good'

15. *ˀahanmačin xotai iwolla ošem hik'onda,*
ˀahanmačin xotai iwolla ošem h-ik'o-nda
year three sit-DEP good 3-talk-ASP
'In three years she talked good.'

16. *xawi čʰušehektasun, sinda*
xawi čʰ-ušehe-k-tasun si-nda
Redwood.Indians 1SG.P-take.along-DIR-PST say-ASP
"The bad Indians took me to this country", the woman said'

17. *č'imar it akʰoteˀn*
č'imar it akʰo-teˀ-n
person lots kill-DER-ASP
'The bad Indians killed lots of people'

18. *noˀot čʰušehemdeˀwšur hit akʰodeˀw č'imara*
noˀot čʰ-ušehe-m-deˀw-šur hit akʰo-deˀw č'imar-a
1SG 1SG.P-take-DIR-DER-formerly many kill-DER person-?
'They took me off my folks, [they killed many people]'

19. *noˀot čušehemdeˀw k'oṭihut*
noˀot č-ušehe-m-deˀw k'oṭi-hu-t
1SG 1SG.P-take-DIR-DER run.away-CONT-ASP
'They took me off, I fled'

20. *ˀawa hida imamda ˀamaq'eˀta*
ˀawa hida i-mam-da ˀama-q'e-ˀ-ta
house lots 1SG.A-see-ASP country-die-1SG.A-ASP
'I saw lots of houses, I will die in this country'

21. *čitxa lulihčaxat q'eˀxanan, ˀamaq'eˀni,*
čitxa lul-ih-čaxa-t q'e-ˀ-xana-n ˀama-q'e-ˀ-ni
blanket drop-1SG.A-COMP-ASP die-1SG.A-FUT-ASP country-die-1SG.A-ASP
'I lost all my blankets, I am going to die, [I will die in this country]'

22. *nunuˀ yuwam, nunuˀ čʰak'oxan,*
nunuˀ y-uwa-m nunuˀ čʰa-k'o-xan
? 1SG.A-go-DIR ? 1PL.P-talk-FUT
'I am going to go, [we are going to talk]'

23. *ˀamaq'eˀni, hisiˀta č'imara, masunu ˀiwoxanˀi, hisikinda*
ˀama-q'e-ˀ-ni hisiˀta č'imar-a masunu ˀ-iwo-xan-ˀi hisik-inda
land-die-1SG.A-ASP good person-? always 1SG.A-stay-FUT-ASP good-PROG
'[I will die here, the people are good], I am going to live here all the time'

24. *č'imarot hisikinda, hisikni č'imara nunuˀ,*
č'imar-ot hisik-inda hisik-ni č'imar-a nunuˀ
person-DEF good-PROG good-ASP person-? ?
'Good folks, [the people are good]'

25. *ˀiwo hita č'awund amew,*
ˀ-iwo hita čʰ-awu-nd amew
1SG-A-stay lots 1SG.P-give-ASP food
'I'll stay here, they gave me[lots of] food'

26. *ˀawaˀi sumusunda, nunuˀ ˀiwoxan,*
ˀawa-ˀi sumu-su-nda nunuˀ ˀ-iwo-xan
house-POSS like-be-ASP ? 1SG.A-stay-FUT
'It's like my own house, I am going to stay'

27. *hamew ita yeman, hopew*
hamew ita y-ema-n hopew
food lots 1SG.A-eat-ASP acorn-soup
'I eat lots, lots of acorn-soup'

28. *hiwanda, čitx isiˀ isiˀdaˀn, ˀičinšoll isiˀ yoxaˀidaˀn*
h-iwa-nda čitx isiˀ isiˀ-daˀn ˀičinšoll isiˀ y-oxaˀi-daˀn
3-go-ASP blanket good good-INF dress good 1SG.A-make-INF
'[She went, good blanket, it must have been good], I am going to make a good dress'

29. *č'imar heyˀewinda, kumičin čʰuk'oˀnan*
č'imar heyˀew-inda kumičin čʰ-uk'o-ˀna-n
person ?-PROG all 1SG.P-talk-APPL-ASP
'The people are good,they all talk to me good'

30. *ˀimikot sumusut čʰuk'oˀnanda*
ˀimikot sumu-su-t čʰ-uk'o-ˀna-nda
friend like-be-ASP 1SG.P-talk-APPL-PROG
'Like friends, they talk to me,'

31. *ˀamaš hisiˀtinda,hik'otinta č'imariko*
ˀamaš hisiˀ-tinda h-ik'o-tinta č'imariko
country good-PROG 3-talk-PROG Chimariko
'She was o.k., talked Chimariko'

32. *kimot č'imarot niwo sudadinda,*
kimot č'imar-ot n-iwo su-da-dinda
this person-DEF IMP.SG-stay be-?-PROG
'The man told her to stay there'

33. *hisik ik'onda ˀawami sumusudinda, ˀ-imiˀna-n*
hisik ik'o-nda ˀawa-mi sumu-su-dinda ˀimiˀnan
good talk-PROG house-POSS like-be-PROG 1SG.A-want-ASP
'He talked nice, [it's like your house, I like it]'

34. *ˀama ˀimiˀnan, hisikinda, č'imarot niwo, sinda*
ˀama ˀ-imiˀna-n hisik-inda č'imar-ot n-iwo si-nda
country 1SG.A-want-ASP good-PROG person-DEF IMP.SG-stay say-ASP
'[I like this country, the good folks told her to stay]'

35. *qʰosumut naˀiš ˀiwoxandinda, ˀamaš, ˀik'otinda,*
qʰo-sumu-t naˀiš ˀ-iwo-xan-dinda ˀamaš ˀ-ik'o-tinda
2PL-like-ASP but.me 1SG.A-stay-FUT-PROG country 1SG.A-talk-PROG
'[But I am like you], I am going to stay here, [I talk like in this country]'

36. *ˀamaš čʰusiˀtinda ˀik'ot, č'imariko ˀiko'tinda*
ˀamaš čʰ-usiˀ-tinda ˀ-ik'o-t č'imariko ˀ-iko'-tinda
country 1SG.P-good-PROG 1SG.A-talk-ASP Chimariko 1SG.A-talk-PROG
'Now I talk good, [I talk Chimariko]'

37. *noˀot xukeenadinda, ˀikeedinda, ˀiwoxandinda noˀot kimalla*
noˀot x-ukee-na-dinda ˀ-ikee-dinda ˀ-iwo-xan-dinda noˀot kimalla
1SG NEG-know-NEG-PROG 1SG.A-hear-PROG 1SG.A-sit-FUT-PROG 1SG here
'[I don't understand, I understand that I will stay here]'

38. *kumičin č'imar isiˀtinta, ˀimikot sumusut*
kumičin č'imar isiˀ-tinta ˀimikot sumu-su-t
all person good-ASP friend like-be-ASP
'[All people are good, they were] like my friends'

39. *kimot ˀiṭirot č'imar hit, ˀimikot č'imara, ˀiṭixaˀideˀw sumusut*
kimot ˀiṭir-ot č'imar hit ˀimikot č'imar-a ˀiṭixaˀi-deˀw sumu-su-t
this man-DEF person lots friend person-? chief-DER like-be-ASP
'[This man, lots of people, this friend was like a chief]'

40. *masunu ˀiwodinda, č'imar it uwaktat*
masunu ˀ-iwo-dinda č'imar it uwa-kta-t
always 1SG.A-sit.down-ASP person lots go-DIR-ASP
'I am going to stay, [lots of people will come]'

i.iv. Mrs Bussell (Source: Harrington 021-0002)

1. *masunu huwaktanhut šunuhullot,*
masunu h-uwa-kta-nhu-t šunuhull-ot
always 3-go-DIR-CONT-ASP old.woman-DEF
'Mrs. Bussell goes around all the time'

2. *huwaktat masunu šunuhullot pʰaˀmot*
h-uwa-kta-t masunu šunuhull-ot pʰaˀmot
3-go-DIR-ASP always old.woman-DEF that
'She goes around all the time, that old woman'

3. *ˀawaidače xowonat, šičel hiwontat*
ˀawa-ida-če x-owo-na-t šičel h-iwonta-t
home-POSS-LOC NEG-stay-NEG-ASP horse 3-ride-ASP
'She does not stay at home, she goes around on horseback'

4. *huwaktat, ˀiṭi sumusut, hopew ˀičʰuˀnan*
h-uwa-kta-t ˀiṭi sumu-su-t hopew ˀ-ičʰuˀna-n
3-go-DIR-ASP man like-be-ASP acorn.soup 1SG.A-eat-ASP
'She goes around, like a man, I would like to eat acorn soup'

5. *sinda, yuṭiˀi paačʰikun, kimass uwatkun, huwomni welmu*
si-nda yuṭi-ˀi paačʰikun kimass uwa-tku-n h-uwo-m-ni welmu
say-ASP acorn-POSS no.more today go-DIR-ASP 3-go-DIR-ASP quickly
'She says, but my acorns are none, today she came, she went back home at once'

6. *welmu uwomni, hamew xewunan, xok'oˀnanan*
welmu uwo-m-ni hamew x-ewu-na-n x-ok'o-ˀna-na-n
quickly go-DIR-ASP food NEG-give-NEG-ASP NEG-talk-APPL-NEG-ASP
'At once she returned, I did not give her dinner, I did not speak to her'

i.v Hollering at New River (Sources: Harrington 021-0110)

1. *č'imar hepatta čeminčani, ˀakʰa ṭewut*
č'imar h-epat-ta čeminčani ˀakʰa ṭewu-t
people 3-sit-ASP across.the.river water big-ASP
'The people were living on the other side of the river, the water was high.'

2. *k'owin č'imar, kowni mamot nunuˀ, kowmiˀna*
k'ow-in č'imar kow-ni mamot nunuˀ kow-miˀ-na
holler-ASP person holler-IMP 2SG ? holler-?-NEG
'Somebody hollered, you yell (in answer) no, don't yell (another person ev. said)'

3. *himisamdu koowidinda, mamot kowmiˀnat*
himisamdu koowi-dinda mamot kow-miˀ-na-t
devil holler-PROG 2SG holler-?-NEG-ASP
'It is a devil hollering, don't you yell'

4. *kowmilot himisamtu hapukʰeˀxanat, himisamdu k'unoˀop*
kow-mi-lot himisamtu h-apukʰeˀ-xana-t himisamdu k'un=oˀop
holler-POSS-NOM devil 3-steal-FUT-ASP devil NEG=COND
'The devil will steal your voice, if it is not a devil'

5. *ˀap hišektakon, č'imarsoˀop, xošektanakon*
ˀap h-išekta-kon č'imar=soˀop x-ošekta-na-kon
fire 3-make-FUT person=COND NEG-make-NEG-FUT
'He will make a fire, if a person, he does not make a fire'

6. *himisamdu tiˀakon, č'imalsoˀop hišektakon*
himisamdu tiˀa-kon č'imal=soˀop h- išekta-kon
devil MOD-FUT Indian=COND 3-make-FUT
'It is a devil, if it is an Indian he will make a fire'

7. *himedašur ˀapu pačʰigut, ˀawa qʰoqʰ huhooidat*
himedašur ˀapu pačʰigut ˀawa qʰoqʰ h-uhooida-t
next.morning fire no.more house two 3-?-ASP
'The next morning there was no fire, there were two houses here too'

8. *ˀapu xošektanat, himisamdudaˀn sideˀw,*
ˀapu x-ošekta-na-t himisamdu-daˀn si-deˀw
fire NEG-make-NEG-ASP devil-INF say-DER
'He made no fire, it must have been the devil, they said'

9. *himedašur hisumitta pačʰigut ˀapu, himisamdudaˀn sideˀw*
himedašur h-isu-mi-tta pačʰigut ˀapu himisamdu-daˀn si-deˀw
next.morning 3-be-DIR-DER no.more fire devil-INF say-DER
'They looked across the river to this side the next morning, there was no fire, it must have been the devil they said'

Harrington provides additional information for this story: Harrington 021-110: 'Here at New River the New River Indians said that if a person hollers and you don't know who it is you should not answer, for it may be a *himisamdu* 'devil' hollering and if you answer he will steal your voice (inf. word's) and thus cause your death. There were two Indian houses here on this side of the river (Mrs Noble apparently refers to the vicinity of her ranch) and they on the other side and yet in the morning saw no smoke rising from the houses, which proved that it was an Indian devil who had been hollering. The above relates to the Indian 'ranch' that was formerly across here from Mrs. Noble. Is a spring ?? there and one could raise a ??. There were three houses there and on this side of the river by informant's barn but at bank of the river were four houses. These were all big dark houses, Indian houses.'

i.vi Dailey Chased by the Bull (Source:Harrington 020-0586)

1. *ˀisiyakutni haˀačʰakinta mušmuš ṭewu,*
ˀ-isiyakut-ni haˀa-čʰa-kinta mušmuš ṭewu
1SG.A-?-ASP ?-1SG.P-PROG bull big
'I looked back, the bull was taking after me'

2. *čʰuwetxanan čisit ˀimumni*
čʰ-uwet-xana-n či-si-t ˀ-imum-ni
1SG.P-hook-FUT-ASP ?-say-ASP 1SG.A-run-ASP
'I said: he is going to hook me, I ran'

3. *Dailey hik'ot mušmuš čʰuwetni, yečučutapmun, hiṭiytew yuc'uˀtamun*
Dailey h-ik'o-t mušmuš čʰ-uwet-ni y-ečuču-tapmun hiṭiytew y-uc'uˀ-tamun
Dailey 3-say-ASP bull 1SG.P-hook-ASP 1SG.A-?-DIR fence 1SG.A-?-DIR
'Dailey said: the bull hooked me, I dodged, I jumped over the fence'

4. *haˀačʰamta, hipikmut Dailey, hixomet, hiṭiyteˀw hiwetta,*
haˀa-čʰa-m-ta h-ipik-mu-t Dailey h-ixome-t hiṭiyteˀw h-iwet-ta
?-1SG.P-DIR-ASP 3-?-DIR-ASP Dailey 3-?-ASP fence 3-hook-ASP
'He took after me, he took after Dailey, he missed, he hooked the fence'

5. *moxowetnan, p^{h}a^{ʔ}yit p^{h}uncarye,*
mo-x-owet-na-n *p^{h}a^{ʔ}yit* *p^{h}uncar-ye*
2SG-NEG-hook-NEG-ASP thus.say woman-POSS
'He didn't hook you, thus said his wife'

6. *muwette^{ʔ}ta mak^{h}omet,*
m-uwet-te^{ʔ}ta *m-ak^{h}o-me-t*
2SG-hook-COND 2SG-kill-MOD-ASP
'If he had hooked you, he would have killed you right'

7. *moxowetnatinta, hawitomta, č^{h}uwetni sit,*
mo-x-owet-na-tinta *h-awi-tom-ta* *č^{h}-uwet-ni* *si-t*
2SG-NEG-hook-NEG-ASP 3-afraid-?-ASP 1SG.P-hook-ASP say-ASP
'He didn't hook you. He was scared, he hooked me he said'

8. *hawitomta, xowetnat, hek'omatta,*
h-awi-tom-ta *x-owet-na-t* *h-ek'o-ma-tta*
3-afraid-?-ASP NEG-hook-NEG-ASP 3-say-?-DER
'He was scared, but he did not hook him, he told'

9. *p^{h}a^{ʔ}yit č^{h}uwetni sit*
p^{h}a^{ʔ}yit *č^{h}-uwet-ni* *si-t*
thus.say 1SG.P-hook-ASP say-ASP
'Thus he said, he hooked me he said'

10. *xowetnat, p^{h}uncarye p^{h}a^{ʔ}yit*
x-owet-na-t *p^{h}uncar-ye* *p^{h}a^{ʔ}yit*
NEG-hook-NEG-ASP woman-POSS thus.say
'But it did not hook him, so his wife said'

i.vii On Grandmother Getting the Hiccups (Source: Harrington 020-0638)

1. *puneš ṭamma hiput, ha^{ʔ}umkilo^{ʔ}ta sanke^{ʔ}nop*
puneš ṭamma *h-ipu-t* *h-a^{ʔ}umkilo^{ʔ}-ta* *sanke^{ʔ}n-op*
once salmon.meal 3-work-ASP 3-?-ASP basket-DEF
'Once (my grandmother) took a mouthful of salmon-meal, she uncovered it, the pack basket'

2. *hisi^{ʔ}ta hixotat, hipuhunmut, hisekmimi^{ʔ}nat, lečit, lečit,*
hisi^{ʔ}ta *h-ixota-t* *h-ipu-hunmu-t* *h-isekm-imi^{ʔ}na-t* *leči-t* *leči-t*
good 3-look-ASP 3-work-DIR-ASP 3-swallow-want-ASP hiccup-ASP hiccup-ASP
'She looked at it, she put some in her mouth, she tried to swallow it, she hiccoughed'

3. *pačʰaˀ qʰosumsiˀ, pačʰi misekmuˀ,*
pačʰaˀ qʰ-osumsi-ˀ pačʰi m-isekmu-ˀ
what 2PL-do-Q what 2SG-swallow-Q
'What did you all do, what did you swallow'

4. *ˀaqʰa nawum, luˀni, ˀaqʰa luˀit haṭu*
ˀaqʰa n-awum luˀ-ni ˀaqʰa luˀ-it haṭu
water IMP.SG-give drink-IMP.SG water drink-ASP then
'Give her water, drink, she drank then [water]'

5. *hisekmut, hisiˀta haṭu hita hisekmutaˀ*
h-isekmu-t hisiˀ-ta haṭu hita h-isekmu-taˀ
3-swallow-ASP good-ASP then lots 3-swallow-INF
'She swallowed, and then she was all right. I guess she took a little too much.'

6. *ˀisekmu čisit, xakimnan, xotalla hipuhunmateˀqʰ, sit.*
ˀ-isekmu či-si-t x-akim-na-n xotalla h-ipu-hunma-teˀqʰ si-t
1SG.A-swallow ?-say-ASP NEG-?-NEG-ASP a.little 3-work-DIR-ADM say-ASP
'I tried to swallow it, but it wouldn't go down, a little one should put, she said'

7. *mamot maš mipuhunmat hita, mamuš hita mipuhunmuˀ,*
mamot maš m-ipu-hunma-t hita mamuš hita m-ipu-hunmu-ˀ
2SG but 2SG-work-DIR-ASP lots but.you lots 2SG-work-DIR-Q
'But you took lots, but did you take lots'

8. *himow, hita ˀipuhunmut.*
himow hita ˀ-ipu-hunmu-t
yes lots 1SG.A-work-DIR-ASP
'Yes, I took lots.'

i.viii Cutting Finger When Cleaning Salmon (Source: Harrington 020-0469)

1. *čʰuṭa ṭeyta yekʰutni čʰiselimtu, ˀumul yekʰutaˀče*
čʰu-ṭa ṭe-yta y-ekʰut-ni čʰiseli-mtu ˀumul y-ekʰut-aˀče
POSS-hand ?-POSS 1SG.A-cut-ASP knife-INST salmon 1SG.A-cut-ASP
'I cut my thumb with a knife, when I was cleaning a salmon'

2. *ˀumul yekʰutaˀče čʰuṭa ṭeyta yekʰutni,*
ˀumul y-ekʰut-aˀče čʰu-ṭa ṭe-yta y-ekʰut-ni
salmon 1SG.A-cut-ASP POSS-hand ?-POSS 1SG.A-cut-ASP
'Cleaning the salmon I cut my thumb'

3. *masolaˀi hataqmun*
masola-ˀi h-ataqmu-n
daughter-POSS 3-tie-ASP
'My daughter tied it up'

4. *kimaˀase ˀuluytaˀi huwatkun, čʰuxotayetkut, hiwonta xanim*
kimaˀase ˀuluyta-ˀi h-uwa-tku-n čʰ-uxota-ye-tku-t h-iwo-nta xanim
today sister-POSS 3-go-DIR-ASP 1SG.P-look.at-?-DIR-ASP 3-stay-ASP still
'My sister (Martha) came over today, she came to visit me, she is still here'

i.ix Cutting Navel (Source: Grekoff 004.008)

1. *hinoˀyta, hisuma nitix, xalallop, nakʰohoshu k'una*
h-inoˀy-ta hi-suma n-itix xalall-op n-akʰohoshu k'una
3-bear-ASP POSS-face IMP.SG-wipe baby-DEF IMP.SG-cut NEG
'She bears it, wipe his face, (of) that baby, don't cut it'

2. *nunuˀ, ˀaweye hinoˀylala hatu, nihuy, nataqmu honapu,*
nunuˀ ˀaweye h-inoˀy-lala hatu n-ihuy n-ataqmu honapu
? sac 3-bear-? thereupon IMP.SG-wash IMP.SG-tie.up navel
'Let it be, she bears the sac thereupon, wash him, tie the navel'

3. *keˀčʰulala, malla nakʰohoshu, xočʰulla xoliˀtinta, hičʰu nexaˀy*
keˀčʰulala malla n-akʰohoshu xočʰulla xoliˀ-tinta hičʰu n-exaˀy
this.long there IMP.SG-cut short bad-PROG long IMP.SG-cause
'This long (gesture), there you cut it off, it is bad short, make it long'

4. *hisiˀxan, nitxoˀma wenčʰu*
hisiˀ-xan n-itxoˀma wenčʰu
good-FUT IMP.SG-put cradle
'(So) it will be good, put it in the cradle'

i.x Postnatal Seclusion (Source: Grekoff 004.008)

1. *hačiˀnatat ˀeloh, ˀeloh hexaˀyta, p'un hixopektat pʰuncar*
h-ačiˀnata-t ˀeloh ˀeloh h-exaˀy-ta p'un h-ixopekta-t pʰuncar
3-lie-ASP hot hot 3-make-ASP one 3-watch-ASP woman
'She lies on a hot (rock, place), she makes it hot, she watches the woman'

2. *hamew hawut, ˀelohqʰut luˀit, hopew,*
hamew h-awu-t ˀeloh-qʰut luˀ-it hopew
food 3-give-ASP hot-liquid drink-ASP soup
'She gives her food, she drinks a hot liquid, soup'

3. *ˀelohqʰut luˀit, ˀešoh xamanat,*
ˀeloh-qʰut luˀ-it ˀešoh x-ama-na-t
hot-liquid drink-ASP cold NEG-eat-NEG-ASP
'She drinks the hot liquid, she does not eat cold'

4. *ˀelohaikulla hamat, ˀalla p'un, sumusut hiwot, p'olalla*
ˀeloh-aikulla h-ama-t ˀalla p'un sumu-su-t h-iwo-t p'olalla
hot-only 3-eat-ASP month one like-be-ASP 3-stay-ASP alone
'She only eats hot, for one month, she lives like this, alone'

5. *hamat, ˀaˀa xamanat, paačʰikut*
h-ama-t ˀaˀa x-ama-na-t paačʰikut
3-eat-ASP meat NEG-eat-NEG-ASP no.more
'She eats, (but) she does not eat meat, not any more'

i.xi Hopping Game (Source: Harringto 020-0576)

1. *hiceˀpʰ upʰo hucumṭuket čimar xačile hapimtat pʰaˀaasinni*
hiceˀpʰ upʰo h-ucu-m-ṭuket čimar xačile h- apim-ta-t pʰaˀaasinni
? foot 3-hop-DIR-? Indian children 3-play-?-ASP that.way
'They hop on foot, the Indian children play that way'

2. *pusuwa hiṭaˀtamta mall uwatmut hitxan punmutu*
pusuwa h-iṭaˀta-m-ta mall uwa-tmu-t h-itxa-n pun-mutu
stick 3-chop-DIR-ASP there go-DIR-ASP 3- put-ASP one-INST
'They lay down a stick (on the ground), they hop on it'

3. *lawinta wečʰup himantamut, lawinta hupʰu hiceˀpʰemtu*
law-inta wečʰup h-iman-tamu-t law-inta hupʰu hiceˀpʰe-mtu
?-PROG some 3-fall-DIR-ASP ?-PROG foot ?-INST
'Some of them give out and fall down, with one foot they couldn't stand it'

4. *pusuw iṭaˀṭarop malla p'un huwatmut, map'un*
pusuw iṭaˀṭa-rop malla p'un h-uwa-tmu-t map'un
stick chop-DEP there one 3-go-DIR-ASP that.one
'One gets to the stick, he gets to stick'

5. *hucumeˀkʰamta, himantamorop map'un, hiˀamta*
h-ucu-meˀkʰam-ta h-iman-tamo-rop map'un h-iˀam-ta
3-hop-?-ASP 3-fall-DIR-DEP that.one 3-?-DER
'He beats, those fellows that went down got beaten.'

i.xii Crawfish (Source: Harrington 020-0550)

1. *šur txol hetat*
šur txol hetat
formerly crawfish they.were.many
'Formerly there were many crawfish;

2. *ˀaqʰaqʰut hiˀektaˀxat, hetat*
ˀaqʰaqʰut h-iˀekta-ˀxa-t hetat
river 3-swim-COMP-ASP they.were.many
'They swam all in the river, they were many'

3. *hiničxeˀkut, pʰiˀalop, hiničxeˀkut,*
h-iničxeˀku-t pʰiˀal-op h-iničxeˀku-t
3-smell-ASP bacon-DEF 3-smell-ASP
'They smelled it, that bacon, they smelled it'

4. *ˀaqʰa yeˀaqʰtut čitxayamulla,*
ˀaqʰa y-eˀa-qʰtu-t čitxa-yamu-lla
water 1SG.A-?-liquid-ASP blanket-without-DEP
'I went immersingly into the water being naked'

5. *pʰiˀa yehatat, hiničxeˀkut, ˀičiˀta,*
pʰiˀa y-ehata-t h-iničxeˀku-t ˀ-ičiˀ-ta
grease 1SG.A-have-ASP 3-smell-ASP 1SG.A-catch-ASP
'I had grease, they smelled it, I caught them'

6. *puqʰela ˀitxaˀmat, ˀaqʰa ˀelohqʰut ˀixaˀyta*
puqʰela ˀ-itxaˀ-ma-t ˀaqʰa ˀeloh-qʰut ˀ-ixaˀy-ta
basket 1SG.A-put-?-ASP water hot-liquid 1SG.A-cause-ASP
'I put them in a basket, I made the water hot'

7. *memat txolop ˀiwinqʰutta*
memat txol-op ˀ-iwin-qʰut-ta
alive crawfish-DEF 1SG.A-dump.liquid-ASP
'I dumped them alive, the crawfish, immersingly'

8. *hikuytam hupʰo ˀaqʰuye hikuyta,*
h-ikuytam hupʰo ˀaqʰuye h-ikuyta
3-taste.good leg tail 3-taste.good
'The leg tails taste good, they taste good'

9. *hoputeˀw ˀama, txol makumčaxat q'ehčaxat*
hopu-teˀw ˀama txol makum-čaxa-t q'e-h-čaxa-t
mine-DER land crawfish perish-COMP-ASP die-3-COMP-ASP
'They mined the land, all crawfish perished all, they died all'

ii. *Transcript of sound recording*

Smithsonian Institution, National Anthropological Archives
Local number: NAA INV 00001297
#1297 J. P. Harrington Audio Collection, John Paul Marr Collector
CHIMARIKO – Martha Ziegler (13 min.)
Original: Aluminium Disc (digitized from Audio Cassette)

The recording consists of a set of Chimariko words elicited by John Paul Marr from Martha Ziegler. The exact year of the recording is unknown; most likely it occurred in the 1930s or 1940s. Many of the Chimariko words and expressions are repeated upon Marr's request. Given the quality of the recording, it is not possible to offer an accurate narrow phonetic transcription. However, the stress can be identified in most instances. It has been indicated with an accent mark over the vowel in the transcript. Where the recording is unintelligible # indicates a word or syllable. Questionable or unclear parts of the transcript are indicated with a subsequent (?). A time stamp of the recording has been placed every 30-60 seconds throughout the transcript.

Transcript:

	Marr:	Yes, anything.
	Ziegler:	Aha.
	Marr:	Anything that you think it's gonna be valuable.
	Ziegler:	You want to show the word to me?
	Marr:	#.
	Ziegler:	What makes the decision?
	Marr:	Where are we? End of it.
	Ziegler:	You know.
00:49		
	Ziegler:	I just had it on my mind, but, but quickly it dropped.
	Marr:	Pig.
	Ziegler:	Ha?
	Marr:	Pig.
	Ziegler:	*Kálu*, but *šíwi* was some dog.
	Marr:	But pig, pig.
	Ziegler:	*Šinčéla.*
	Marr:	Dog?
	Ziegler:	It's the same, dog.
	Marr:	Say it over.
	Ziegler:	*Šimále*, no, *šinčéla.*
	Marr:	Bear?
01:15		
	Ziegler:	Hm, *šinšémbla.*
	Marr:	Deer.
	Ziegler:	*ˀáˀa.*
	Marr:	Say this one over.
	Ziegler:	*ˀáˀa.*

Marr: Pork?
Ziegler: Hm, hm, hm, *šinčéla*. I mean, they're all called *šinčéla*.
Marr: And what's the word for man?
Ziegler: Hm. Hm, I don't know.

01:42

Ziegler: They would come to my town.
Marr: What's the word for house?
Ziegler: Hm, there is a word, too.
Marr: How about the word for water?
Ziegler: *Áq*^{h}*a*.
Marr: *Aka*?
Ziegler: *Áq*^{h}*a*.
Marr: Say that one over: water.
Ziegler: *Áq*^{h}*a*.
Marr: And, do you know the word for lake?
Ziegler: No, I don't.
Marr: River?
Ziegler: Hm, I don't know. *Áq*^{h}*aq*^{h}*ut. Ax, áq*^{h}*aq*^{h}*ut.*
Marr : Mountain?
Ziegler : Hm. ##. What about the mountain?
Marr: How about the word for tree?
Zieger: That word mountain again will come to me cause I don't hear it so much so long ago.

02:52

Marr: Now say the word for bird?
Ziegler: *Tíṭa*^{ʔ}.
Marr: Say it again. Say that one over.
Ziegler: *Tíṭa*^{ʔ}.
Marr: You know that, the word for grass?
Ziegler: Hm. Do you know what, I can't think.
Marr: How about snake.
Ziegler: *Káluh.*
Marr: Say that one over.
Ziegler: *Káluh Káluh.*
Marr: Pig?
Ziegler: Hmm. It's a long time when the words have come to me, you know, that means when you don't really talk so long that my mother's been dead from there, you know, for some years now. You know her.

03:41

Marr: How about the word for fire?
Ziegler: ^{ʔ}*áp*^{h}*u.*
Marr: Say that one again.
Ziegler: ^{ʔ}*áp*^{h}*u.*
Marr: How about the word for acorn.
Ziegler: Hm. I don't know.

Marr: You don't know the word for tree?
Ziegler: No, I don't.
Marr: ###
Ziegler: It takes a long time that it'll come back to me, when one doesn't think about it, you know.
Marr: When you say it in a tense, is it all?
Ziegler: Hm?
Marr: Do you know how to say it in tenses?
Ziegler: No.
Marr: What about the word for apple?
Ziegler: ### talk about, they might would have liked to talk to you.
Marr: I can help you (?).

04:51

Ziegler: Hm, do you know the family?
Marr: Yeah.
Ziegler: Pomo (?). You know it's their eagle.
Marr: What?
Ziegler: The word *ulusuf.*
Marr: Yeah, eagle.
Ziegler: Hm. *Káwah.*
Marr: How about the word for water snake.
Ziegler: I don't know. Hm.
Marr: And the word for a salmon?
Ziegler: Hm.

05:12

Marr: beavers (?)?
Ziegler: I don't know.
Marr: Say the word for fightbear (?)?
Ziegler: That's what the word means, a *čintóqa* .
Marr: Say it. It's still a word (?).
Ziegler: *Čintóqʰa.*
Marr: Well, that's the word for Indian.
Ziegler: *ˀaku* (?). Yes, this is the last one. *Čintóqʰa wááqa wóqa.*
Marr: Say it again.
Ziegler: *Čintóqʰa wóóqa.*
Marr: That's a (?) ?
Ziegler: That's just on my mind, you know. Hm. That's such a nice word. *Šóhokohčéu.*
Marr: Say it again.

06:08

Ziegler: *Šóhokohčéu.*
Marr: Do know the word for blackbird?
Ziegler: Hm.
Marr: How about for ###?
Ziegler: No, I don't know how you call that. *Éšoh. Éloh.*
Marr: Say the word for cold again.

	Ziegler:	*Éšoh.*
	Marr:	And now the word for hot.
	Ziegler:	*Éloh. Mutákweh .*
	Marr:	Say the word for rain again.
	Ziegler:	I said *mutákwe.*
	Marr:	*Mutákwe.*
	Ziegler:	*ˀípo.*
	Marr:	Smell.
	Ziegler:	Yes, *ˀípo. Pučéli.*
	Marr:	Sit down.
	Ziegler:	No, I said live in.
	Marr:	Live in.
	Ziegler:	*Nimóqačoh.*
06:54		
	Ziegler:	*Nímačeh.* Yeah.
	Marr:	Mountain (?).
	Ziegler:	Yes, I know.
	Marr:	Acorn soup.
	Ziegler:	*Húpehupéu.*
	Marr:	Now say the word for acorn alone.
	Ziegler:	*Húṭe.*
	Marr:	Now say the word for soup alone.
	Ziegler:	*Háṭu.*
07:29		
	Ziegler:	[...] I can't say that.
	Marr:	Say the word old man again.
	Ziegler:	*ˀíčunčálah.*
	Marr:	Bird
	Ziegler:	*uélaˀ.*
	Marr:	Say it again, bird.
	Ziegler:	*uélaˀ.*
	Marr:	*##.*
	Ziegler:	*mutákwe.*
	Marr:	rain, say it again.
	Ziegler:	*mutákwe.*
	Marr:	What about, small.
	Ziegler:	I don't know that that ## to.
	Marr:	The word head.
	Ziegler:	*Hímaˀ.*
	Marr:	Say it again.
	Ziegler:	*Hímaˀ. húšot.*
	Marr:	Again.
	Ziegler:	*Húšot.*
	Marr:	The word for leg.
	Ziegler:	Hm.
	Marr:	You don't know.

Ziegler: Hm. *Áp^{h}u.*
Marr: Fire, say it again.
Ziegler: *Áp^{h}u.*
Marr: Dog.
Ziegler: *Šinčéla.*
Marr: Coyote, say it again.
Ziegler: That's not what I was saying.

08:34

Marr: Bear.
Ziegler: *Šinšémbla.*
Marr: Wolf.
Ziegler: I don't know.
Marr: Deer.
Ziegler: *ˀáˀah.*
Marr: Water.
Ziegler: *Áq^{h}a.*
Marr: The word man.
Ziegler: Hm. I don't know how to say that.
Marr: River.
Ziegler: Hm. *Áq^{h}aq^{h}ut.*
Marr: Mountain. You don't know.
Ziegler: Mm.
Marr: Bird.
Ziegler: The words I don't know, all of them mean again so much to me, you know. Salmon.
Marr: Yes, say it.
Ziegler: *Úmul.*
Marr: Watersnake.
Ziegler: Hm. Hm, I don't know.
Marr: acorn soup say.
Ziegler: Hmm, I would call it *čalamu.*
Marr: Bird.
Ziegler: No, I said house.
Marr: Oh, house.
Ziegler: Hm, *ˀáwah.*
Marr: Say it again
Ziegler: *ˀáwah.* But there's only this small house, *tsoˀu* (?).
Marr: Say it again.
Ziegler: *Dénah.*
Marr: Again.
Ziegler: *Dénah. Pópčel.*
Marr: ### again.
Ziegler: *Poptiah pópčel. Aq^{h}ahúút huut.*
Marr: Again.

10:38

Ziegler: *Áq^{h}a Huut. Šíwaléčoh.*

Marr: That's the meaning of size.

Ziegler: Mhm. *ˀáˀah.*

Marr: That was deer.

Ziegler: Mhm.

Marr: How about coyote?

Ziegler: Hm, that's what I don't know.

Marr: Oh yeah, that's right. Bird.

Ziegler: *Šišémblah.*

Marr: Water. Water.

Ziegler: *Áqʰa.*

Marr: River

Ziegler: I don't know this. I didn't say that I belongs to me if I don't know. River is *áqʰaqut.*

Marr: Pig. Salmon.

Ziegler: *Úmul* is salmon.

Marr: There's another word for 'trout' maybe.

Ziegler: Mhm. Yeah, that's a word *ixóp*. That's the word for trout. That's a little trout, like a little fish, you know.

Marr: Aha. How about the word for cold?

Ziegler: *Éšoh.*

Marr: Hot.

12:06

Ziegler: *Éloh.*

Marr: ###.

Ziegler: Yes, *héšqoh.*

Marr: Again.

Ziegler: *Héšqoh.*

Marr: Is that man coming?

Ziegler: Yeah. *Čémprate húwaq néh*?

Marr: Again.

Ziegler: *Čémprate huwáq neh? ˀaˀa huwáq neh.* The deer are coming.

Marr: Bread?

Ziegler: *Četnéuh.*

Marr: Again.

Ziegler: *Četnéuh.*

Marr: Butter. That's flour.

Ziegler: *Yúma.*

Marr: Again, flour.

Ziegler: *Yúma. Ánoqʰeh.*

Marr: Eggs again.

Ziegler: *Ánoqʰeh.*

Marr: Knife?

Ziegler: *Šišélah.*

Marr: Again.

Ziegler: *Šišélah.*

BIBLIOGRAPHY

Aikhenvald, Alexandra Y.

2005 *Grammars in contact: a cross-linguistic perspective*. Position paper for the 2005 International Workshop Grammars in contact: a cross-linguistic perspective. La Trobe University: Research Centre for Linguistic Typology. http://www.latrobe.edu.au/rclt/Workshops/2005/2005page.htm

Aikhenvald, Alexandra Y. and R. M. W. Dixon eds.

2001 *Areal diffusion and genetic inheritance.* Oxford: Oxford University Press.

Anderton, Alice

1991a Kitanemuk: Reconstruction of a dead phonology using John P. Harrington's transcriptions. *Anthropological Linguistics 33: 4.* [Published March 1994]. 437-447.

1991b The Spanish of John P. Harrington's Kitanemuk Notes. *Anthropological Linguistics Vol. 33 No. 4.* [Published March 1994]. 448-457.

1993 *The Spanish of J. P. Harrington's California Field Notes, II.* J. P. Harrington Conference, Washington DC, November 16, 1993.

Bauman, James

1980 Chimariko placenames and the boundaries of Chimariko territory. *Trends in Linguistics 16: American Indian and Indoeuropean Studies: Papers in Honor of Madison S. Beeler.* Kathryn Klar, Margaret Langdon and Shirley Silver eds. New York: Mouton. 11-29.

Beck, David

2000 Grammatical convergence and the genesis of diversity in the Northwest Coast Sprachbund. *Anthropological Linguistics 42.* 147-214.

Berman, Howard

1983 Some California Penutian morphological elements. *International Journal of American Linguistics 49.* 400-412.

1985 Consonant Lengthening in Chimariko. *International Journal of American Linguistics 51:4.* 347-349.

2001a. Notes on Comparative Penutian. *International Journal of American Linguistics 67:3.* 346-349.

2001b. Chimariko Linguistic Material. Victor Golla and Sean O'Neill eds. *The Collected Works of Edward Sapir XIV: Northwest California Linguistics.* New York: Mouton de Gruyter. 1039-1076.

Blevins, Juliette

2003a Yurok Syllable Weight. *International Journal of American Linguistics 69:1.* 4-24.

2003b One Case of Contrast Evolution in The Yurok Vowel System. *International Journal of American Linguistics 69:2.* 135-150.

Bright, William

1954 Some Northern Hokan Relationships. *University of California Publication in American Archaeology and Ethnology.*

1957 *The Karok Language.* University of California Publications in Linguistics Vol. 13. University of California Press: Berkeley.

1976 North American Indian Language Contact. In Thomas A. Sebeok ed. *Native Languages of the Americas, Vol. 1.* New York: Plenum Press. 59-72.

1978 Sibilants and naturalness in aboriginal California. *Journal of California Anthropology Papers in Linguistics* 1. 39-64.

Bright, William and Jane O. Bright

1965 Semantic structures in Northwestern California and the Sapir-Whorf hypothesis. American Anthropologist 67. 249-58.

Bright, William and Joel Sherzer

1976 Areal features in North American Indian languages. *Variation and change in language: Essays by William Bright*, selected and introduced by Anwar C. Dil. Stanford: Stanford University Press.

Buckley, Thomas

1989 Kroeber's theory of culture areas and the ethnology of northwestern California. *Anthropological Quarterly* 62. 15-26.

Bybee, Joan, William Pagliuca, and Revere Perkins

1994 *The evolution of grammar: tense, aspect and modality in the languages of the world.* Chicago: University of Chicago Press.

Callaghan, Catherine A.

1991 Encounter with John P. Harrington. *Anthropological Linguistics Vol. 33 No. 4.* [Published March 1994]. 350-355.

Campbell, Lyle

1985 Areal Linguistics and its Implications for Historical Linguistics. *Proceedings of the Sixth International Conference on Historical Linguistics*, Jacek Fisiak ed. Amsterdam: John Benjamins. 25-56.

1997 *American Indian Languages: The Historical Linguistics of Native America.* Oxford: Oxford University Press.

2005 Areal linguistics. *Encyclopedia of Language and Lingustics* (2nd edition), ed. By Keith Brown. Oxford: Elsevier.

Comrie, Bernard

1976 *Aspect.* Cambridge: Cambridge University Press.

1984 *Tense.* Cambridge: Cambridge University Press.

Conathan, Lisa

2002a Split Intransitivity and Possession in Chimariko. *Survey of California and Other Indian Languages Report 12: Proceedings of the 50th Anniversary Conference.* UC Berkeley, June 8-9, 2002. 18-31

2002b Pragmatic convergence: Person hierarchies in Northern California. *Proceedings from The Workshop on Structure and Constituency in Languages of the Americas.* L. Bar-el, L. Watt and I. Wilson eds. 19-33.

2004 *The Linguistic Ecology of Northwestern California: Contact, Functional Convergence and Dialectology.* Dissertation, University of California, Berkeley.

Conathan, Lisa and Esther Wood

2002 Repetitive Reduplication in Yurok and Karuk: Semantic Effects of Contact. *Papers of the Thirty-fourth Algonquian Conference*, ed. H.C. Wolfart, 19-33. Winnipeg: University of Manitoba.

Crawford, James M.

1976 A Comparison of Chimariko and Yuman. In Margaret Langdon and Shirley Silver eds. *Hokan Studies.* The Hague: Mouton de Gruyter. 177-191.

Curtin, Jeremiah
1940 *Memoirs of Jeremiah Curtin*. Joseph Schafer ed. Madison: The State historical society of Wisconsin.
Dahl, Östern
2001 Principles of areal typology. In Haspelmath, Martin, König, Ekkehard, Oesterreicher, Wulf & Raible, Wolfgang eds. *Language typology and language universals: an international handbook*, vol. 2. Berlin: Mouton de Gruyter. 1456-70.
Delancey, Scott
1981 An Interpretation of Split Ergativity and Related Patterns. *Language 57:3*. 626-657.
Driver, Harold E.
1962 *Indians of North America*. Chicago: The University of Chicago Press.
Dixon, R. M. W.
1994 *Ergativity*. Cambridge University Press.
1995 Complement clauses and complementation strategies. In F. R. Palmer ed. *Grammar and meaning: essays in honor of Sir John Lyons*. Cambridge University Press. 175-220.
Dixon, Roland B.
1910 The Chimariko Indians and Language. *University of California Publications in American Archeology and Ethnology 5:5*. Berkeley: University of California Press. 295-380.
1931 Dr. Merriam's "Tlo-Hom-Tah'-Hoi". *American Anthropologist 33:2*. 264-267.
Dixon, Roland B. and Alfred L. Kroeber
1913 New linguistic families in California. *American Anthropologist* 15. 645-655.
Dryer, Matthew, Martin Haspelmath, David Gil, and Bernard Comrie eds.
2004 *World Atlas of Language Structures*. Oxford: Oxford University Press.
Eatough, Andrew
1999 *Central Hill Nisenan Texts with Grammatical Sketch*. University of California Publications in Linguistics Vol. 132. University of California Press: Berkeley.
Garret, Andrew
2001 Reduplication and infixation in Yurok: Morphology, semantics, and diachrony. *International Journal of American Linguistics 67:3*. 264-312.
Givón, Talmy
1984 *Syntax: A Functional-Typological Introduction, Vol. I*. Amsterdam: John Benjamins.
Goldberg, Adele
1995 *A Construction Grammar Approach to Argument Structure*. Chicago: University of Chicago Press.
Golla, Victor
1970 *Hupa Grammar*. Dissertation, University of California, Berkeley.
1991 John P. Harrington and His Legacy. *Anthropological Linguistics 33:4*. [Published March 1994]. 337-349.
2000 Language history and communicative strategies in aboriginal California and Oregon. In *Languages of the North Pacific Rim*, Vol. 5, edited by O. Miyaoka and

M. Oshima, pp. 43–64. Suita, Japan: Faculty of Informatics, Osaka Gakuin University.

Golla, Victor and Sean O'Neill eds.
2001 *The Collected Works of Edward Sapir XIV: Northwest California Linguistics.* New York: Mouton de Gruyter.

Good, Jeff
2002 *The Vowel System of California Hokan.* Survey Report #12: Papers from the 50th anniversary conference of the Survey of California and Other Indian Languages. http://email.eva.mpg.de/~good/Hokan_vowels.pdf
2004 *A sketch of Atsugewi phonology.* Presented at the annual winter meeting of SSILA. Boston, January 8-11, 2004.

Grekoff, George
1950-1999 Unpublished notes on various topics. Survey of California and other Indigenous Languages. University of California, Berkeley.
1996 Surface-marked Privatives in the Evaluative Domain of the Chimariko Lexicon. *Survey of California and other Indian Languages Report 10: The Hokan, Penutian & J.P. Harrington Conferences.* Leanne Hinton ed. UC Berkeley, June 28-29, 1996. 35-55.

Haas, Mary
1963 Shasta and Proto-Hokan. *Language*, Vol. 39, No. 1.
1964 California Hokan. *Studies in California Linguistics*, ed. by William Bright. University of California Publications in Linguistics 34. Berkeley: University of California Press. 73-87.
1970 Consonant symbolism in Northwestern California: A problem in diffusion. *Languages and cultures of western North America: Essays in honor of Sven S. Lilyeblad*, ed. by Early H. Swanson, Jr. 86-96. Pocatello, Idaho: Idaho State University Press.
1976 The Northern California Linguistic Area. In Margaret Langdon and Shirley Silver eds. *Hokan Studies: Papers from the First Conference on Hokan Languages.* The Hague: Mouton. 347-360.

Harrington, John Peabody
1921 Field notes on microfilm.
1926 Field notes on microfilm.
1928 Field notes on microfilm.

Heine, Bernd and Tania Kuteva
2005 *Language Contact and Grammatical Change.* Cambridge: Cambridge University Press.

Hopper, Paul and Sandra A. Thompson
1980 Transitivity in grammar and discourse. *Language* 56. 251-299.

Hymes, Dell
1981 *'In vain I tried to tell you': Essays in Native American Ethnopoetics.* Philadelphia: University of Pennsylvania Press.
2003 *Now I know only so far: Essays in Ethnopoetics.* Lincoln: University of Nebraska Press.

Jany, Carmen
2004 *Argument Structure and Transitivity in Chimariko.* Masters Thesis. University of California, Santa Barbara.
2007 Is there any evidence for complementation in Chimariko? *International Journal of American Linguistics 73:1.* 94-113.
Johnson, John R., Amy Miller, and Linda Agren
1991 The Papers of John P. Harrington at the Santa Barbara Museum of Natural History. *Anthropological Linguistics 33:4.* [Published March 1994]. 367-378.
Kaufman, Terrence
1988 A research program for reconstructing Proto-Hokan: First groupings. *Papers from the 1988 Hokan-Penutian Languages Workshop.* University of Oregon Papers in Linguistics. Compiled by Scott DeLancey. Eugene: Oregon. 50-168.
Kinkade, M. Dale and William R. Seaburg
1991 John P. Harrington and Salish. *Anthropological Linguistics Vol. 33 No. 4.* [Published March 1994]. 392-436.
Klar, Kathryn
2002 J. P. Harrington's Field Work Methods in his own words. *Survey of California and Other Indian Languages Report 12: Proceedings of the 50th Anniversary Conference.* UC Berkeley, June 8-9, 2002. 9-17.
Kroeber, Alfred
1911 *The languages of the coast of California north of San Francisco.* University of California Publications in American Archeology and Ethnology 9.
1925 *Handbook of the Indians of California.* Bulletin of the Bureau of American Ethnology 78.
1959 Possible Athabascan influences on Yuki. *International Journal of American Linguistics* 25:59.
Ladefoged, Peter and Ian Maddieson
1996 *The Sounds of the World's Languages.* Oxford: Blackwell.
Landar, Herbert
1974 Bibliographic Note: Chimariko. *International Journal of American Linguistics 40:3.* 247-8.
Langdon, Margaret
1974 *Comparative Hokan-Coahuiltecan studies.* The Hague: Mouton.
Langdon, Margaret And Shirley Silver
1984 California t/ṭ*. *Journal of California and Great Basin Anthropology Papers in Linguistics 4.* Banning, California: Malki Museum Inc. 139-165.
LaPena, Frank
1978 Wintu. *Handbook of North American Indians,* William Sturtevant ed. Vol. 8. 324-340.
Lee, Dorothy
1944 Categories of the Generic and the Particular in Wintu. *American Anthropologist 46:3.* 362-369.
Macaulay, Monica
1993 Reduplication and the Structure of the Karuk Verb Stem. *International Journal of American Linguistics 59:1.* 64-81.

Masica, Colin
1976 *Defining a linguistic area.* Chicago: University of Chicago Press.
McLendon, Sally
1964 Northern Hokan (B) and (C): A comparison of Eastern Pomo and Yana. *Studies in California Linguistics*, ed. by William Bright. University of California Publications in Linguistics 34. Berkeley: University of California Press. 126-144.
Merlan, Francesca
1985 Split intransitivity: functional oppositions in intransitive inflection. In Johanna Nichols and Anthony C. Woodbury eds. *Grammar inside and outside the clause.* Cambridge University Press.
Merriam, C. Hart
1930 The New River Indians Tlo-Hom-Tah'-Hoi. *American Anthropologist 32:2.* 280-293.
1979 *Indian Names for Plants and Animals among Californian and other Western North American Tribes by C. Hart Merriam.* Assembled and Annotated by Robert F. Heizer. Socorro, NM: Ballena Press.
Mills, Elaine L. ed.
1985 The Papers of John Peabody Harrington in the Smithsonian Institution 1907-1957 Vol. 2: A Guide to the Field Notes : Native American History, Language and Culture of Northern and Central California. New York: Kraus International Publications. 49-56.
Mithun, Marianne
1986 On the nature of noun incorporation. *Language 62.* 32-37.
1987 The 'Passive' in an Active Language. In James E. Redden ed. *Papers from the*
1987 *Hokan-Penutian Languages Workshop.* Occasional Papers on Linguistics Nr 14. Department of Linguistics: Southern Illinois University at Carbondale.
1990 Language obsolescence and grammatical description. *International Journal of American Linguistics 56.* 1-26.
1991 Active/Agentive Case Marking and Its Motivations. *Language 67:3.* 510-546.
1992 The substratum in grammar and discourse. In Ernst Hakon Jahr ed, *Language Contact: Theoretical and Empirical Studies.* New York: Mouton. 103-115.
1994 Hokan Languages. In R.E. Asher ed. *The Encyclopedia of Language and Linguistics.* Oxford: Pergamon. 1588-1590.
1999 *The Languages of Native North America.* Cambridge: Cambridge University Press.
2000a Valency-changing derivation in Central Alaskan Yup'ik. In R. M. W. Dixon and Alexandra Y. Aikhenvald Eds. *Changing Valency: Case Studies in Transitivity.* Cambridge University Press.
2000b *Our California Linguistic Heritages: What Was, What Is, and What Can Be.* Paper presented at the Program on Tradition and Community Orality and Ethnic Identity at the University of California, Berkeley, May 2000.
2003 Why prefixes? In: *Acta Linguistica Hungarica.* Hungarian Academy of Sciences. Hungary: Budapest.

2004a *How stable are core argument categories?* Paper presented at the Typology of Argument Structure and Grammatical Relations in Languages Spoken in Europe and North and Central Asia Meeting in Kazan, May, 2004.

2004b *The Non-universality of Obliques*. Paper presented at the Syntax of the World's Languages Conference in Leipzig, August, 2004.

2004c Typology across the Americas: Sounds. Handout from Seminar, Fall 2004.

2005 Beyond the Core: Typological Variation in the Identification of Participants. *International Journal of American Linguistics*, volume 71. 445–472

2006 Voice without subjects, objects, or obliques: Manipulating argument structure in Agent/Patient systems (Mohawk). In Yoshihiro Nishimitsu, Taro Kageyama, and Tasaku Tsunoda eds. *Voice and grammatical relations.* Typological Studies in Language 65. Amsterdam: Benjamins. 195-216.

2008 The emergence of agentive systems. *The typology of semantic alignment systems.* Mark Donohue and Søren Wichmann, eds. Oxford University Press.

in press Core argument patterns and deep genetic relations: Hierarchical systems in Northern California. Typology of argument structure and grammatical relations. Bernard Comrie, ed. *Studies in Language Companion Series.* Amsterdam: John Benjamins.

Nichols, Johanna

1983 On direct and oblique cases. *BLS 9*. 170-192.

Noonan, Michael

1985 Complementation. In Timothy Shopen ed. *Language typology and syntactic description Vol. II.* Cambridge University Press. 42-139.

Olmsted, D.L.

1966 *Achumawi Dictionary.* University of California Publications in Linguistics Vol. 45. University of California Press: Berkeley.

1984 *A Lexicon of Atsugewi.* Reports from the Survey of California and Other Indian Languages. Wallace Chafe and Leanne Hinton eds. Report 5.

Payne, Thomas E.

1997 *Describing Morphosyntax: A guide for field linguists.* Cambridge University Press.

Pitkin, Harvey

1984 *Wintu Grammar.* University of California Publications in Linguistics Vol. 94. University of California Press: Berkeley.

1985 *Wintu Dictionary.* University of California Publications in Linguistics Vol. 95. University of California Press: Berkeley.

Pitkin, Harvey and William Shipley

1958 Comparative Survey of California Penutian. *International Journal of American Linguistics 24:3.* 174-188.

Poser, William J.

1995 Binary comparison and the history of Hokan comparative studies. *International Journal of American Linguistics 61:1.* 135-144.

Powell, John Wesley

1891 *Indian linguistic families of America north of Mexico.* Annual Report of the Bureau of American Ethnology 7:1-142.

Powers, Stephen
1877 Tribes of California. *Contributions to North American Ethnology3.* 439-613. Washington, D.C.
Robins. R.H.
1958 *The Yurok Language: Grammar, Texts, Lexicon.* University of California Publications in Linguistics Vol. 15. University of California Press: Berkeley.
Sapir, Edward
1911 [1990] Review of Roland B. Dixon: The Chimariko Indians and Language. *The Collected Works of Edward Sapir V: American Indian Languages.* William Bright ed. New York: Mouton de Gruyter. 185-187.
1920 [1990] A Note on the First Person Plural in Chimariko. *The Collected Works of Edward Sapir V: American Indian Languages.* William Bright ed. New York: Mouton de Gruyter. 245-249.
Sapir, Edward and Morris Swadesh
1960 *Yana Dictionary*. University of California Publications in Linguistics Vol. 22. University of California Press: Berkeley.
Sawyer, Jesse O. and Alice Schlichter
1984 *Yuki Vocabulary*. University of California Publications in Linguistics Vol. 101. University of California Press: Berkeley.
Scheibman, Joanne
2002 Point of View and Grammar: Structural patterns of subjectivity in American English conversation. Amsterdam: John Benjamins.
Schlichter, Alice
1981 *Wintu Dictionary*. Reports from the Survey of California and Other Indian Languages. Wallace Chafe, Leanne Hinton, and Alice Schlichter eds. Report 2.
Sherzer, Joel
1976a *An areal-typological study of American Indian languages North of Mexico.* Amsterdam: North Holland Publishing Co.
1976b Areal Linguistics in North America. In Thomas A. Sebeok ed. *Native Languages of the Americas, Vol. 1.* New York: Plenum Press. 121-174.
Shipley, William F.
1963 *Maidu Texts and Dictionary*. University of California Publications in Linguistics Vol. 33. University of California Press: Berkeley
1964 *Maidu Grammar*. University of California Publications in Linguistics Vol. 41. University of California Press: Berkeley.
1973 California. In Thomas A. Sebeok ed. *Current Trends in Linguistics Vol. 10: Linguistics in North America.* Mouton: The Hague. 1046-1078.
Silver, Shirley
1964 Shasta and Karok: A binary comparison. *Studies in California Linguistics*, ed. by William Bright. University of California Publications in Linguistics 34. Berkeley: University of California Press. 170-81.
1966 *The Shasta Language*. Dissertation, University of California, Berkeley.
1976 Comparative Hokan and Northern Hokan Languages. In Langdon and Silver, *Hokan Studies: Papers from the First Conference on Hokan Languages.* The Hague: Mouton.

1978a Chimariko. *Handbook of North American Indians*, 8 California. Robert F. Heizer ed. Washington D.C.: Smithsonian Institution. 203-210.

1978b Shastan Peoples. *Handbook of North American Indians*, 8 California. Robert F. Heizer ed. Washington D.C.: Smithsonian Institution. 211-224.

Silverstein, Michael

1976 Hierarchy of features and ergativity. In R.M.W. Dixon, *Grammatical Categories in Australian Languages*. Canberra: Australian Institute of Aboriginal Studies.

Stirling, M. W.

1963 John Peabody Harrington. *American Anthropologist 65*. 370-381.

Swanson, Earl H. Jr. ed.

1970 *Languages and Cultures of Western North America*. Pocatello, ID: The Idaho University Press.

Teeter, Karl V.

1964 *The Wiyot Language*. University of California Publications in Linguistics Vol. 37. University of California Press: Berkeley.

Thomason, Sarah Grey and Terrence Kaufman

1988 *Language Contact, Creolization, and Genetic Linguistics*. Berkeley: University of California Press.

Thompson, Sandra A.

1997 Discourse Motivations for the Core-Oblique Distinction as a Language Universal. In Akio Kamio ed. *Directions in Functional Linguistics*. Studies in Language Companion Series. John Benjamins: Amsterdam. 59-82.

2002 Object complements and conversation towards a realistic account. *Studies in Language 26:1*. 125-164.

Thompson, Sandra A., Joseph Sung-Yul Park, and Charles N. Li

2006 *A Reference Grammar of Wappo*. University of California Publications in Linguistics 138.

Thompson, Sandra A. and Paul J. Hopper

2001 Transitivity, clause structure, and argument structure: Evidence from conversation. In Joan Bybee and Paul Hopper eds. *Frequency and the Emergence of Linguistic Structure*. Typological Studies in Language 45. John Benjamins: Amsterdam.

Tozzer, A. M. and A. L. Kroeber

1947 Roland Burrage Dixon. *American Anthropologist 47*. 104-118.

Wallace, J. William

1978 Hupa, Chilula, and Whilkut. *Handbook of North American Indians*, 8 California. Robert F. Heizer ed. Washington D.C.: Smithsonian Institution. 164-179.

Winter, Werner

1973 *Areal Linguistics: Some general considerations*. Diachronic and typological linguistics, T. Sebeok ed. The Hague: Mouton. 135-47.

Wood, Esther and Leanne Hinton

2000 A Report on George Grekoff's Collection of Chimariko (and other) Materials. *Survey of California and other Indian Languages Report 11: Proceedings of the Meeting of the Hokan-Penutian Workshop*. Laura Buszard-Welcher ed. UC Berkeley. 109-11.

www.ingramcontent.com/pod-product-compliance
Lightning Source LLC
Chambersburg PA
CBHW082146230426
43672CB00015B/2850
9780520098756